Nation-building in Turkey and Morocco

Why do some ethnic groups live peacefully with the states that govern them, whereas others develop into serious threats to state authority? Through a comparative historical analysis, this book compares the evolution of Kurdish mobilization in Turkey with the Berber mobilization in Morocco by looking at the different nation-building strategies of the respective states. Using a variety of sources, including archival documents, interviews, and memoirs, Senem Aslan emphasizes the varying levels of willingness and the varying capabilities of the Turkish and Moroccan states to intrude into their citizens' lives. She argues that complex interactions at the ground level – where states have demanded changes in everyday behavior, such as how to dress, what language to speak, what names to give children, and more mundane practices – account for the nature of emerging state–minority relations. By taking the local and informal interactions between state officials and citizens seriously, this study calls attention to the actual implementation of state policies and the often unintended consequences of these policies.

SENEM ASLAN is Assistant Professor of Politics at Bates College. She has published articles in the *International Journal of Middle East Studies*, *Nationalism and Ethnic Politics*, and the *European Journal of Turkish Studies*.

Nation-building in Turkey and Morocco

Governing Kurdish and Berber Dissent

SENEM ASLAN
Bates College, Lewiston, Maine

CAMBRIDGE
UNIVERSITY PRESS

32 Avenue of the Americas, New York NY 10013-2473, USA

Cambridge University Press is part of the University of Cambridge.

It furthers the University's mission by disseminating knowledge in the pursuit of education, learning and research at the highest international levels of excellence.

www.cambridge.org
Information on this title: www.cambridge.org/9781107054608

© Senem Aslan 2015

This publication is in copyright. Subject to statutory exception and to the provisions of relevant collective licensing agreements, no reproduction of any part may take place without the written permission of Cambridge University Press.

First published 2015

A catalogue record for this publication is available from the British Library

Library of Congress Cataloguing in Publication data
Aslan, Senem, 1975– author.
Nation-building in Turkey and Morocco: governing Kurdish and Berber dissent / Senem Aslan, Bates College, Lewiston, Maine.
pages cm
Revised version of the author's dissertation–University of Washington, Seattle, 2008.
Includes bibliographical references and index.
ISBN 978-1-107-05460-8 (hardback)
1. Kurds–Turkey–Ethnic identity.   2. Kurds–Turkey–Government relations.   3. Nationalism–Turkey–History–20th century.   4. Turkey–Ethnic relations.   5. Berbers–Morocco–Ethnic identity.   6. Berbers–Morocco–Government relations.   7. Nationalism–Morocco–History–20th century.   8. Morocco–Ethnic relations.   9. Nation-building–Social aspects.   I. Title.
DR435.K87A83 2014
322.4′209561–dc23
2014032036

ISBN 978-1-107-05460-8 Hardback

Cambridge University Press has no responsibility for the persistence or accuracy of URLs for external or third-party internet websites referred to in this publication, and does not guarantee that any content on such websites is, or will remain, accurate or appropriate.

*To my parents, Berin and Ahmet Aslan,
and my husband Jason Scheideman.*

Contents

List of figures		ix
Acknowledgments		x
1	Governing "areas of dissidence"	1
	Areas of dissidence	5
	Central arguments	15
	Organization of the book	34
2	Policies of "extreme makeover": state–Kurdish relations in the early Turkish Republic	36
	State versus the local elites: state-building and Kurdish resistance	41
	Forgotten Turkishness: assimilation policies in the early republic	56
	Policies of Westernization in the Kurdish areas	69
	Conclusion	78
3	State-building and the politics of national identity in Morocco	80
	Political actors of the post-independence period	84
	Tribes against state expansion: rebellions in post-colonial Morocco	92
	Rural leaders as allies and the retraditionalization of symbolic space	97
	Moroccanness and Berber identity	106
	Conclusion	110

4	The making of an armed conflict: state–Kurdish relations in the post-1950 period	114
	1950–1970: state–Kurdish relations in transition	117
	1970–1980: radicalization of Kurdish activism	127
	Post-1980: the return of the transformative state and the rise of the PKK	130
	The fragmented state: contention over expressions of Kurdishness	139
	The controversy over naming	143
	The controversy over Kurdish music	151
	Attempts at reconciliation? State–Kurdish relations in the post-2000 period	156
	Conclusion	162
5	The rise of the Amazigh movement and state cooptation in Morocco	164
	The rise of the Amazigh activism and the initial repression	167
	The era of political openings and the discursive recognition of Berber identity	171
	Contained contention: strategic concessions to placate the state	178
	Accommodation of Amazigh demands	181
	Conclusion	194

Conclusion 196
Bibliography 206
Index 226

Figures

1 A meeting in the People's House in Urfa. 68
2 People's Chamber in Karakoçan. 72
3 An official ceremony in Urfa. 75
4 A brass band in Siverek. 76
5 A sports team going hiking in Elazığ. 77
6 The new building of IRCAM. 165
7 The symbol of the Amazigh movement on a wall in Rabat. 175
8 A cartoon from *Le Monde Amazigh*. 188

Acknowledgments

This book has grown out of my dissertation at the University of Washington, Seattle. I have had the privilege of studying with two exceptional scholars, Joel Migdal and Reşat Kasaba, whose never-ending intellectual enthusiasm and guidance were my constant sources of motivation. This book owes its existence to their formative influence on me, their generous support, and friendship. I am indebted to both. I would also like to thank my other committee members, Mary Callahan and Ellis Goldberg, for their careful and critical readings of my dissertation drafts, for pushing me to think through some tough questions, and for providing me detailed suggestions. Ellis played a key role in teaching me the history and politics of the Middle East. Mary introduced me to the exciting literature on nation-building in Southeast Asia and inspired me with her own work.

I conducted the research for this book in Turkey, Morocco, and briefly in France, during the eighteen months from March 2006 until August 2007. I also made follow-up visits to Turkey and Morocco in the summers of the following years. My major fieldwork was funded by the Jennings Randolph Peace Scholar Dissertation Fellowship of the United States Institute of Peace, with additional funding from the University of Washington – the Graduate School's Chester Fritz Fellowship and the Maurice and Lois Schwartz Grant from the Department of Near Eastern Languages and Civilization. The period I spent as a postdoctoral fellow in the Near Eastern Studies department at Princeton University was crucial in revising this study for publication. I thank Michael Cook and Şükrü Hanioğlu for giving me this opportunity. Research funds from Princeton University and Bates College allowed me to conduct additional research

Acknowledgments

in Turkey and Morocco. Bates College Faculty Development Fund also covered the publication costs of this book. I am grateful for these.

I have known so many fascinating and interesting people during the course of my field research. It was thanks to them that it was one of the most exciting periods of my life. I interviewed over fifty Kurdish and Berber activists, journalists, scholars, and state officials. A list of my interviewees can be found in the Bibliography. They were very generous in sharing their time and sources with me, including court decisions and publications of activist organizations, that would otherwise be impossible or very hard to find. In Turkey, special thanks to Ali Fuat Bucak, Nilgün Toker, Mehmet Kuyurtar, Nedret Bilici, Sezgin Tanrıkulu, Ümit Fırat, and Tanıl Bora, who helped me establish many contacts and shared their deep knowledge about the Kurdish question. Müslüm Akalın was very generous in sharing his large collection of photographs of Urfa and allowing me to use two of these images in this book. I would like to thank Bruce Maddy-Weitzman, who put me in contact with a number of scholars and Amazigh activists in Morocco. I am also grateful to Adria Lawrence, who helped me find an assistant in Rabat and offered me invaluable practical suggestions about doing research in Morocco. I am indebted to Ahmed Boukouss, Mounir Kejji, Meryem Demnati, and Hassan Id Belkassm in Morocco for talking to me at length about the Amazigh movement, making connections for other interviews, and for sharing their resources. I am very grateful to Mounir Kejji, who opened up his private library to me and provided me many dissertations, journals, and books on the Amazigh movement. Mustapha Qadéry helped me use the National Library in Rabat and shared his academic work. Special thanks to Younes Amehraye. He was a lifesaver in Morocco, helping me with almost every detail during the field research process, from finding an apartment to transcribing the interviews. He was not only an assistant to me but also a good friend. I was fortunate to make other wonderful friends in Morocco. Dilek Eroğlu, Emin Tüzün, Manuel Viegas, Sawssan and Najwa Belkziz, and Françoise Hradsky advised me about the intricacies of daily life in Morocco and made my stay much more enjoyable. I would like to thank Seçkin Sertdemir for helping me find accommodation in Paris and keeping me company.

Over the course of my research I have used various libraries and archives. I thank in particular the staff at the Republican Archives in Yenimahalle, Ankara, whose help was crucial for this research. The administration of the National Library in Ankara allowed me to save time by going through the newspapers and periodicals myself in their closed stacks. The staff of the Turkish Human Rights Association, in its Diyarbakır, Istanbul, and Ankara branches, were very generous in opening their libraries to me and allowing me to use any source that they had. In Morocco, I did research at the National Library in Rabat as well as the libraries of the Institut Royal de la Culture Amazighe (IRCAM), Association Marocaine de Recherche et d'Échange Culturel (AMREC), and Centre Tarik Ibn Zyad. In Paris, where I spent a month of my fieldwork, I used the library of the Kurdish Institute of Paris along with the libraries of Sciences Po and the Institut National des Langues et Civilisations Orientales (INALCO). I am grateful to the staff at all these institutions.

Over the course of the research and writing of this project I benefited enormously from conversations with colleagues and friends. During my graduate studies at the University of Washington I benefited from the discussions in the Turkish Studies Circle, organized by Reşat Kasaba. I would like to thank its participants, particularly Selim Kuru, Maureen Jackson, Işık Özel, Arda İbikoğlu, Tuna Kuyucu, Ahmet Kuru, and Turan Kayaoğlu, for helping me clarify this project and its arguments. I particularly thank Ceren Belge and Nicole Watts. Throughout the fieldwork in Turkey, my path frequently crossed theirs. We worked in several libraries together, shared data, exchanged contacts, and spent long hours during dinners discussing the Kurdish issue. Having them around made the research process much more pleasurable than it would otherwise have been. I learned a lot from reading their work and benefited from their critical insights and suggestions during the research and writing process. I am grateful to Maureen Jackson, Başak Kuş, Pascal Ménoret, Henri Lauzière, and Ali Yaycıoğlu for their friendship and support. Maureen and Pascal answered my numerous questions during revisions with patience. I also thank Thomas Pierret, Ben White, Sean Yom, Yüksel Sezgin, George Gavrilis, Kristin Fabbe, Jonathan Wyrtzen, Arang Keshavarzian, Amaney Jamal, Elise Massicard, Gilles Dorronsoro, Şener Aktürk, Mohammed Daadaoui, Jon Mercer, and Elizabeth Kier for their comments, questions, and advice along the way.

I had the opportunity to present parts of this work in the Near Eastern Studies department at Princeton University; the Center for Democracy, Toleration, and Religion at Columbia University; the Council on Middle East Studies at Yale University; the Center for Middle Eastern Studies at Harvard University; the Conference on the New Middle East at the University of Illinois at Urbana-Champaign; at the "Nationizing the Dynasty – Dynastizing the Nation" Conference at UCLA as well as at the conferences of the Middle East Studies Association, International Studies

Association, and American Political Science Association. I thank the participants of these conferences for asking questions that helped sharpen my ideas.

My colleagues in the Politics Department at Bates College provided invaluable assistance through their encouragement and mentorship. Jim Richter, Áslaug Ásgeirsdóttir, Danny Danforth, Francesco Duina, Stephen Engel, Caroline Shaw, and Benjamin Moodie read parts of this work and gave me insightful feedback. I thank them all. It was a pleasant surprise to meet John Hall when he came to Bates to teach a class during the short term. I am grateful to him for reading and commenting on the draft manuscript.

I thank my editor, Will Hammell, at Cambridge University Press for his interest in my work and guidance during the publication process. I am grateful to two reviewers for their careful reading of the manuscript, criticism, and suggestions. I would also like to thank Georgina Boyle for her meticulous copy-editing.

Parts of this work previously appeared in two articles and a book chapter: "Incoherent State: The Controversy over Kurdish Naming in Turkey," *European Journal of Turkish Studies* 10 (2009); "Everyday Forms of State Power and the Kurds in the Early Turkish Republic," *International Journal of Middle East Studies* 43, no. 1 (2011): 75–93; and "Negotiating National Identity: Berber Activism and the Moroccan State," in *The Everyday Life of the State: A State-in-Society Approach*, edited by Adam White, 176–188, Seattle, University of Washington Press, 2013. I thank the *European Journal of Turkish Studies*, Cambridge University Press, and the University of Washington Press for permission to reprint those parts.

Finally, I would like to express my gratitude to my family. In Ankara the Ersoy family, in particular Günseli Ersoy, showed me immense hospitality I will never forget. In Urfa, Sevinç and Emin Aslan opened their apartment to me. Ben and Jack Scheideman deserve special thanks for their patience and giving me quiet space during the writing process. I have been very lucky to have my brother Çağrı and my sister-in-law Simge in Seattle, offering me relief whenever I needed a break. My father set an example of being a serious academic with his diligence, curiosity, and passion. My mother reminded me to always take better care of myself and have pleasure in life, before being a scholar. Even though my parents do not particularly like that I live thousands of kilometers away, they are always very encouraging. I am grateful to them for what they have taught me and for their support. To my husband Jason Scheideman, thanks is not enough. He was always by my side at the most stressful moments, tolerating my idiosyncrasies with patience and humor. He read and edited several drafts, challenged me with his tough questions (sometimes at the expense of creating a fight), and pushed me to think more theoretically. I benefited enormously from his engagement with my work. It is to my parents and to Jason that I dedicate this book.

I

Governing "areas of dissidence"

Creating a common national identity and binding society's allegiance to central authority have been important objectives of the modern state. Particularly in the Middle East and North Africa, formation of a national identity took a more state-led character than in the Western context. While in Western Europe, the process of linguistic and cultural homogenization extended over centuries as a result of industrialization, capitalism, urbanization, and increased literacy, in the Middle East and North Africa, the pressures of centralizing and expanding state authority have led rulers to undertake more top-down strategies to achieve social homogeneity in a shorter time span. Ethnic groups that are different from the state's ideal image of the citizen have been affected by these homogenization policies in various ways. Some ethnic identities politicized and became the basis for full-fledged nationalist mobilization. Some ethnic groups, however, entered into uneasy, and yet peaceful, relations with the state. Why do some ethnic groups live peacefully with the states that govern them, whereas others develop into serious threats to state authority? What sorts of nation-building policies breed violent ethnic mobilization and which policies lead to state–minority reconciliation? Why do states pursue different strategies to build their nations? This book tackles these questions through a comparative study of Morocco and Turkey, where nation-building and state–minority relations have followed very different trajectories.

In both countries, authorities faced "areas of dissidence" in the early and mid-twentieth century in which Kurds in Turkey and Berbers in Morocco presented huge challenges to the new states attempting to establish dominance in their territories. Kurds and Berbers held the capacity for resistance to state domination and control. Geographically, these communities were located in rough terrain with inaccessible mountains and difficult climates. Socially, they were organized into tight clans or tribes, as a result of which a strong local hierarchy competed with central rulers for social control. Finally, a distinct culture, marked by a separate language, created a powerful basis for autonomy in the areas of dissidence. Initially, Berbers and Kurds posed similar challenges to the Moroccan and Turkish state rulers in centralizing their states and creating a national identity. However, the complex, often volatile, relations between the Berber and Kurdish societies in Morocco and Turkey, respectively, and the states in which they live have taken very different turns. While the Kurds have resisted the Turkish state, sometimes violently, Moroccan Berbers have worked out an uneasy accommodation with the state. This book explores the reasons behind the relatively peaceful relationship between the Berbers and the Moroccan state and the sometimes violent and confrontational relationship between the Kurds and the Turkish state.

In Turkey, Kurds constitute the largest ethnic minority and are estimated to be between 15 and 20 percent of the population (Watts 2010, xi). Since the foundation of Turkey as a nation-state, Kurdish protest has increasingly radicalized and became the primary challenge that threatened Turkish security. In time, the Kurdish activists' demands for cultural rights were progressively replaced by demands for secession and national liberation. In other words, Kurdish ethnic activism has gradually evolved into a nationalist movement.[1] Since 1984, the movement has resorted to violence and the armed wing, the PKK (Kurdistan Workers' Party), has succeeded in becoming a hegemonic power within the movement, dictating the strategies and demands of Kurdish activists at large. The insurgency also managed to gain considerable support from Kurdish society, succeeding in becoming a mass movement. Successive political parties and several nongovernmental organizations have formed the political wing of this movement.

The Berber movement followed a distinct path. Estimates put Berber-speakers in Morocco at around 40–45 percent of the population (Maddy-Weitzman 2011, 1) and they form the second largest ethnic group in Morocco after the Arabs. Like the Kurdish movement in Turkey, Berber activism emerged as a cultural movement, advocating linguistic and cultural rights. Unlike the Kurdish movement, however, there has been little

---

[1] The difference between an ethnic and a nationalist movement is that the latter asks for self-determination or regional autonomy (Olzak 2006, 40–41).

change in its demands and strategies over the years. Today the Berber activists' demands primarily revolve around acceptance of difference and cultural recognition. It is an ethnic identity movement. Berber mainstream activists take a conciliatory stance in their relations with the state and refrain from challenging the political system of Morocco, let alone territorial unity. The Berber movement also has shown considerable diversity in its structure as it is composed of more than 100 associations with different agendas, ranging from doing social work in rural areas to publicizing Berber rights abuses by state authorities. Despite the large number of organizations working for a pro-Berber agenda, the movement's support has been limited to the urban areas, largely to the educated strata, such as lawyers, students, and intellectuals. As David Crawford (2001, 364) points out, there is no one unique sense of Berberness that appeals to the larger Berber-speaking society in Morocco and the rural Berbers remain outside the scope of this ethnic movement.

Through a comparative historical analysis, this book explains the different evolutions of Kurdish and Berber dissent by looking at the different nation-building strategies of the respective states, which varied, I argue, because of these states' different paths to state formation. Nation-building refers to state attempts to create a common national identity within its borders. States vary in their willingness and capabilities to seek social homogeneity and to intrude into their citizens' lives to build a common identity. Language policies, states' attitudes towards expressions of ethnic identity – such as dress, naming, and music – and official discourses on national identity indicate how states draw the boundaries of national membership. I argue that complex interactions at the ground level, where states have demanded changes in everyday behavior, such as how to dress, what language to speak, what names to give children, and more mundane practices, account for the nature of emerging state–minority relations, particularly the possibility of violent confrontation between ethnic groups and the state. Differences in the everyday intrusiveness (the extent to which the state interferes in the private sphere of individuals that it aims to transform) and the comprehensiveness of nation-building policies (the extent to which the state seeks a wide range of changes in behavior, values, habits, lifestyles) go a long way in explaining whether state–ethnic group relations end up as confrontational or not.

Why do states' nation-building strategies differ? This book contends that a state's nation-building is influenced by the type of its state-building strategies. State-building is the process of establishing monopoly of rule by a central authority over a bounded territory. The relative autonomy of the state vis-à-vis local centers of power, such as tribal leaders, religious sheikhs, and landed notables, affects the state's ability to intervene in society and seek social transformation for the sake of building a common identity. I argue that variation in state autonomy from social centers of power is critical for the formulation of nation-building strategies.

In Turkey, a military-bureaucratic elite, which inherited a large state apparatus from the Ottoman Empire, founded the Turkish Republic and consolidated the central state at the expense of local authorities, more specifically the tribal leaders and religious sheikhs. In their attempt to create a homogeneous nation, these political elites aimed at an "extreme makeover" of the society and sought a wide range of changes in people's behavior, values, habits, and lifestyles. As the largest minority and living in areas that are hard to control, Kurds became the main targets of this social-engineering project. The Kurdish protest in Turkey, I maintain, rests on the everyday experiences of the Kurdish masses as a result of the state's policies to push such a "makeover" and to interfere in their private lives. In Morocco, on the other hand, the monarchy needed the support of the local authorities in centralizing and consolidating its state institutions. Due to the high level of interdependence between the state and local authorities, the state followed a cautious nation-building strategy and refrained from undertaking a transformative state project to homogenize the society. The Moroccan state's interference in the Berber areas was minimal and gradual as a result of the monarchy's alliance with, and cooptation of, Berber power centers. Due to the absence of a social-engineering project and a low level of state intrusion, the Berber activists' demands did not radicalize and the appeal of Berber mobilization remained limited.

This chapter is composed of three parts. In the first part, I elaborate on the concept of "areas of dissidence" to discuss the similarities between the Berber- and Kurdish-speaking areas and to highlight the puzzling aspects of my question.[2] This section also presents a brief discussion of the earlier relations of the Kurdish and Berber communities with the Ottoman and Moroccan dynasties and provides a historical background to the study. The central arguments of the book, along with a discussion of how they conform to and diverge from some of the main arguments

---

[2] I borrowed this term from the academic literature on Morocco, which divides the country into *bilad al-makhzen* (government land) and *bilad al-siba* (land of dissidence). Further discussion on these concepts in the Moroccan context can be found below.

of the state- and nation-building literatures, constitute the second part of this chapter. The final section presents a brief outline of the book.

AREAS OF DISSIDENCE

The Turkish Republic was founded in 1923 following the disintegration of the Ottoman Empire in the aftermath of World War I, after a four-year War of Independence. Morocco became independent from French colonial rule in 1956. During these states' struggle against the Western powers, the Kurdish and the Berber populations largely supported the nationalist military campaigns. In the Turkish case, most Kurdish leaders sided with the Ankara government in its resistance against the Allies. In the Moroccan case, Berbers and Arabs fought against the French under the Liberation Army. These strategic alliances, however, did not immediately pave the way for peaceful relations between the Berbers and the Kurds and their respective states in the aftermath of independence.

The Kurdish and Berber communities initially presented similar challenges to the Turkish and Moroccan state-builders at the time of their countries' establishment as modern nation-states. This was largely because both ethnic groups shared certain characteristics as residents of "areas of dissidence," or areas that present a higher capacity for resistance to state domination and control. I do not conceptualize the characteristics of "areas of dissidence" as constant features. Neither do I take it for granted that these areas' relations with the central power will always be contentious. In this section, my objective is to clarify the main characteristics of these areas that pose similar challenges to centralizing states. The outcome of such challenges depends on state strategies to rule over these areas.

One important characteristic of "areas of dissidence" is the presence of a strict social hierarchy or of communities governed by local elites with high authority and legitimacy. Tribal chiefs, large landowners, warlords, and religious authorities are examples of such local centers of power that enjoy authority to mobilize collective action within their community. The literature on modern states conceives of these strong local elites as potential impediments to state centralization and expansion (Tilly 1992; Hechter 2000). Predecessors of modern states, such as empires and feudal states, are characterized by indirect rule and rely on the intermediacy of local elites to rule their subjects. No central ruler was able to enforce his will over the territories he ruled before the advent of modern communications technology. While the regions that were closest to the center were ruled directly by the central ruler, the peripheries could only be controlled through some form of indirect rule. Central rulers had to cooperate with powerful local intermediaries in order to extract from and control these peripheral regions. The local centers of power were allowed to enjoy autonomy in governing their own territory in return for compensating the central ruler in taxes and supplying military service in times of war (Hechter 2000). Modern states, nevertheless, are defined by direct rule, administrative centralization, clear territorial boundaries, monopoly of binding rule-making, and the monopoly over the means of physical violence (Mann 1986). As states' capacities to administer distant territories increased with improvements in transportation and communication, central rulers began to claim monopoly of rule over their territories, without any intermediaries. As a result, the increasing attempts by central states to rule directly over their territories tend to challenge the authority of local elites. This increases the likelihood of conflict between the central state and local elites. In line with these expectations, Wimmer *et al.* (2009) find that secessionist mobilizations are more likely to occur in regions with previous autonomy and long histories of indirect rule.

For modern state-builders tribal regions are potential "areas of dissidence." Tribal societies are built upon a hierarchical structure and their leaders can compete with central states for social control. A tribe can be defined as "a political entity, bound by shared conceptions of patrilinear kinship serving as a basis for solidarity, and oriented toward the collective defense of itself as a group" (Charrad 2001, 9).[3] Tribal social organizations may seriously threaten modern state rulers' intentions to monopolize the use of violence, to extract surplus, and to impose a uniform law. Tibi (1990, 130) suggests: "Any state structure, being a centralized monopoly of power, runs counter to all kinds of segmentary tribal social organization insofar as a distinctiveness and a certain degree of autonomy are basic features of any tribe." Tribal leaders enjoy considerable authority over their tribesmen and have strong bargaining power in dealing with the state, largely due to their ability to mobilize collective action. They combine a certain moral authority, usually based on a combination of religious and customary authority, over their societies. Tribal leaders' authority is also derived from the amount of wealth they possess

---

[3] Tribal forms are immensely diverse in terms of their political leadership, cultural attributes, number of members, and mode of production. For instance, some tribes may contain only a few hundred people while others may be composed of hundreds of thousands. While some tribes are nomadic pastoralists, others are settled cultivators. For more on the complexity of the tribal systems in the Middle East, see Tapper (1990).

and their legitimacy depends on a continuous flow of goods and services to their followers (Khoury and Kostiner 1990, 9). Historically, tribes usually retained a certain degree of autonomy from central power, depending on their military power. Aside from the existence of a highly authoritative leadership, tribal norms and customs may also challenge states' law and ideology. Fragmented tribal identities may threaten modern states' attempts to build unmediated, direct rule and their ideals of constructing equal citizenship and a common national identity (Tibi 1990).

The Berber and Kurdish societies were largely tribal at the time of Turkish and Moroccan independence. As such they posed three basic challenges to their respective states. Both societies were traditionally ruled by powerful local authorities, namely, the tribal chiefs and religious leaders. Both communities enjoyed a long history of different degrees of autonomy from central rule. And, finally, they were both well-armed societies, which directly threatened states' claims to the monopoly of means of violence. These factors made collective action against a centralizing power easier for the Berbers and Kurds.

During the Ottoman period, the Kurdish areas formed a frontier region along the eastern border between the Ottoman and the Safavid Empires. Before the Ottoman conquest, the Kurds were organized either under nomadic tribes that were free from central control or in confederations of tribes, called emirates (Özoğlu 2004, 46–47). The Kurdish leaders' loyalty was crucial for the Ottoman rulers in curbing Safavid expansion. The Ottoman Empire incorporated these emirates in the sixteenth century and, in return for their loyalty to the Ottomans against the Safavids, accorded them an autonomous status. When the Ottoman state was strong, the Kurdish leaders fulfilled their military and financial obligations. But such fulfillment was irregular. Many times they could simply refuse to pay tribute or send military support to the center (Van Bruinessen 1992, 158–159). As Özoğlu (2004, 59) states: "Although the Ottoman state oversaw the function of the Kurdish emirates, organized as districts or sancaks, Kurdish rulers enjoyed de facto autonomy, particularly in the late eighteenth and early nineteenth centuries; the strong emirates were almost in complete control of their own internal affairs, paying only lip service to Istanbul."

The main confrontation between the Kurdish emirates and the Ottoman state started in the nineteenth century with the centralization efforts of the state. As a result of a series of political and military actions, the Ottoman state managed to abolish the Kurdish emirates and centrally appointed governors began to rule over these territories. In practice, nevertheless, the governors' authority was quite limited. The removal of the emirates fragmented authority in the Kurdish regions, resulting in several tribal authorities being in conflict with each other. The governors' authority was not adequate to prevent tribal conflicts. The sheikhs, leaders of religious brotherhoods, gained political power as they began to mediate between tribes: "This was because sheikhs were the only figures whose influence exceeded the limits of the tribes. Eventually, the sheikhs became the new political leaders after the defeat of the Kurdish emirs. Beginning in the late 1800s, most Kurdish rebellions were led by Kurdish sheikhs" (Yeğen 1996, 219). As Kasaba (2009, 103–104) argues, paradoxically, Ottoman reforms of centralization also strengthened local authorities. For instance, the new land code of 1858, which aimed to break up communal tenure by registering land in the name of individuals, ended up benefiting tribal chiefs and sheikhs. People's fear of new taxation and conscription led them to avoid registering their land in their names. In the end tribal chiefs and sheikhs, who knew how to deal with state officials, registered large conglomerates of land in their own names and became powerful landowners. In addition, the state rulers' concern over Russian occupation and the rise of Armenian nationalism led them to recruit many Kurdish tribal leaders into the Ottoman army or to create tribal militias to police the Eastern provinces. As a result, loyal Kurdish tribes were supplied with arms by the Ottoman state (Kasaba 2009, 119–122; Van Bruinessen 1992, 185). While the Ottoman state went a long way in centralizing its institutions over the course of the nineteenth century, tribes continued to survive (Kasaba 2009, 120). When the Turkish Republic was established in 1923, the state founders encountered economically, politically, and morally strong tribal leaders and sheikhs, who would not be happy with losing their privileges to state power. Hence the majority of the revolts in the early years of the republic arose in the Kurdish tribal areas as a reaction to the expansion of state authority.

The Berber tribes' historical relationship with the state exhibited many similarities to the Kurdish case. The Alawite dynasty ruled Morocco from the mid-1600s. The literature on pre-colonial and colonial Morocco divides the country into two conceptual areas. *Bilad al-makhzen* (government land) refers to the areas that were under the control of the central authority and that paid taxes to it.[4] *Bilad al-siba* (land of dissidence)

---

[4] *Makhzen* literally means "storehouse," denoting the state treasury where collected revenues were kept. In current use it refers to the governing elite that is centered around the king.

was composed of dissident tribes that did not recognize the *makhzen's* authority and did not pay taxes. It was largely the Berber-speaking tribes that constituted the majority of the *bilad al-siba* (Gellner 1972a; Hart 1999).[5] The relationship between the central power and the tribal areas fluctuated continuously. Whenever the sultan had the military means, he could bring the dissident tribes into the orbit of central authority and weaken their autonomy. At other times, mutual alliances brought tribal support for the sultan's rule. Local chiefs acted as intermediaries between the central authority and tribal groups. While the sultan achieved some social control, the local chiefs could keep part of the taxes that they collected for the sultan.

In the nineteenth century the Moroccan countryside was characterized by "regional pockets of power" ruled by local elites with their own armies (Charrad 2001, 104–107). When the French started their colonial conquest of Morocco, they encountered the strongest resistance in the mountainous Berber areas. It took the French more than two decades to pacify the Berber countryside. French colonial rule (1912–1956) expanded the reach of the central authority and modernized the political structure, but its influence on state–tribe relations was mixed. On the one hand, the French built a modern administrative apparatus, pacified and disarmed the dissident Berber tribes, and strengthened the central state. On the other hand, they found it easier to rule over the countryside indirectly through a number of loyal tribal chiefs, whom they appointed as *qaids*, or rural administrators, leaving the tribal structure intact. When compared to the earlier periods, the French weakened the Berber tribes' previous power to challenge the central state, but as part of their divide-and-rule strategy the French also sought to create clear-cut boundaries between Arab and Berber identities, tried to strengthen customary law and tribal councils, and allowed certain tribal leaders to accumulate enormous amounts of wealth and enjoy autonomy in exchange for their support for colonial authority (Maddy-Weitzman 2011, 60–61; Wyrtzen 2011, 228–232). Charrad (2001, 129) writes that some tribal chiefs received arms to conquer areas and rule them in the name of the French. Ben Kaddour (1972, 260) points out that some tribal notables received land and were transformed into feudal landlords during the colonial period.

---

[5] This dichotomy has been recently criticized as being overly simplistic. Scholars emphasize that the relations between the central authority and rural areas were constantly negotiated and that there was a continuum of relations between the *siba* and the *makhzen*, rather than a rigid distinction between the two areas (Maddy-Weitzman 2011; Wyrtzen 2011).

When Morocco gained independence from colonial rule in 1956, Berber chieftains presented a strong challenge to state rulers' aspirations of further centralization and social penetration. As in Turkey in the first years after independence, the Moroccan state encountered a series of tribal uprisings in the Berber-speaking regions.

A second feature of "areas of dissidence" is the difficult geography that makes the intrusion of state authority difficult. These areas have historically been "zones of refuge," in James Scott's (2009) terms, and enjoyed varying degrees of autonomy from central control. Peripheral regions, deserts, mountainous areas, swamps, and jungles are examples of such rough terrain. The states' inability to reach and exercise effective rule in these areas allows the communities residing in them to form their own political structures and enjoy considerable autonomy. Fearon and Laitin (2003) find that rough terrain is significantly related to higher rates of civil war because these areas give a crucial advantage to rebels fighting states. The Berber and Kurdish areas at large presented such rough terrain for state-builders. The Eastern and Southeastern provinces of Turkey, where the majority of the Kurdish-speaking populations lived (and still live even after years of internal migration), are known for their rugged mountains and severe climate. As Van Bruinessen (1992, 11) writes: "The heart of Kurdistan consists of forbidding mountains that have always deterred invading armies and provided a refuge to the persecuted and to bandits." In Morocco, the Berber regions similarly constitute the geographically less accessible part of the country with their high mountains. The Moroccan Berber-speakers are traditionally concentrated in the Northern Rif mountains, High and Mid-Atlas mountains, the Anti-Atlas mountains in the southwest, and the Souss Valley in Southern Morocco. One important consequence of difficult geography is the low economic integration and development of these populations, which is also seen as a potential source of conflict (Gurr 2000). The difficulties of states to bring public services to these areas is usually perceived as discrimination by their residents and creates grievances that may push them to mobilize against the state. In both Morocco and Turkey, the rural, mountainous Berber and Kurdish areas have been the least developed areas with the highest levels of poverty compared to other parts of the two countries (Crawford 2002, 64–65; Kirişci and Winrow 1997, 122). In fact, until the late 1990s the Turkish state considered the economic underdevelopment of the Kurdish regions to be the root of the Kurdish unrest (Yeğen 2007) and invested heavily in developing its infrastructure and improving its socio-economic situation. The public non-military expenditure in Eastern and Southeastern Anatolia has been much higher than the public revenue extracted from these regions and above the national average of public investment (Mutlu 2001). In Morocco, however, the Berber areas have not seen a similar level of public investment.

Finally, areas of dissidence are characterized by their inhabitants' distinct culture, different from the culture of the surrounding society or the one endorsed by the state. As Scott (1998) suggests, a distinct cultural feature, such as religious beliefs, language, and social norms, complicates the state's efforts to make the society more "legible" in order to establish social control. Modern states aim at "rationalizing and standardizing what was a social hieroglyph into a legible and administratively more convenient format" (Scott 1998, 3). A distinct culture makes achieving the objective of controlling and manipulating the society hard for state officials. Particularly, difference in language presents an effective barrier to state officials' access to local communities. That is why linguistic homogenization has been an important part of state-building processes (Scott 1998, 72). The Berber and Kurdish populations are distinguished from the majority of the population in Morocco and Turkey by their unique languages. The Berber language in Morocco is composed of three oral dialects, Tashelhit, Tamazight, and Tarifit, of the Hamito-Semitic family (Marley 2004, 26). The Kurdish language is an Indo-European language related to Persian. Two major dialects, Kurmanji and Zazaki, are spoken by the Kurdish communities in Turkey. As linguistic minorities, Kurds and Berbers have become the main targets of language policies in their states. Both the Moroccan and the Turkish state elites aimed at linguistic centralization and expected every citizen to learn the official language, Modern Standard Arabic and Turkish, respectively. The choice of an official language is likely to create conflict between states and linguistic minorities as it identifies the "core nation," in Brubaker's terms (1996, 103), as distinct from the citizenry. Language policy choices affect prospects for a group's survival along with affecting who has access to schools and public services, who is treated fairly by state officials, who has opportunities for economic advancement, and who can participate in politics. As William Safran (2004, 4) states, languages are not only states' tools for national integration but also their means of political control. As I will explain in the following chapters, in both countries a major source of tension between these ethnic groups and their states emerged out of language policies.

The similarities between the two ethnic groups, in terms of their culture and historical relations with the central authority, make the issue of the different trajectories of each ethnic movement puzzling. In both countries neither Kurds nor Berbers have been subject to formal discrimination in public office or employment. They have enjoyed equal rights of citizenship and could enter high-ranking state positions, as long as they did not advocate a distinctive Kurdish or Berber identity. In both countries the labor markets were not segmented along ethnic lines, and access to public resources were not determined based on ethnic identity (Miller 2013, 194; Mutlu 2001). In short, both states provided similar incentives to Kurds and Berbers to learn the official languages and integrate into the Turkish and Moroccan societies.

The outcomes in my cases also run counter to some of the expectations that can be derived from the ethnic conflict literature. Especially in Morocco, the development of Berber activism as a non-violent movement is counterintuitive given some of the conditions that make the chance of violent conflict likely in the post-colonial period.[6]

Many scholars (Brown 1997, 525–527; Kapferer 1988; Malkki 1995) emphasize the link between ethnic conflict and colonialism. Colonial regimes have been influential in constructing rigid ethnic categories and redefining the content of ethnic identities through their divide-and-rule policies. By categorizing people into ethnic groups with clear-cut boundaries and defining these identities as mutually exclusive, antagonistic, and hierarchical categories, the colonial powers planted the seeds of ethnic conflict. Such constructions of identities, along with favorable treatment of one group over the other, could politicize ethnic differences and create the potential for conflict. In Morocco, the French colonial administrators imagined a clear-cut separation between the Berber and Arab identities. They considered the Berbers to be more democratic and less Islamized than the Arabs. They hoped to thwart the Arabization and Islamization of the Berbers by institutionalizing ethnic differences through the creation of a separate educational and legal system for the Berbers. For example, a series of decrees (the most famous of these was the Berber Dahir of 1930) gave the right to the Berber tribal councils to apply local customary law, rather than the Sharia, within their jurisdiction.[7] Special

---

[6] Also see Byman (1997–1998) for a discussion of why ethnic peace in Morocco is surprising given the assumptions of the ethnic conflict literature. While my analysis intersects with Byman's, he underlines that the absence of an ethnic conflict is particularly puzzling given the weakness of the Moroccan state, with its low coercive and institutional capacity at independence. In contrast, my argument emphasizes that such weakness is at the heart of explaining the ethnic peace in Morocco.

[7] The Berber Dahir triggered a series of demonstrations in Morocco as well as in other Muslim countries and was condemned as a colonial attempt to attack Islam and to divide

French schools were set up in Berber rural areas. One of these schools, the Collège d'Azrou, aimed at creating a loyal indigenous elite by educating the children of local notables for administrative posts (Miller 2013, 100). Such divide-and-rule policies did not lead to a communal conflict between the Arabs and the Berbers after independence. The Moroccan case presents an important chance to analyze under what conditions colonial constructions of identities create the potential for conflict.

Another factor that makes the Moroccan and Turkish outcomes surprising is their political systems. Regime type has been cited as an important factor that affects the forms taken by ethnic protest. For instance, Gurr (2000, 154) finds that ethnopolitical groups in democratic societies are more likely to use strategies of protest than rebellion, while in nondemocratic settings they are more likely to rebel. Similarly, Brown (1997, 548–549) argues that while democracies resolve ethnic tensions in the long run, authoritarian regimes are successful in repressing and controlling ethnic dissidents only in the short term.[8] But the Moroccan and Turkish cases run counter to the expectations of much of the literature on the ethnic consequences of regime types. While Turkey has been a democracy, albeit an imperfect one, since 1950, Morocco has been authoritarian with the monarch as the supreme decision maker.

Finally, a number of scholars point out that ethnic groups that span borders are more likely to demand secession to form their own nationstates (Brass 1991; Horowitz 1985). "The most intense and complex spillover effects in ethnopolitical conflict happen among groups that straddle international boundaries – intense and complex, because they draw in a multiplicity of ethnic and state actors. Of the 275 groups currently in the Minorities at Risk study, nearly two-thirds have kindred in one or more adjacent countries," writes Gurr (2000, 91). According to this argument, ethnic activists benefit from the support and sanctuary of their brethren in other countries. In addition, when an ethnic group becomes politically active, their members' demands and strategies also influence their brethren across state borders. It has been argued, for instance, that Kurdish mobilization in Iraq in the 1960s led by Mustafa Barzani was highly

---

the Moroccan Muslim community into Arabs and Berbers. Many scholars date the beginning of a unified nationalist movement in Morocco to the declaration of the Berber Dahir. For more on the French Berber policy, see Wyrtzen (2011) and Burke III (1972).

[8] The democratic regimes' record of preventing communal conflict between different ethnic groups, nevertheless, is highly mixed. For instance, Snyder (2000) argues that bloody ethnic conflicts are associated with a period of democratization in places where political institutions are too weak to protect individual liberties.

influential in the emergence of a separate ethnic consciousness among the Kurds in Turkey. Similarly, Gurr (2000, 91) points out that there has always been cooperation between the Kurdish leaders, activists, and guerrillas in Turkey, Syria, Iraq, and Iran.

The influence of ethnic brethren living on the other side of the border on radicalizing the demands of ethnic mobilization, however, should not be exaggerated. One important problem with this argument is that it takes cooperation between ethnic brethren for granted. This perspective conforms to the primordialist assumption that ethnic groups are unitary and ignores intra-ethnic tensions and disagreements. It assumes that there is a monolithic sense of ethnic identity that is shared by every member of an ethnic community. In fact, the definition and boundaries of cultural groups are fluid and dynamic. Ethnic identities are in a constant state of flux; they are contextual. Members of the same ethnic group may imagine and formulate their identities in very different ways in different locations, time periods, and circumstances. As Paul Brass (1985) argues, the literature largely ignores the internal struggles within an ethnic group for control over the meanings of the values and symbols of the group and over its boundaries. In fact, in the Kurdish case, competition and conflict between different Kurdish groups both within and across countries have been as common as cooperation. Different levels and forms of Berber ethnic mobilization across North Africa is another example that runs counter to the emphasis on ethnic brethren solidarity. The existence of a vibrant and confrontational Berber activism in Algeria since the 1980s along with a transnational Berber activism were influential in creating an ethnic consciousness and mobilization among Berber intellectuals in Morocco. Compared to the Algerian and Paris-based Berber movements, Moroccan Berberists were latecomers to the movement. But the gradual radicalization of the Algerian Berber movement hardly transformed the Moroccan Berber activists' demands and strategies. In fact these two movements evolved in quite different ways from each other. An analysis of the larger transnational Berber movement and the Algerian Berber activism is beyond the scope of this book. However, it is important to note here that the Algerian state policies towards its Berber minority were much more assimilationist and repressive than the Moroccan state's (Willis 2012, 212) and resembled the Turkish state policies towards the Kurds. The earlier politicization and radicalization of the Berber movement in Algeria support the general argument of this book.[9]

---

[9] For more on the transnational and Algerian Berber activisms, see Maddy-Weitzman (2011).

The cultural and geographical commonalities between Morocco's Berbers and Turkey's Kurds, which gave way to their similar historical relations with the central authority, make the different evolutions of their ethnic mobilizations in the twentieth century puzzling. In addition, the forms that these ethnic mobilizations took contradict some of the main assumptions of the ethnic conflict literature. The next section will elaborate on my central arguments explaining the different evolutions of Kurdish and Berber dissent in light of the literatures on state- and nation-building.

CENTRAL ARGUMENTS

In this book I examine the breadth and depth of policies that states formulate to create a common national identity and their effects on the development of ethnic movements. In other words, I examine the degree of comprehensiveness and intrusiveness of nation-building policies. While comprehensiveness denotes the level of the state's ambitions for a wide range of changes within society, intrusiveness stands for the extent to which the state manages to interfere in the private sphere of individuals that it aims to transform. I argue that the gradual nationalization and expansion of the Kurdish movement was a consequence of a highly comprehensive and intrusive nation-building process in Turkey. In contrast, the Moroccan state's much less ambitious and less intrusive policies to build a common national identity hindered the development of Berber identity into a nationalistic one and limited the Berber movement's appeal within the Berber population at large.

In Turkey, the state's attempt to create a homogeneous nation went beyond the creation of an official national history, the dissemination of one common language, and the creation of certain national symbols such as national holidays. The Turkish state endorsed a thick definition of national belonging and aimed at an "extreme makeover" of the society, dictating the dos and don'ts for daily behavior. The state's ambitions turned out to be the most comprehensive for the Kurdish citizens as they represented not only the largest linguistic minority within the boundaries of the Turkish Republic but also a society that the state elite perceived to be in most need of modernization. As I will explain in the next chapter, the founders of the new state perceived the Kurds as a "primitive," feudal society that was not familiar with state law and authority. The existence of such a large community within the borders of the republic was considered a danger to Turkey's modernization as a unitary Western state. The state's nation-building policies in the Kurdish areas turned into a massive civilizing mission that aimed at transforming Kurdish values, language, dress, tastes, and habits.

The Moroccan state's nation-building policies, in contrast, were much more limited in scope. The manner in which the monarchy articulated and implemented its nation-building agenda was cautious and incremental. The boundaries of Moroccanness, as defined by the monarchy, were quite fluid, ambiguous, and in a state of flux. There was neither a firm nationalist ideology propagated by the state nor a set of policies that were passionately followed to change people's lifestyles, customs, and values. While the monarchy aimed at linguistic unification in administration and education, it refrained from undertaking an aggressive nation-building project to forcefully mold its population into a well-defined category of Moroccanness. The central state's minimal interference in the Berber areas and the absence of a comprehensive and coercive state project of homogenization thwarted a large-scale ethnic resistance from the Berber community that a more coercive and intrusive state might have produced.[10]

What explains the different nation-building strategies of these states? The literature on states in the Middle East emphasizes differences between republican and monarchical strategies in national identity construction. Lisa Anderson underlines that unlike republics, which seek social homogeneity, monarchies support social diversity. Monarchs, she writes, "thrive on multiplicity and avail themselves of considerable ambiguity and nuance in defining the members of their realm" (2000, 56). Different nation-building strategies originate from different ideas of legitimacy. Republican rule is based on popular sovereignty, which requires citizens' interchangeability and equality. Monarchies, by contrast, rest on kinship, inequality, and social hierarchy. Monarchs play the role of mediators, balancing and manipulating different groups within their societies, and present themselves as the representatives and the uniting symbols of their nation (Anderson 2000, 59–60). A similar distinction between different governing strategies of monarchies and republics is also made by Lust-Okar and Jamal (2002). Their analysis of electoral rules in different regime types in the Middle East suggest that monarchies promote

---

[10] Unlike in Morocco, the Algerian state undertook policies of Arabization and modernization that were broad in scope and intrusive into the everyday lives of Berber communities, particularly in the 1960s and 1970s. These policies helped form a quite confrontational Berber (Kabyle) movement in the 1980s and provoked occasional violence between the Algerian state authorities and Berber activists. For more on the Algerian Berber movement, see Maddy-Weitzman (2011).

political fragmentation and in republics the ruling party seeks to maintain its monopoly in the legislature. Their finding is analogous to Anderson's understanding of how different regimes rule. Monarchies benefit from social diversity and fragmentation while republics favor social homogeneity and unity. Monarchical durability depends on a flexible form of rule. A monarch should be able to form coalitions with any group to manage opposition. Such flexibility necessitates the absence of a strong official ideology that guides state behavior (Lucas 2004).

This description of nation-building strategies fit the cases of Turkey and Morocco well. While the Turkish Republic endorsed a strong nationalist ideology and sought cultural homogenization, the Moroccan monarchy has been more tolerant of linguistic and cultural diversity within its realm and refrained from undertaking a transformative state project to homogenize the society. Yet, when the broader Middle East is taken into account, nation-building strategies do not vary uniformly with regime type. The Iranian monarchy's nation-building policies and state–minority relations resembled the Turkish Republic's to a great extent. Reza Shah undertook a massive social-engineering project to turn Iran into a homogeneous Persian state. He closed down minority schools and printing presses, outlawed traditional ethnic clothing, and replaced many place names with Persian names (Abrahamian 1982, 143, 163). Muhammad Reza Shah continued his father's policies. He established the Literacy Corps to disseminate a sense of national identity and the Persian language in the countryside (Sabahi 2001). As in Turkey, he banned the Kurdish language from the public and private spheres. Both shahs did not encourage social diversity and did not endorse a gradualist approach to modernization. Neither has Saudi Arabia been tolerant of diversity within its realm. On the contrary, the Saudi monarchy has propagated a strong official ideology, Wahhabism, and undertook a massive social-engineering effort to shape its society, even at the level of everyday behavior, in line with the norms of Wahhabism. Therefore, regime type alone falls short of explaining the nation-building strategies that states endorse. To understand how far states can go in their attempts at social transformation, one needs to take into account the relative autonomy of the state, which refers to state's ability to formulate and implement policies independent of societal interests and pressures.

One of the primary arguments of this book is that nation-building is influenced by the type of state-building strategies, which has serious consequences in shaping state autonomy. State-building refers to the process of establishing monopoly of rule by a central authority over a bounded territory.[11] In this process, depending on the state rulers' military and administrative capacity and ideological orientation, they coopt, bargain with, or coerce social groups, in varying degrees, to make them recognize and abide by the central authority's monopoly of rule. The extent of state rulers' alliances with and cooptation of social groups to centralize and consolidate the central authority shapes the level of state autonomy. These bargains and alliances with society in turn constrain states' choices to seek social transformation and national identity formation. While the Turkish state's relative autonomy from local authorities helped the political elite to implement a comprehensive and intrusive social-engineering project to create a homogeneous nation, the Moroccan monarch's consolidation of authority through alliances with and cooptation of local authorities precluded an ambitious nation-building policy that sought social uniformity.

When compared to the Moroccan state rulers, the founders of the Turkish state enjoyed an important advantage in establishing the Turkish nation-state. They inherited a well-organized and professional bureaucratic and military apparatus, which had gone through a series of reforms of rationalization and centralization as part of Ottoman modernization during the nineteenth century. These reforms strengthened and modernized Ottoman state institutions and made them more efficient in administering society than in earlier periods. Some of the most important nineteenth-century Ottoman reforms included the imposition of direct taxation, weakening of the power of provincial administration and tribalism, sedentarization of nomadic populations, professionalization of the army, introduction of conscription, secularization and codification of laws, and the introduction of secular and Western-type schools.[12] As a result, state power was increasingly concentrated within the Ottoman civilian and military bureaucracy, from which the founders of the Turkish state originated.

A comparison of the raw figures of military manpower between Morocco and Turkey, which had roughly similar population figures around the time when they emerged as nation-states (12.6 million in 1964 in Morocco and 13.6 million in 1927 in Turkey), points to the contrast between these states' coercive capacities.[13] In the middle of World

[11] For two good reviews of different theories of state-building, see Vu (2010) and Spruyt (2002).
[12] For more on the Ottoman reforms of the nineteenth century, see Hanioğlu (2008) and Kasaba (2009).
[13] I obtained the population figures for Morocco from Waterbury (1970, 10) and the Turkish population figures from Dündar (1999).

War I, the Ottoman army had around 800,000 soldiers, though the number had reduced to 100,000 men at the end of the war (Zürcher 2004, 100). Before World War II, the number of soldiers in the Turkish army ranged between 100,000 and 120,000 men in the single-party era. The Turkish government increased its army to 1.5 million during World War II (Zürcher 1998, 207). Even in its weakest condition, the Turkish army was almost four times larger than the Moroccan army of 28,000 men in 1956 (Hurewitz 1969, 343). When Morocco gained independence in 1956, Turkey's force level had reached 400,000 (Hurewitz 1969, 227).[14]

Zürcher (2007, 103) emphasizes the institutional links between the empire and the republic to explain the success of Mustafa Kemal and his followers in establishing the Turkish Republic and undertaking their reformist, ideological program: "It was the army, and certainly also the gendarmerie, which allowed the republican regime to extend its control into every corner of the land and into every village, to a degree the empire had never achieved." He points out that both the army of the national movement and the civilian bureaucracy remained intact and continued practically without change under the republic. Similarly, Karen Barkey (1997, 104) calls attention to the advantages of being a rump state, that is, a state that broke off from the core imperial domain. She argues that the main continuity between the Ottoman Empire and the Turkish nation-state was in the state apparatus: "The rump state remains more confident and united by imperial legacy than the periphery, gaining its strength from its previous imperial domination; it has better developed institutions and state apparatus." The military-bureaucratic elite and particularly Mustafa Kemal emerged from World War I and the following War of Liberation with unrivalled supremacy and legitimacy vis-à-vis the Ottoman monarchy, which they could overthrow swiftly. As Hale Yılmaz (2013, 13) underlines, the military and diplomatic victories that Mustafa Kemal and the nationalist forces won during the War of Liberation gave them credibility and legitimacy. The social, demographic, and economic devastation that resulted from years of war created a society vulnerable to a state intent on radically transforming it. Endowed with the ideas of positivism, modernism, reformism, Jacobinism, and Turkish nationalism, which they had been discussing for a long time as solutions to the

---

[14] The gap between the coercive capabilities of these states continued in the following years. In 1980, the size of the military in Morocco was 117,000 men while in Turkey it was 567,000. The size of the police force was 3.6 times larger in Turkey than in Morocco in 1990: 87,160 in Turkey and 24,133 in Morocco. To compare historical data on military capabilities, see King and Zeng (2001).

decline of the Ottoman Empire, this military-bureaucratic elite conceived of itself as having the necessary instruments to establish direct rule over the society. Relative to the Moroccan nationalists after independence, the Turkish state leaders had higher infrastructural capabilities in the form of military, bureaucratic, and ideological resources that allowed them to concentrate state authority at the expense of local power centers. Building a state autonomous of religious orders and tribal networks gave the state elite the ability to undertake nation-building measures that aimed at a complete transformation of Kurdish society.

The intention to centralize the state by weakening the local power centers did not necessarily preclude strategic alliances with certain tribal leaders in the region as opposed to others, particularly during the turbulent times of rebellion in the first decades of the republic. There were tribal and landed notables who served within the ranks of the single party as local party representatives or parliamentarians from the Kurdish regions. As I show in Chapter 2, many of the state policies formulated at the state's center to detribalize the region also had unintended consequences and failed to transform the social structure. Nevertheless, the state's deep suspicion of local power centers and its general policy to eliminate their authority and prestige continued throughout the single-party period. While the republican power structure and institutions were taking shape, the founding elite made decisions without concern for the interests of local power centers, even those who were loyal to the republican regime. Many tribal leaders and their families who were deported and resettled during the single-party era included government loyalists (Üngör 2011, 136).

This book builds on the "state-led nationalism" model, which sees the emergence of nationalism and its spread among the masses as a process that is directly linked to modern state formation (Tilly 1994). According to this model, modern states require the cultural homogenization of the population and the creation of a uniform sense of nationhood for two reasons. First, linguistic standardization and homogenization are crucial for bureaucratic efficiency. States can ensure legal uniformity, collect taxes more efficiently, and control their populations more easily when there is one common language spoken within their borders (Laitin 1992; Tilly 1992, 100). Second, modern state-building requires cultural homogenization because of its increased need for social compliance and loyalty. As Hobsbawm (1989, 149) states,

> The state not only made the nation, but needed to make the nation. Governments now reached down directly to each citizen in their territory in everyday life, through modest but omnipresent agents, from postmen and policemen to teachers

and (in many countries) railway employees. They might require his, and eventually even her, active personal commitment to the state: in fact their "patriotism".

As states' demands from their populations increase – in the form of taxes, military mobilization, and conformity to the states' norms and laws – and as they penetrate more into people's everyday lives, they need to legitimize this more intense form of rule. The modern state binds the allegiance of its population to itself by claiming to represent the will of its people. The modern state rulers have incentives to define boundaries of their society through ethno-national criteria because "the principle of ethnonational representativity of government – that like should rule over likes – became de rigueur for any legitimate state" (Wimmer 2008, 991). The state-centered explanations of nation-building see the formation of a national consciousness among the people living within the state's boundaries and their cultural homogenization as an outcome of a state's large-scale and coercive nation-building process. States define their nation by determining who is included and who is excluded, by shaping the form of a nationalist ideology, by making the rules of conduct for the society, and by identifying the national norms and culture. As explained by Weber's (1976) classic study of the French nation-building process, compulsory military service and the school system play the key roles in imposing a sense of nationhood and cultural uniformity. In Turkey, too, conscription and schooling have been major tools of the state to disseminate the official nationalist ideology and the Turkish language to the masses. The creation of a common sense of nationhood and a nationalist ideology gives states the tools to justify their rule in the name of their nations and ensure their populations' compliance. States ask their citizens to join the military and, when necessary, to die for their states out of a commitment to their nations. They seek to impose a sense of solidarity and unity among their citizens and to divert their loyalties from local centers of power to the state. To this end, they promote their citizens' cultural distinctiveness vis-à-vis other nations and invent or revive traditions, symbols, and rituals. As Tilly (1994, 138) argues, modern state rulers adopt programs of "normative indoctrination" to stimulate people's commitment to the state. Similarly, Corrigan and Sayer (1985, 4) associate modern state formation with "moral regulation," which they define as an attempt to shape people's customs, thinking, behavior, and the way they perceive their place in the world. Although today's states have more say over their citizens' lives and all claim to be nation-states, there have been variations in states' aspirations and capabilities to seek social control and transformation. In other words, there have been important differences in the scope of state intrusion into people's everyday lives. Some states have asked for radical transformations from their societies – including changes in people's physical appearance, the language they speak at home, even the names they give their children – to inscribe a national look on them, while others demand more modest changes to build their nations. The state-centered approaches to nationalism do not problematize these variations and explain why states pursue different strategies to build their nations. In this book, I call attention to how differences in state centralization are crucial for nation-building policies and levels of state intrusiveness.

Much of the literature on state- and nation-building expects an increased likelihood of conflict between state and social actors as a direct result of the state's centralization and cultural manipulation. As Nugent (1994, 335) points out, the state-centered approach conceptualizes nationalism "as a movement outward from the state's centers of power, in which the state incorporates territory by coercive means and attempts to assimilate culturally alien groups into a unified, national consciousness, likewise by force." Such a coercive process, according to the literature, almost always leads to increased political unrest and reaction. Hechter (2000, 56), for instance, emphasizes the conflict-producing effects of the transition from indirect to direct rule. Indirect rule entails the existence of separate governance units for different groups in society. Local authorities enjoy great autonomy in administering their communities. They collect taxes, recruit men for their own armed forces, and make their own communal laws. According to Hechter (2000, 37), indirect rule does not lead to a nationalist project because it makes each governance unit congruent with culturally homogeneous societies, or nations. Transition to direct rule, however, threatens both the power of the local authorities and the cultural autonomy of minorities. Hechter (2000, 60) conceives of authority as a zero-sum commodity. The central state can gain control only by weakening local authorities. As the central state's rule expands, it increases local authorities' interest to engage in "peripheral nationalism," to protect their rights and privileges. "Political centralization thus entails fearsome conflict," he concludes (2000, 60).

Yet, the assumption that state centralization creates an inevitable conflict between state and local authorities or ethnic groups is not always true. The historical trajectories of my two cases, Turkey and Morocco, point in different directions. As expected, sometimes, modern state-building leads to strong reactions from local power centers and ethnic minorities and weakens the state's capacities to control and penetrate its society, or at least parts of it. This explanation fits the relationship between the Turkish state and the Kurds. However, in other cases, state centralization may go hand in hand with the preservation of local power centers and can be achieved through their support. In other words, areas of dissidence can turn into areas of support for the state. The Moroccan case suggests that authority may not be a zero-sum commodity. It shows the multiplicity of forms of state- and nation-building, which the literature does not take into adequate account, and offers a good case study to extend the discussion on nation-states and conflict. As Karen Barkey (1994) underlines in her work on Ottoman state centralization, theories of state formation largely rely on the processes of Western European state development and give the impression that there is a uniform direction for state-building. This book underlines that there are different paths to state- and nation-building, which have different consequences for state–minority relations. The European model of the nation-state was not simply exported to non-European contexts. The Moroccan trajectory of state centralization presents an alternative model.

Modern state formation may not necessarily be carried out in opposition to local authorities, such as tribal leaders or rural notables, as many scholars of the literature assume (Hechter 2000; Tilly 1992; Waldner 1999). The clash of interests between local authorities and the central state should not be taken for granted. In fact, state centralization can be achieved through the support of local power centers if conditions are created to ensure that they also benefit from this process. One such strategy is the integration of local power centers into the central state's structure, thus making them into state agents. Such a state-building strategy transforms and redefines the role and power of local authorities but does not necessarily weaken them. The local authorities are granted new power and privileges (especially in the form of wealth to distribute to their constituencies) in state institutions.

This strategy differs from indirect rule associated with pre-modern forms of the state, as it does not allow an autonomous status to local authorities. The central state can enjoy the monopoly over the use of violence, can unify its legal system, and can regularly extract taxes from its society. Nevertheless, state decisions have to be made while keeping an eye on the interests of local authorities. This state-building strategy creates an interdependent relationship between the central ruler and local authorities. While the central ruler depends on the support of the local authorities to extend his rule over the peripheries, the local authorities rely on his cooperation to benefit from the spoils of the regime and to enjoy their privileges, albeit in redefined ways. In other words, each side's actions are constrained by the other's presence. State rulers need to consider the local authorities' reactions while making decisions and the local authorities, who are now state agents, have to take into account how their acts could affect the patronage networks formed between themselves and the central state.

Such state structures fit Eisenstadt's (1973) definition of "neopatrimonialism" closely. Eisenstadt characterizes neopatrimonial regimes as paternalistic central states that concentrate power mostly through a dense network of personal patronage and less through ideology, coercion, or mass political participation. The political system is built upon the access of the peripheral groups to the center through cooptation, by gaining access to the sources of distributive policies or bureaucratic positions. The rulers of these regimes also emphasize their mediatory role between different factions of the society. The mediatory-distributive functions are crucial for these regimes (Eisenstadt 1973, 14–15). Neopatrimonial regimes, according to Eisenstadt (1973, 11), are different from patrimonial regimes, which are also highly personalistic, because they contain many elements of modern states, such as territorial unification, universalistic administration, and legal claims. They also have complex and differentiated institutions, such as political parties and well-developed bureaucracies. Parties and parliaments in neopatrimonial regimes function as spaces for competition over positions controlling the distribution of resources and patronage networks (Eisenstadt 1978, 277). Finally, these regimes encounter the growth of new political demands, another characteristic that is different from patrimonial systems. The stability of neopatrimonial regimes, therefore, largely depends on the ability of the state to broaden new political groups' access to the center, to expand the clientelistic networks to them, and to incorporate the new elites within their central political framework (Eisenstadt 1973, 50–51). In short, these regimes have to be highly adaptable ideologically and in practice in order to deal with new political challenges.

If modern states can take the neopatrimonial form in which local authorities are coopted within the state institutions, rather than eliminated or weakened, then how would such a system build its nation to increase people's commitment to the state? Because these states are based on a different state–society relationship from that of the European model, which much of the literature discusses, their nation formation also takes a different form. Due to the high level of interdependence between the state and social centers of power, the state's ability to act as a transformative actor or to take up the role of an agent of social makeover to mold people into a homogeneous unit turns out to be highly limited. In fact, such state formation is likely to bring a thinner and fuzzier conception of nationhood that can accommodate social diversity and a flexible nationalist ideology that allows for negotiation and compromise, when necessary.

Two reasons can be given to explain why nation-building in these regimes tends to be more accommodative of social and cultural diversity. First, these regimes favor incremental social change over sudden and far-reaching changes because they would not want to upset the stability of their regimes, which largely depends on the central rulers' alliance with local centers of power, such as leaders of tribes, ethnic and religious communities, big landlords, and the like. As Eisenstadt (1973, 14) argues: "In most of these countries, the distinctiveness of the center did not become connected ... with attempts to a structural and ideological transformation of the periphery or with effecting far-reaching changes in the periphery's basic conception of social order." Therefore, they tend to refrain from interfering into the daily, private lives of their citizens. Second, because these regimes' continuity depends on their ability to coopt potentially threatening groups with new political demands, the official ideologies propagated by these states tend to be fuzzier and more flexible. Their conceptions of nationhood, therefore, tend to be thinner, more inclusive, and tolerant of cultural diversity in order to allow for negotiation and adjustment when new challenges arise.

The Moroccan trajectory of modern state-building and national integration followed this pattern. In 1956, when Morocco emerged as an independent state, the political elite encountered a society that was highly fragmented along linguistic as well as tribal lines. According to estimates, around 40 percent of the population spoke Berber (Hart 1972) and more than two-thirds of the population belonged to tribes (Charrad 2001, 152). This highly fragmented social structure was a heritage of the Moroccan pre-colonial state structure, which was quite weak in dominating its society. As Charrad (2001, 104) points out, the Moroccan state had neither a stable bureaucracy nor a standing army as late as the end of the nineteenth century. Gellner (1972a, 364) writes that in the pre-colonial era almost half of the territory of the country was inhabited by tribes that were outside the political order and did not pay taxes to the central authority. Although French colonial rule strengthened central state institutions and put an end to tribal dissidence, it did not attempt to transform the social structure. Rather, as part of their divide-and-rule policies, the French played on the social fragmentation and exacerbated it. The departure of the French also left state institutions brittle. After the departure of the French, the replacement of French administrators with Moroccans proved to be a long and painful process. A year before independence almost three-fifths of the civil servants in the bureaucracy were French (Ashford 1961, 119), and the training and recruitment of Moroccan personnel to fill the administrative posts took years.[15]

The Moroccan state-building experience relied heavily on the cooptation of tribal authorities and rural notables to tie them to the central authority. Faced with a highly fragmented society and a weak state structure in 1956, the nationalist Istiqlal Party's efforts to consolidate state authority by attacking the tribal power base and its homogenization attempts failed in the immediate aftermath of independence. Playing on the growing resentment against Istiqlal in the rural areas, the king consolidated his power through an alliance with tribal authorities and rural notables and managed to marginalize the party. Istiqlal's ambitious homogenization policies were reversed. The alliance with rural notables limited the state's capacity to undertake nation-building based on any large-scale social-engineering project, especially in the countryside where kin-based solidarities were strong and where tribal authorities, most of whom were Berber-speakers, enjoyed a high level of social prestige. While the monarchy aimed at linguistic unification in administration and education, it refrained from undertaking an extreme makeover project to forcefully mold its population into a well-defined category of Moroccanness. In other words, there was neither a clear-cut nationalist ideology propagated by the state nor a set of policies that were passionately followed to change people's lifestyles, customs, values, and behavior. The central state's minimal interference in the Berber areas and the absence of a comprehensive and coercive state project of homogenization obstructed the radicalization of the Berber ethnic movement and limited its appeal among the Berber population at large and limited its appeal among the Berber population at large.

This does not mean that the Moroccan state was not involved in a nation-building project. It certainly was. Nevertheless, the manner in which the monarchy articulated and implemented its nation-building

[15] On estimates regarding the growth of the bureaucracy in the first decade following independence, see Waterbury (1970, 279). The need to fill the administrative posts left vacant by the French gave the monarchy an important tool for establishing patronage networks. According to Waterbury, the king's control of the administration became his major instrument of rule. For more on the development and Moroccanization of the bureaucracy, see Waterbury (1970, 275–280) and Ashford (1961, 116–124).

agenda was cautious and incremental. The state sought to homogenize its population linguistically and pursued Arabization policies to expand the use of Modern Standard Arabic. It also presented Arabic culture as the high culture to define Moroccan national identity and neglected Berber culture. The boundaries of Moroccanness, however, as defined by the monarchy were quite fluid, ambiguous, and in a state of flux. As Rémy Leveau (1993, 252–253) notes: "While the very concept of the monarchy, and of the boundaries of the state and of the public observance of Islam, must be respected, everything else is negotiable." When the Berber ethnic movement began to pressure the state for recognition of difference, the monarchy could adjust its discourse to accommodate Berber identity without having to refute its earlier narrative on Moroccan identity. Its previous discourse on Moroccan national identity was vague and adjustable enough to allow for such discursive transition and compromise. The regime's adaptability to new demands from the Berbers, I argue, has been influential in preventing the nationalization of the Berber protest.

The Moroccan monarchy's adjustment to new Berber demands was not only at the discourse level. The monarchy also extended its patronage network to coopt the Berber activists. The response of the monarchy to the growing demands of the Berber movement was in line with its response to the rise of other political groups in society. In general, the monarchy has been successful in extending its clientelistic networks to political actors to thwart their rising challenge to the regime. The Moroccan state's initial weakness in the earlier years of independence, namely, its need for accommodation with alternative centers of power in society, pushed it to become a highly adjustable regime in the face of new challenges and new political actors. Such adaptability to new circumstances gave the regime its major strength, providing it with stability and durability. With regards to the Berber movement, for instance, the monarchy's cooptation of certain Berber activists by integrating them into the state structure fragmented the movement and weakened its capacity to challenge the regime in radical ways.

My argument, however, does not necessarily suggest that the Moroccan state strategies of nation-building have always been inclusive of different cultures or accommodative of the Berber movement's demands. Nor do I argue that gradual recognition and integration of Berber ethnic identity was a result of the Moroccan state's commitment to liberal multiculturalism and minority rights. The Moroccan state's relations with the Berber movement were not always defined by compromise and the state has also sought to repress and silence Berber activists. Until the mid-1990s the

Berber issue was a sensitive topic. However, the Moroccan state has been more adaptable to changing circumstances and new challenges. Its fuzzy imagining of national identity led it to consider more options than the Turkish state did in dealing with growing ethnic demands and to respond quicker to the rise of the Berber movement before it radicalized.

Due to its rigid nationalist ideology, the Turkish state's reaction to the emergence of a Kurdish ethnic movement, whose demands initially revolved around cultural rights, was marked by intolerance and indiscriminate suppression. Even at a time when the Kurdish movement looked very similar to the Berber movement in terms of its structure, strategies, and demands, the Turkish state elite chose to exclude the movement from the legal sphere of contention. It was this exclusion along with the state's meticulous prohibitions of Kurdish cultural expression that gradually led to the Kurdish movement's radicalization and nationalization. As Wimmer (2008, 991) points out, political exclusion along ethnic lines provides incentives to the elites of the excluded minority to emphasize ethnic rather than other divisions. State policies can transform minorities into "nations." This book avoids the assumptions of nationalist teleologies, which see national movements as inevitable consequences of ethnic movements or ethnic identities.[16] It does not take for granted a pre-existing understanding of Kurdish nationhood that was reawakened by modernization processes. In line with Brubaker's argument (1996, 19), this study contends that nationhood should be studied as a "contingent, conjuncturally fluctuating, and precarious frame of vision," rather than a "real entity" that can be objectively defined. It examines how particular policies of the Turkish state led to the construction of Kurdish nationhood in Turkey as a "cognitive frame" (Brubaker 1996, 16), informing the narrative and strategies of Kurdish activists.

This study is focused on the consequences of state strategies on ethnic movements. It is not my intention to suggest that the Moroccan strategies that produced ethnic stability have yielded better outcomes in other areas as well. The Moroccan approach to state-building has curtailed incentives for a state-led development agenda. Today Morocco ranks quite low in measures of socio-economic development compared to Turkey. In the Human Development Index, out of 186 countries, Turkey ranks 90th, positioning in the high human development category, while Morocco ranks 130th in the medium development category. Morocco has lower

---

[16] For a critique of nationalist teleologies and a discussion of national indifference in the context of the Austro-Hungarian Empire, see Judson (2006) and Zahra (2008).

literacy rates (67 percent compared to Turkey's 94 percent), a lower rate of urbanization (57 percent compared to Turkey's 72 percent), and much lower GDP per capita ($2,902 compared to $10,666 in Turkey).[17] While the Moroccan state has so far dealt well with its social diversity, preventing serious conflict, this ethnic stability did not necessarily open the way for political or socio-economic development. Turkey's achievements in modernization and development came at the cost of serious social conflict, including but not limited to the Kurdish conflict that hurt its democratization process and has cost the economy between $300 billion and $450 billion since 1984 (International Crisis Group 2012, 1).

Four broader implications can be derived from this comparative analysis of Turkey and Morocco. First, there are different paths to state- and nation-building, which have different consequences for state–minority relations. As the Moroccan case shows, modern state-building does not necessarily have to entail the elimination or weakening of local power centers as well as different cultural and ethnic identities. In other words, modern state-building may not have to be a process that takes place in opposition to society, which in the end leads to a high degree of social resistance, as most of the literature assumes. What the literature in general does not take into account is the possibility of high interdependence between the central authority and local communities. In these cases state centralization and nation-building may not take a solely coercive form but may proceed in cooperation with local communities, without presenting a serious challenge to their interests.

Second, this study challenges the functionalist approaches to state- and nation-building processes. State-centric, functionalist approaches to nationalism take it as axiomatic that building a national identity and a homogeneous nation is essential to building an effective state. The Turkish case shows that such an intrinsic relationship between state-building and nation-building should not be exaggerated. As the Turkish example shows, the state's attempts at building a national identity and a culturally homogeneous population can in fact weaken its ability to exercise effective social control and to legitimize its rule, at least within certain parts of its population. The Turkish state's capacity to exercise social control and to attract Kurdish loyalties to the state declined at times when the state-led

---

[17] See UNDP (2013) for the Human Development Index. The literacy rate is from 2011 and rate of urbanization and the GDP figures are from 2012. See World Development Indicators of the World Bank at http://data.worldbank.org/indicator (accessed January 3, 2014).

nation-building project was most fervently implemented. Today, almost nine decades after its establishment, the Turkish state still struggles to command the loyalties of its Kurdish citizens, its control over the Kurdish areas is far from complete, and its ability to resolve the Kurdish conflict is not certain. State-led nationalisms can take many different forms. Therefore, rather than thinking of state- and nation-building as positively correlated, it is more important to specify what types of nation-building help states achieve social control and increase their legitimacy.

Another implication of this study relates to states' capacities. Michael Mann's conceptualization of state power is one of the most cited in the modern state literature. Mann (1986, 113) assesses state power in two dimensions. Despotic power refers to state autonomy and indicates "the range of actions which the elite is empowered to undertake without routine, institutionalized negotiation with civil society groups." The second dimension, infrastructural power, indicates the state's institutional capacity to penetrate society and enforce its decisions. In general it is measured through the "resources at the disposal of the state," such as the extent of the military and police forces, its administrative network, and state revenue and expenditure (Soifer 2008, 237).[18] While these two conceptualizations are analytically distinct, in practice they are related. For a state to enjoy high autonomous power, it needs high infrastructural power, or the necessary resources to enforce its policy (Mann 1986, 115).

This study contends that despotic power (or state autonomy) and infrastructural power are poor predictors of a state's ability to control its society. The Turkish state's higher autonomy from local power centers and its higher level of penetration in the Kurdish areas, relative to the Moroccan state, did not necessarily lead to a seamless enforcement of state policies or higher levels of social control in the Kurdish areas. Neither state autonomy nor a state's institutional resources guarantee a state's ability to enforce decisions and control society. As John Brewer (1990, xx) suggests

---

[18] See the December 2008 issue of *Studies in Comparative International Development* 43 (3–4) for a detailed discussion of Michael Mann's conceptualization of state power. Hillel Soifer's article in this issue highlights two other conceptualizations of infrastructural power than the national capabilities approach that complicates the concept of state power. The "weight of the state approach" assesses power by focusing on the impact of state actions on society and the ability of the state to achieve the intended effects of its policies. The "subnational variation approach" takes the uneven reach of the state into consideration and looks at the variations of state power across its territory. These two aspects are very important but more challenging to assess. In the following chapters I try to take into account these two aspects of state capacity in my discussions of state policies if there is data available.

in his work on the building of the British fiscal-military state, neither autonomy nor a large state apparatus are necessary for state strength: "The effective exercise of power is never merely a matter of logistics, a question of whether or not a state has the requisite bureaucracy or military cadres. States are not just centres of power; they are also sources of authority whose effectiveness depends on the degree of legitimacy that both regimes and their actions are able to command."

Furthermore, in the Turkish case, the state's strength, which initially derived from an autonomous military and a well-developed and centralized bureaucratic structure, has created a more inflexible official approach to nation-building, which narrowed down the range of options that was available to the Turkish state elites in dealing with Kurdish protest. Such rigidity contributed to the Turkish state's failure to resolve conflicts with the Kurdish population. Although Turkish state actors equate the use of military power against Kurdish dissent as a sign of state strength, its frequent use during the history of the Turkish Republic is actually a sign of limited state control in the Kurdish areas. In Morocco, what appears as weakness in the form of the state's need for support from social power centers and its limited resources to penetrate the everyday life of its society, may turn out to be its major strength. Such weakness may force the state to be more flexible and can make it more capable of preventing conflict and sustaining stability than states that are considered to have higher institutional/coercive and autonomous power. As the following chapters will show, in the face of the emergence of a new Berber elite and a growing Berber movement, the Moroccan state resorted to a wider range of policies than the Turkish state, which helped it to manipulate and control the movement better, curtailing its potential to present a major challenge to the regime. The examples of Morocco and Turkey show the highly contextual and relative character of states' capacities and the difficulty of assigning fixed labels to states.

Finally, this study underlines that the institutional and ideological legacies of states from previous periods matter for the forms of state and nation formation. Despite the Turkish state's emphasis on a radical break from the Ottoman past, the Ottoman reforms of state centralization and Westernization had significant consequences for the ability of the founders of the Turkish state to undertake a series of reforms in accordance with the vision they had for society. That vision, of a strictly homogeneous nation that "would speak one single language, think and feel alike," was also shaped by the lessons that the founders of the Turkish Republic took from the rapid disintegration of the multi-ethnic and multi-religious

Ottoman Empire.[19] In Morocco, the historical legacy was a weak dynasty and a strong tribal society coupled with the colonial experience. The monarchy's alliance with and cooptation of tribal power centers, its endorsement of gradual social change, and its recreation of Moroccan authenticity and traditional values were very much related to the institutional and social configurations that were inherited from the pre-colonial and colonial periods.

My approach draws on the "state in society" approach (Migdal 2001; Migdal *et al.* 1994), which calls for a more ethnographic study of the state and a more balanced account of the relationship between state and society. Although the theoretical framework of this study is built on the state-centered understanding of national identity formation, my analysis departs from the literature in one important aspect. Major theoretical models of state-led nationalism reify the state and take it as a coherent actor. During my research I was sensitive to the non-monolithic nature of the state and examined the practices of officials at different levels of the state. As Hansen and Stepputat (2001, 16) suggest: "As modern forms of governmentality penetrate and shape human life in unprecedented ways, the practices and sites of governance have also become ever more dispersed, diversified, and fraught with internal inconsistencies and contradictions." I tried to understand these internal contradictions, whenever my data allowed. Rather than paying attention to only the decisions of state leaders and legislators at the state's center, I examined how local officials implemented policies, sometimes in ways that were unintended by the state elite. I realized that how policies were implemented on the ground was as influential as decisions made at the state's center in shaping the general nation-building process.

During my fieldwork I realized the importance of the interactive process between state and social actors and their mutually transformative relationship. Policies are shaped as a result of the conflicts, struggles, and negotiations between different state actors as well as between local officials and citizens on the ground. Minority groups influence the formulation and implementation of state policies as they interact with the state, through their demands and strategies. For instance, I show how the seemingly continuous Turkish state policies changed in subtle but important ways as a result of the Kurdish response over the years. My assertion does

---

[19] The quotation is from a speech that Şükrü Kaya, the minister of the interior, gave in parliament in 1934. For the whole speech, see *TBMM Zabıt Ceridesi*, June 14, 1934, pp. 140–141.

not necessarily mean that the Kurdish activists could change state policies in accordance with their own demands. On the contrary, as I discuss in the fourth chapter, Kurdish resistance that turned violent in the 1980s played an important role in turning the military-bureaucratic establishment into a more powerful political actor to the detriment of the civilian politicians, which in turn increased state oppression or impeded political solutions to the problem. Similarly, the support that the Moroccan state gave to the development of the Berber language in recent years had a lot to do with the informal interactions of Berber activists with people close to the palace circles. This study underlines the effects of complex and informal interactions at the ground level on the general formation of nation-building policies.

I take the concept of identity as a dynamic and fluid one. When I use the term "ethnic minority," I do not take it as a fixed entity with clear boundaries. As Brubaker (1996, 60) argues: "A national minority is not simply a group that is given by the facts of ethnic demography. It is a dynamic political stance, or, more precisely, a family of related yet mutually competing stances, not a static ethno-demographic condition." Not every individual speaking Kurdish or Berber would claim to be a member of a distinct minority. Similarly, not every ethnic activist demanding recognition of a distinct Kurdish or a Berber identity necessarily carries such a distinct identity. In addition, there is not a fixed claim to what it means to be a Kurd or a Berber. The content of ethnic identities is in flux, although they are perceived as real and given by those who hold them.[20]

This study examines Turkish and Moroccan state- and nation-building practices since the emergence of Turkey and Morocco in the international state system as independent nation-states, in 1923 and 1956, respectively. I chose these dates as starting points because it is after these dates that we see a systematic effort on the part of these states, through mass education, conscription, and the like, to foster national integration and homogenization. In both countries, I examine two major periods. The first involves the initial state- and nation-building period, which covers the years before the emergence of well-developed ethnic movements. While there were Kurdish and Berber rebellions in this period, they were temporary events rather than sustained and organized efforts with broad goals of social and political change. These periods are between 1923 and

---

[20] Laitin (1998, 20) writes about the "Janus-facedness" of identities that accounts for both the constructed and the primordialist nature of identities. Identities seem natural and given to those who hold them but they are adopted and constructed depending on social opportunities.

1950 in Turkey and between 1956 and 1980 in Morocco. In the second period, I examine state responses to the emergence of well-organized ethnic movements with identifiable goals. In the Turkish case, this covers the post-1950 era, while in the Moroccan case it covers the post-1980 period.

ORGANIZATION OF THE BOOK

In the next chapter I examine the Turkish state- and nation-building strategies during the single-party era (1923–1950) and the ways in which state intrusion into Kurdish daily life escalated into military conflict. Drawing heavily on the local administrative reports coming from the Kurdish areas, this chapter analyzes the state's attempts to establish authority in Kurdish areas, its attacks on Kurdish local authorities, and its project of transforming the Kurds into "civilized, secular Turks." I analyze day-to-day interactions of local bureaucrats with Kurdish leaders and society, the state's detribalization efforts, and its responses to Kurdish revolts. It underlines how the Turkish state's project of molding the Kurdish society and individuals in a highly comprehensive manner, from language and dress to people's tastes, daily behavior, loyalties, and values, planted the first seeds of Turkish state–Kurdish conflict.

In Chapter 3, I examine the Moroccan monarchy's consolidation of power and its strategies of social control in the first decades after its independence, from 1956 to 1980. I discuss how these strategies of state-building shaped its relations with the Berber-speaking population and its approach to nation-building. I argue that the monarchy's alliance with Berber rural power centers foreclosed the possibilities of a large-scale transformative nation-building project and a high level of state intrusion into the Berber areas. I also discuss the ways in which the monarchy imagined its nation, its ambivalence about ethnic diversity, and what its discourse and policies about Moroccanness implied for the Berber-speakers. The monarchy defined Moroccanness primarily by Muslim identity and left room for the expression of Berber identity in private and in public, as long as such expression did not imply a political project. Such an approach, I argue, delayed the politicization of Berber identity and kept it within the confines of a cultural movement.

The second half of the book examines the evolutions of modern Kurdish and Berber ethnic movements and the states' responses to them. The main aim of Chapter 4 is to explain how and why the Kurdish movement gradually radicalized, found appeal with the Kurdish masses, and became a major threat to the Turkish Republic. It first discusses the abandonment of the "makeover" project and the state's withdrawal from regulating Kurdish daily life with the transition to multi-party politics in 1950. The low level of state intervention in the Kurdish areas brought relative quiet among the Kurdish masses. The Kurdish mobilization during the two decades after the transition to democracy resembled today's Berber movement: it was highly fragmented, its demands largely revolved around cultural rights, and its appeal remained limited among the majority of Kurds. The turning point in state–Kurdish relations was the 1980 military coup. The chapter discusses the effects of another set of "extreme makeover" projects coupled with increased state intrusion and indiscriminate repression in the Kurdish areas after the coup. It analyzes how everyday bans on the cultural expressions of Kurdishness, in dress, speech, music, and the like, increasingly politicized their meaning and helped transform the Kurdish movement into a full-fledged form of nationalism with support from the Kurdish masses. The chapter concludes with a discussion of the Turkish state's accommodations of Kurdish linguistic and cultural demands in the 2000s and their mixed consequences.

In Chapter 5, I examine how the Moroccan state's response to the rise of the Berber ethnic movement from the 1980s onward preserved its conciliatory tone and limited aims for cultural rights. I discuss the Moroccan state's use of selective repression, cooptation, and accommodation of the movement's basic demands. I argue that the ambiguity of the nationalist ideology made official concessions, at least at the discursive level, easier than in the Turkish case. The incremental concessions to the movement, mostly in the form of symbolic gestures rather than real policy changes, worked to lower the tension between the state and the Berber activists. The activists' increasing hopes that their demands were negotiable led them to be much more open to conciliation than the Kurdish activists. The chapter also discusses the monarchy's attempts at cooptation of the Berber movement by integrating its representatives into state channels. Such cooptation helps the monarchy to control the movement and to weaken and marginalize its more radical faction.

The Conclusion summarizes the main arguments of the book, discusses recent developments in Turkey and Morocco that relate to the Kurdish and Berber movements, and reviews the book's main theoretical implications.

2

Policies of "extreme makeover"

State–Kurdish relations in the early Turkish Republic

One day in the mid-1940s, Sıdıka Avar, accompanied by members of the Turkish gendarmerie, visited a small Kurdish village in the mountains to convince the villagers to send their daughters to her boarding school. Avar was the director of the Elazığ Girls' Institute, which was founded on Atatürk's orders after the Kurdish rebellion in Dersim in 1937. Its mission was to educate girls and to disseminate the Turkish language in a region where the majority of girls were not sent to school and the majority of the population did not speak Turkish.[1] She began explaining to a group of villagers the purpose of the school. A man interrupted her: "They will be given to men in Ankara and Elazız without marriage," referring to why he thought the state wanted to recruit the girls to the school. Avar explained that this was impossible, showing them the students she brought with her as examples. "The government takes them to defile the Kurdish seed," said another. Avar tried to convince them that the state did not interfere in issues related to marriage, considering it a private matter that was the decision of the parents. She said:

> The government sent me so that you see who educates your girls. In our school in Elazız, there are 16 female teachers like me. A big school with its doctor, cook, and workers is established for your girls. The state finances it completely, sends us to you to introduce the school, and you are still reluctant to give your girls. The city folks beg us to take their girls.

A villager replied, "We are satisfied with our condition. What will the state do by educating our girls?" Avar explained the importance of

---

[1] The school also recruited many girls who were orphaned during the Dersim rebellion.

educating girls for the well-being of families. "What is the government's advantage out of this?" asked another. "Why does the state care if I live well or not?" Irritated, Avar explained, "Each household is a child of the state, the government. If there is no family, can there be a nation? If there is no nation, can there be a state? Therefore, states are based on nations, nations on families, and families on individuals." After a while, Avar's students started to explain their school in two different Kurdish dialects. Seeming unconvinced, one villager said, "Well, lady, we don't have any girls in this village. Will the state take them by force?" Another jumped in, "Don't they think that if the state tries to take our girls by force, there will be a rebellion here?" These remarks infuriated Avar. She reminded her audience of the army's power and how it crushed the previous rebellions in the region. The next morning, Avar found an empty village, as all the villagers had gone to work in the fields before she woke up. She left without recruiting any girls for the school (Avar 2004, 168–172).

Avar's encounter with the villagers gives an accurate glimpse of state–Kurdish relations in the early republican period. During the authoritarian single-party era, which lasted from 1923 until 1950, this relationship can be defined as an uneasy encounter between a modernist, transformative state, which strove to regulate and reform the daily lives of its citizens, and a minority ethnic group, which was accustomed to a considerable degree of autonomy in managing its affairs. After the establishment of the republic in 1923, the Turkish state under the leadership of Mustafa Kemal Atatürk and his party, the Republican People's Party (RPP), carried out an ambitious program of state centralization and nation-building. The state aimed at imposing its direct rule over the society, to dominate it without any intermediaries. It also aimed to create a homogeneous nation, but this attempt went beyond the creation of an official, national history, the dissemination of one common language, and the creation of certain national symbols such as national holidays. The state elite sought an "extreme makeover" of the society, dictating the dos and don'ts of daily life, in accordance with the norms of Western modernism, to create the new national subject. As the state elite adopted a thick definition of Turkishness, how people dressed, how they looked physically, what language they spoke, and how they presented themselves in public space became objects of state regulation in the early republican era.

The state's objectives turned out to be the most ambitious and comprehensive in the Kurdish areas compared to the other regions as it encountered not only the largest linguistic minority there, but also deeply rooted tribal and religious solidarities. Kurds held the capacity for resistance to state domination as the local hierarchy made collective action against the state easier. The rough terrain of the Kurdish regions presented another layer of challenge to state expansion. Yeğen (2007, 123) underlines "that their political loyalty was to the tribe; that they would not perform military service; that they were not so enthusiastic in paying taxes to the central power; that they were ignorant. These were the 'facts' perceived by Turkish nationalism when it looked at the Kurds and the territory inhabited by them." The state rulers perceived the strong authority of the local leaders such as religious sheikhs and tribal chiefs over the population to be an indication of backwardness as well as a serious constraint against establishing state authority. In the eyes of the state elite, these regions were associated with religious conservatism and reactionary politics, economic underdevelopment, socio-cultural backwardness, lawlessness, and an unruly population that was not familiar with state authority. In a typical manner, one state official described the Kurds in 1941 as "a population, which the sheikhs of religious brotherhoods and sects and tribal aghas deprived of human law and kept away from civilization by attaching them to superstitions, false beliefs, and totems for centuries."[2] An RPP deputy wrote that Kurds had a character that "is brusque, selfish, timid, gets angry easily, kills easily, and worships only power."[3] In many official reports the Kurdish areas were referred to as "culturally underdeveloped areas" or as "provinces of deprivation." To achieve control, the state elite saw it as necessary to emancipate this population from the bondage of tribal and religious loyalties and to assimilate them into Turkishness. Therefore, Kurds became the main targets of the state's transformative project.

Turkish state policies aimed at a wide range of changes in Kurdish self-perception, behavior, values, habits, and lifestyles during the first three decades of the Turkish Republic. The highly comprehensive and intrusive nature of Turkish nation-building policies and the superiority in force that was displayed in its quashing of rebellions, however, does not mean that the government was successful in putting every policy into practice. What the Turkish state enjoyed in the Kurdish areas during the first three decades of the republic was at best a "dispersed domination," in Joel Migdal's words (2001, 100). There was clearly a wide gap between

---

[2] BCA 490.01-1003.874.1, Hozat People's House Report, Muş Region Inspector Münir Soykam to RPP General Secretariat, April 21, 1941, p. 23. Quotations from Turkish state documents throughout the chapter have been translated by the present author.

[3] BCA 490.01-1015.916.4, Maraş Deputy H. Reşit Tankut to RPP General Secretariat, October 16, 1940, p. 2.

what the state wanted to do and what the state actually *could do* in the Kurdish regions. Some of the policies dictated from the state's center were completely ignored and others were, at best, half-heartedly followed at the local level. The center neither had complete control over its officials nor had the necessary quality of manpower and financial resources to transform the region. Many policies had unintended results. However, this failure does not mean that the policies were inconsequential. The Kemalist civilizing mission inspired many state bureaucrats and the urban, educated strata of the population, who acted as the eager missionaries of Kemalism.[4] Their enthusiasm, active mobilization, and efforts to disseminate the new official ideology in institutions like the People's Houses made the state a visible, intrusive, and, most of the time, a distasteful entity in people's daily lives. The single party founded the People's Houses in 1932 as cultural centers that would spread the ideals of the regime to the masses. From 1940 onward these institutions were established in the rural areas under the name of "People's Chambers." By 1946, there were 76 People's Houses and 759 People's Chambers operating in the Eastern and Southeastern provinces.[5]

Coupled with increased coercive measures as a result of the militarization of the Kurdish regions after the rebellions, the Turkish state managed to intervene much more in the private sphere of Kurdish society than the Ottoman state had. The comprehensive transformative policies and increased state intrusion deeply challenged the authority of local power centers and the dominant value system of Kurdish society. The consequence was a highly confrontational relationship between the Kurds and the Turkish state in the first decades of the republic and the formation of a collective memory that rests on the everyday grievances and fears of the Kurdish masses.

Kurdish nationalism was not an already existing, significant political force at the beginning of the Turkish Republic. Although the idea of Kurdish nationalism emerged at the end of the Ottoman Empire as a response to the empire's disintegration, it was neither a prevalent

---

[4] Kemalism refers to a set of principles that Mustafa Kemal Atatürk and his circle developed in guiding the establishment of the new Turkey. There were six main principles: republicanism, nationalism, populism, étatism, secularism, and reformism. The Turkish constitutions define Kemalism as the official doctrine of the political system. For a discussion on Kemalism, see İnsel (2001).
[5] The numbers were compiled from Erdem and Erez (1963). By the end of 1951, the year that the Democratic Party dissolved them, there were a total of 478 Houses and 4,322 Chambers all over the country (Zürcher 2004, 107).

ideology among the Kurdish masses nor constituted a coherent set of ideas and aims. As Janet Klein (2007) emphasizes, the Kurdish societies and clubs that were formed at the end of the Ottoman Empire used the language of nationalism without necessarily meaning secession or autonomy based on a separate Kurdish identity. Most Kurdish organizations were Ottomanists and advocated the preservation of the multi-ethnic character of the Ottoman Empire. While the Kurdish elites who lived and organized in the center of the empire aimed at the education and modernization of Kurdish society and at countering the negative image of the Kurds, the Kurdish clubs in the provinces were formed to revive the local Kurdish notables' power that was threatened by the growing centralization of the empire. According to Klein (2007, 146), "Kurdish nationalism emerged as one possible future political arrangement for the Kurds, neither as a cause nor a direct result of imperial disintegration, but rather, as one of several responses to it, and particularly to its state-building aftermath." It is the contention of this study that Kurdish demands became nationalist over time and Kurdish nationalism became a mass political movement after the establishment of the Turkish Republic, as a reaction to the type of policies that the Turkish state pursued. This is not to deny that the Turkish state policies at the beginning of the republic were informed by the state elite's fear of Kurdism and the possible separatist tendencies among the Kurds. The state elite was concerned about the nationalist potential of the Kurdish ethnic identity, along with other ethnic identities in the country, and formulated policies in response to such concern. But Kurdish nationalism was not the natural outcome of Kurdish ethnic identity and was not a full-fledged force when the republic was established. As Brubaker and Laitin (1998, 428) point out, there is a tendency among scholars to see "ethnicity at work everywhere," to overestimate the ethnic factor in explaining violent conflicts: "Today, the ethnic frame is immediately and widely available and legitimate; it imposes itself on, or at least suggests itself to, actors and analysts alike ... Today, we – again, actors and analysts alike – are no longer blind to ethnicity, but we may be blinded by it." In this chapter, I call attention to the multiple arenas of the Kurdish–state conflict and argue that the confrontation during the initial periods of the Turkish Republic was much more complicated than being solely an ethnic problem. Apart from being a conflict related to the forceful assimilation of an ethnic group, it was also related to attempts to establish state authority in a hierarchical rural society that had a long history of autonomy, that was heavily armed, and that lived in rough areas that were hard for the state to reach.

This chapter begins with an analysis of how the Turkish state consolidated power by trying to eliminate local centers of power in the Kurdish regions. It then focuses on state intrusions in Kurdish private life to transform Kurds into modern, Westernized Turks. The analysis here relies on an extensive use of primary documents from the Prime Minister's Republican Archives in Ankara. Some of these documents are reports written by RPP parliamentarians, who traveled in the Eastern provinces to inspect the working of state institutions and to gather information about the general political atmosphere of the region. Others consist of reports and letters sent to the state's center by the members of the People's Houses, the Inspectors General, and citizens living in the Eastern provinces.[6] These documents provide invaluable information to understand the range of state objectives and practices in different levels of the state. As they were mostly internal documents, they contain detailed information on the extent to which the state officials could implement the policies they had in mind and the several problems they encountered in pursuing their aims.

STATE VERSUS THE LOCAL ELITES: STATE-BUILDING AND KURDISH RESISTANCE

The problem of establishing state sovereignty and ensuring people's conformity to state laws was a much more difficult task in the Kurdish regions than in other parts of the country. The official aim of the new regime was to establish an unmediated relationship with its citizens. This required weakening of local autonomy, which proved to be a difficult and conflict-prone process due to a combination of certain characteristics of the Kurdish areas. The strong local centers of power, such as the tribal leaders and religious sheikhs, the region's long history of autonomy, its rough and sparsely settled territory, and the existence of an armed population posed serious constraints on the ability of the central authority to reach these areas and achieve state centralization. Furthermore, the region included frontiers with Turkey's neighbors. Making people recognize the newly drawn state boundaries after the dissolution of the Ottoman Empire was a problem that the new regime had to deal with

---

[6] Inspectorates General were regional governorships that presided over all military and civilian institutions. They ruled over areas that were considered to present a threat to state security. The Kurdish areas were administered by Inspectorates General from 1928 until their dissolution in 1953. For more, see Koçak's (2003) study on the Inspectorates General.

in the region. Kurdish economic interaction that used to exist with cities such as Aleppo, Damascus, and Baghdad in the pre-republican period continued in the form of smuggling (Yeğen 1996, 222–223). Illegal border crossings by nomadic tribes, bandits, fugitives, and even ordinary citizens who wished to see their family members on the other side of the border were quite common in the Eastern provinces. Many of the state reports written during this period raised the issue of Kurdish rebels and outlaws who could easily cross the boundaries and find refuge in neighboring states, where they were supported by kin groups or relatives. Turkish authorities also suspected that the French and the British used the smugglers for espionage.[7]

During the first two decades of the republic, the founders of the state worked hard to impose direct rule and establish the state's monopoly of law over the Kurdish regions. The state elite saw the presence of strong local leadership in the Kurdish regions as the root cause of the state's low administrative capacity in Eastern Turkey. Despite the policies of the Ottoman state, particularly of the government of the Committee of Union and Progress after 1908, to empower the central state at the expense of tribal leaders, the Eastern provinces hardly went under the total control of the government. At the beginning of the republican era, the Kurdish tribal leaders still could maintain their pockets of self-rule with their own laws and well-armed militias. The long history of autonomy in the region, the ability of tribal leaders and religious sheikhs to mobilize armed forces and collect tribute from the peasants, as well as the relative insecurity of the region caused by tribal conflicts, banditry, and arbitrary and private use of violence, were major concerns for the state elite (Üngör 2011, 12, 24). Many official reports prepared during the single-party era portrayed the Kurdish regions as feudal and the authority of tribal leaders and sheikhs over the population to be much stronger than the state's.[8] An inspector sent to the Kurdish regions reported: "These ignorant people respect and follow the tribal leaders and are bound to them like slaves."[9] "Tribesmen consider state officials towards whom they do not feel any allegiance like a temporary trouble. They are always hypocritical towards

---

[7] For instance, see the proceedings of the 1936 meeting of the Inspectorates General in Varlık (2010, 41, 95, 205, 253–254).

[8] See, for instance, Mustafa Abdülhalik's report titled "Tedkik Seyahati 14 Eylül 1341" in Yıldırım (2011, 10).

[9] BCA 490.01-998.856.1, Report on the inspection of the People's House in Hakkari, Bitlis Region Inspector and Tokat Deputy Hasip Aytuna to RPP General Secretariat, November 10, 1942, p. 87.

state officials. As the government's prestige and power decreases, the tribal leaders' prestige goes up," wrote Kazım Karabekir in 1923 (quoted in Turan 2011, 69). Similarly, the First Inspector-General Abidin Özmen stated in his report in 1936: "A Kurd is not used to a regular state order. For him, the strongest person is the tribal leader, the agha of the village, the man who is the owner of the field that he cultivates and of the ox that he uses" (Varlık 2010, 112). Detribalization, disarming the population, establishing impermeable borders, sedentarization of the nomadic tribes,[10] collecting taxes, and sustaining public order constituted the main objectives of state-building in the region.

The Turkish state elite's deep suspicions of Kurdish social power centers partly stemmed from a widespread anxiety over territorial integrity. The fragmentation of the Ottoman Empire and the increasing involvement of the Western powers in its domestic affairs during the nineteenth century created a sensitivity among the Turkish state elite about the fragility of territorial integrity (Zarakol 2011). The Kurdish tribal leaders' and religious sheikhs' loyalty to the new regime was suspect when the new regime was founded. This was because at the end of the Ottoman Empire, some of the Kurdish chiefs and notables experimented with the idea of establishing an independent Kurdish state or an autonomous Kurdish region with the backing of the British and the French. As Hakan Özoğlu (2001) underlines, the Kurdish leaders' flirtations with the idea of a separate Kurdish state through outside support were attempts to recover their past legacy and power in their regions of influence when the end of the Ottoman Empire seemed inevitable. The Treaty of Sèvres, which was signed between the Ottoman Empire and the Allies at the end of World War I, stipulated the establishment of an autonomous Kurdish region in Anatolia, which strengthened the fears of the founders of the republic. Although during the War of Independence Kurds largely supported the national resistance movement, with the establishment of the republic, the state elite considered an alliance between the Western powers (particularly the French in Syria and the British in Iraq) and the Kurdish local authorities a strong possibility. The Kurdish tribal presence along the Syrian and Iraqi borders exacerbated the state elite's fears and caused them to perceive the existence of Kurdish strongmen as a serious security threat against the regime.

---

[10] The nomadic lifestyle presents a direct challenge to modern states' aims of achieving direct social control and resource mobilization. For more on the history of state attempts to turn Kurdish nomads into settled peasants, see chapter 4 in Kasaba (2009).

Sheikh Said's rebellion in 1925 sent a warning signal to the state elite, confirming their fears of the strength of local power centers. The rebellion was a direct challenge to the abolition of the sultanate and the caliphate in 1923 as well as the new regime's aspirations for centralization and Turkification. Stemming from both religious and ethnic motives, the rebellion was initially planned by a Kurdish nationalist organization named Azadi, which was established in 1923 by a group of Kurdish intellectuals and officers of the Ottoman army. Azadi had nationalistic objectives aiming at an independent Kurdistan with the help of foreign assistance. The organization's dissatisfaction with the new state stemmed from the official emphasis on Turkish identity as well as the abolishment of the caliphate. However, devoid of any strong links with the Kurdish masses, Azadi's ability to undertake a large-scale revolt was highly limited without the support of local centers of power. It was the Kurdish ulema that played the most important role in this revolt. Religious clergy had both the material and spiritual power to mobilize a large number of people. A religious discourse more than a nationalist one was more appealing to the rural Kurdish masses whose resentments were fresh as a result of the recent secularization measures of the state (Van Bruinessen 1992, 281–283). In the eyes of the Kurds, the abolishment of the caliphate removed the most important bond between the Turks and the Kurds and made the state an anti-religious entity.[11]

In the end, it was the influential Nakşibendi sheikh, Sheikh Said, who assumed the leadership of the first Kurdish uprising against the Turkish Republic. His propaganda largely rested on religious rhetoric. He invited Kurdish tribes to join the rebellion in the name of jihad against the Ankara government. "Islam was the basis of unity between the Turks and the Kurds. The Turks broke it. The Kurds now have to secure their own future," he stated (quoted in Bozarslan 1997, 134). He demanded the restoration of the Sharia and the caliphate and declared that killing one Turk was worth more than killing seventy infidels according to the religious law (Kirişci and Winrow 1997, 104). He had a strong influence on the Zazaki-speaking tribes in his area and managed to mobilize around

---

[11] One of the best indicators of how the Kurds perceived the new regime comes from Sıdıka Avar's memoir (2004, 147). She recounts that the Kurdish villagers did not want to send their daughters to school because they thought that the state wanted their girls not for education but to marry them to non-Muslims, particularly to the Russians and the British. This widespread rumor suggests that the Kurds perceived the secularization measures as a betrayal of Muslim fraternity and thought of these measures as an indication of the state's collaboration with European powers.

15,000 men against 52,000 government forces (Olson 1989, 125–126).[12] The rebellion continued for about three months and ended after the capture of Sheikh Said in April 1925. The suppression of the rebellion incurred heavy expenses by the state, as it cost almost one-third of the government's budget (Bozarslan 1988, 121). The alleged involvement of some of the local members of the RPP as well as state officials and members of the gendarmerie in the rebellion amplified the state elite's insecurities and confirmed their fears about the power of the local Kurdish leadership (Turan 2011, 81–94). After the rebellion, central control over state functionaries serving in the Kurdish areas became an issue of crucial importance for the leaders of the state.

The way the government dealt with the Sheikh Said rebellion underlines the official determination to establish the state's absolute authority in the region. The government announced martial law and established Independence Tribunals with the authority to enforce executions of death sentences swiftly. Üngör (2011, 127–129) writes that indiscriminate counter-insurgency warfare resulted in thousands of fatalities among the villagers. Sheikh Said and forty-seven leading Kurds were executed; influential Kurdish families were deported to the West; and the parliament passed the "Law on the Maintenance of Order," which gave the government the right to ban any organization or publication that was considered a threat to law and order. This law allowed the government to consolidate its monopoly of rule and pass its future radical reforms without encountering overt political opposition in the parliament.[13] Amnesty was out of the question. On the contrary, the government tried to intimidate or suppress Kurdish leading figures who might challenge the regime in the future. As a result, many Kurdish elites and intellectuals whose direct involvement in the rebellion could not be established were arrested. The court prosecuted 5,010 people and sentenced 420 to death (Üngör 2011, 130–131). In September, the government undertook a full-scale attack against religious authority and closed down the religious brotherhoods and dervish orders nationwide.

---

[12] The Kurds did not show a unitary response to Said's rebellion. The Alevi Kurds, for instance, did not participate in the revolt, and some Alevi tribes even helped the state forces, as they were highly skeptical of a Sunni sheikh's promises. Non-tribal Kurds and urban notables also did not support the rebellion. For more information, see Van Bruinessen (1992, 293–295). The Alevi community is a heterodox religious minority that is related to Shi'a Islam. The majority of Kurds in Turkey are Sunni, but a significant minority of Kurds are Alevi.

[13] For more on the Law on the Maintenance of Order, see Zürcher (1998, 179–181).

The Sheikh Said rebellion resulted in the new regime turning its attention more to the Kurdish regions. It led to increased state intrusion into the region to weaken the authority of local power centers. The government used the rebellion as an opportunity to deport powerful Kurdish families, tribal leaders, and religious sheikhs from the region to Western Turkey. Even some tribal leaders who supported the state forces against the rebels were deported (Kaya 2003, 52).[14] One official document written on the Kurds soon after Sheikh Said's rebellion underlined that the main cause of the Kurdish unrest had to do with the tribal structure and it was therefore necessary to emancipate people from the bondage of tribal leaders and religious sheikhs in order to draw them closer to the state. The author of the report advocated the necessity to go beyond ad hoc measures through the adoption of a law on tribes.[15] Ahmet Demirel (2011) finds that the profiles of the deputies representing the Kurdish region in the parliament changed drastically after the Sheikh Said rebellion. Before the rebellion three-quarters of the deputies representing the region were born in the region. In the aftermath of the rebellion, the number of deputies who were native to the region dropped sharply. After the 1927 elections, the percentage of the parliamentarians born in the Kurdish areas was 34.7, and it fell as low as 17 percent in the mid-1930s. Demirel (2011, 92) argues that the Sheikh Said rebellion was a turning point in the history of the single-party period. After the rebellion, localism in the parliament sharply declined. The single party increasingly nominated bureaucrats and former military officers who were born in the Western provinces to represent the Kurdish provinces. The change in the parliament indicates the gradual centralization of the state to the detriment of local power holders in the Kurdish areas.

During official deliberations on the formation of administrative cadres in the Kurdish regions, how to minimize the risk of a possible collaboration between state functionaries and tribal leaders constituted an important topic of discussion among the state elite. The bureaucratic expansion came at a cost of not only increased conflict with the locals but also the increased difficulty of controlling the acts of the state employees. In his 1943 report, the First Inspector-General Avni Doğan called attention to development of close relations between state employees and local

---

[14] For a detailed account of the aftermath of the Sheikh Said rebellion and names of some of the deportees, see Üngör (2011, 133–145).
[15] See "Hülasa: Kürtlere Dair," dated May 7, 1926, in Yıldırım (2011, 64). The author of the report is unknown.

authority figures and its detrimental effects on the imposition of state dominance over society:

> Almost all tribal leaders are smart, sociable, and ingenious people. In order to maintain their authority over the people, they induce the state officials to profit from illegitimate activities. In the provinces, they resort to every trick to establish relations with the provincial administrator, public prosecutor, judge, and chief of the gendarmerie and to achieve the friendship of at least one or two of them. If they cannot succeed, they resort to complaints and calumny. The tribal leaders seem loyal to the state in normal times. But a majority of them participated in almost all of the rebellions that took place in the East. They know about foreign propaganda and provocations and always retain their connections with Syria, Iraq, and Iran.
>
> (Quoted in Bayrak 1994, 251)

Among the higher cadres of the administration, there had always been a deep mistrust of state employees who were native to the region. Lower-level bureaucrats' support for Kurdism or for religious opposition movements and their close relationships with influential figures in the region were constant worries of the central authority. Consequently, the state elite tried to fill state cadres in the East with those coming from the Western provinces.[16] Government employees were expected to stay aloof from the societies they governed. It was believed that non-local government officials could preserve state autonomy better than those who were native to the region.

Military suppression of the Sheikh Said rebellion and efforts at strengthening state authority hardly sustained stability in the region. The state's challenge to local authority structures resulted in serious armed conflict that would last more than a decade. Until 1930, fourteen more rebellions followed Sheikh Said's.[17] Among the most serious was a series of three rebellions in the Ağrı province around the region of Mount Ararat. The final phase of the revolt culminated in 1930 and was led by İhsan Nuri, a deserter from the Turkish army, who escaped to Syria at the time of the Sheikh Said rebellion. The revolt was also supported by a Kurdish nationalist organization, Khoybun, based in Syria. The manpower and arms for the rebellion were once more provided by the tribal leaders, who resented the state's encroachment on their authority. The revolt was ultimately suppressed by the army in September 1930 through the mobilization of 66,000 soldiers and the use of 100 airplanes (Van

[16] See Varlık (2010, 73, 115).
[17] For a complete list of the rebellions, see Turan (2011, 78, fn 172).

Bruinessen 1992, 291; Bozarslan 2008, 340). Another wave of deportations followed the Ağrı rebellions. Between 1920 and 1932, 2,774 Kurds were moved to Western Turkey. Although the sheer numbers of people who were deported to the West were limited and based on security concerns until the mid-1930s, the laws led to widespread rumors that the Kurds would share the fate of the Armenians.[18] Harsh security measures increased Kurdish resentment and suspicion towards the state (Çağaptay 2006, 86, 88). As Charles Tilly (1992) has suggested, war-making also expanded the state's bureaucratic apparatus and led to further state intrusion into the Kurdish areas.

The establishment of three Inspectorates General in the Eastern provinces between 1928 and 1936 signified this bureaucratic expansion. These were regional governorships with extraordinary powers over all administrative and military institutions within their regions. The main objective in the establishment of these institutions was to pacify the turbulent areas by creating a centralized administrative apparatus that would only be accountable to the government. The inspectorates were created to act in a swift manner militarily in case of an armed opposition and coordinated the state's efforts to expand its power. The first inspectorate was established after the Sheikh Said rebellion in 1928. In the 1930s three other inspectorates were established and, with the exception of the Thrace Inspectorate, all others operated in provinces heavily populated by the Kurds (Çağaptay 2006, 47–48). One of the main tasks of the Inspectorates General was to establish the state's monopoly of violence by disarming the population. After 1923, the government started to collect arms from tribes, albeit with great difficulty as the Kurds were quite reluctant to surrender them to the state. According to a report sent to the Ministry of the Interior by the First Inspector-General, the tribes still had around 38,000 weapons in 1928. By 1932, the weapons that were collected within the territories of the First Inspectorate reached 23,000 (Koca 1998, 313). Clashes between tribes and security forces took place largely while the arms were being collected (Koca 1998, 376).

The Inspectorates General were also responsible for coordinating official policies that aimed at detribalizing the region. Policies of resettlement constituted the most important attempt to weaken the region's tribal structure. These measures not only aimed at assimilating the Kurds by dispersing them among the Turks, but also were used to uproot the

---

[18] See the 1936 Report of the Fourth Inspector-General Abdullah Alpdoğan in Varlık (2010, 142).

influential landlords and tribal leaders from their homelands to establish an unmediated relationship between the central authority and the Kurdish masses. In 1934, the parliament passed another law of resettlement, but this time it was more comprehensive and ambitious in its objectives than the previous attempts. The law stated that tribes were not recognized as legal entities and that all property rights acquired by the tribal leaders before the enactment of the law were null and void. It aimed at Turkifying, modernizing, and detribalizing the region through a large-scale resettlement policy by dividing tribes and the families of the tribal leaders and by mixing Kurds with Turkish-speakers.

The Resettlement Law of 1934 divided the country into three zones. The first zone was allocated to those who spoke Turkish and who were of Turkish culture and ethnicity/descent. Tribes, nomads, and people who were not part of the Turkish culture, including the Kurds, could not be settled into these areas. The second zone consisted of areas whose "Turkishness" needed to be enhanced and were largely meant for those people who should adopt the Turkish culture. In other words, these were the areas where Kurds, along with tribal populations and non-Turkish immigrants, would be settled. The aim was to spread the non-Turkish populations around to Turkish villages and towns to assimilate them into the Turkish culture. Finally, a third zone was designated as areas that would be closed to settlement for security reasons. Without a decision of the Council of Ministers, no one would be allowed to settle in these areas, which were mainly in Eastern Turkey where the Kurdish rebellions had taken place.[19] The law also banned those whose mother tongue was not Turkish from forming villages or districts. Apart from its assimilationist intent, the law aimed at weakening the tribal structure. It gave the Ministry of the Interior the authority to settle nomadic tribes, to transfer tribal leaders, to confiscate their property, and to provide them with land and accommodations in their new locations of settlement. As a result of the law, the total number of Kurds who were moved to the West in the 1930s reached 25,831 people from 5,074 households (Çağaptay 2006, 90). Members of the same family were sent to different locations, and their property was confiscated and sold to landless peasants, immigrants, and sedentarized nomads (Üngör 2011, 156). The Surname Law that was passed in 1934 was also used to undermine the tribal structure. The law forbade surnames that were particular to tribes. Hüseyin Koca (1998,

---

[19] There is a large literature on the Resettlement Law of 1934. For detailed analyses of the law, see Çağaptay (2006, 88–90), Tekeli (1990), and Ülker (2008).

132) writes that the sons of some tribal leaders were given different last names than their fathers' and that each son received a distinct last name to break up the tribal structure.[20]

It was in the rough and mountainous terrain of Dersim, where the population shared a strong regional identity that set them apart from the rest of the Kurdish regions, that the state had particular difficulty in establishing its authority. The great majority in Dersim were Alevi Kurds who spoke a distinct form of the Zazaki language. Dersim's cultural distinctiveness, dispersed population, and difficult terrain, characterized by rocky mountains, narrow passes, and deep caves, made the expansion of central authority exceptionally hard. Dersim had been known for its defiance of the state and strong regional autonomy. Even though the Ottoman state attempted to take Dersim under central control through several military operations starting in the second half of the nineteenth century, it failed to achieve permanent domination as a result of its weak infrastructural power and World War I. After the Sheikh Said rebellion, the state elite began to show increasing concerns about Dersim and generated plans to control the region. Even the neutrality of the Alevi Kurds of Dersim or their active support of the Turkish army during Sheikh Said's rebellion did not curtail the state's aim to expand its direct control over the region. Government reports written on Dersim identified the region's well-armed population, long history of autonomy, strong tribal and religious leadership, poverty, lack of infrastructure, and general lawlessness as severe problems for the state (Watts 2000).

A book that was prepared by the General Command of the Gendarmerie underlines how seriously the top echelons of the state considered the Dersim question in the early 1930s.[21] The book provided a detailed survey of Dersim's history, geographic characteristics, and economic situation and discussed the condition of the state institutions operating in the region. It signified the state's attempt to gather systematic data on Dersim, or to make Dersim more "legible," in James Scott's (1998) terms, in order to prepare a major program of transforming the region. It listed Dersim's tribes with brief information on tribal leaders, their attitudes towards the state and their relations with other tribes as well as the amounts of arms each tribe held.[22] It also included several administrators' reports

---

[20] A local historian in Urfa, Müslüm Akalın, confirmed that at times sons of tribal leaders took different last names (email message to author, February 8, 2009). Nevertheless, no systematic data are available on how extensively and evenly this practice was enforced.
[21] This book is published in Yıldırım (2010, 1–266).
[22] According to the estimates of different state institutions, the total number of guns that the tribes of Dersim held ranged between 8,616 and 19,870. Ibid., pp. 122–123.

that contained their proposals to pacify the region. Deportation of the tribal and religious leadership to Western Turkey, redistributing their confiscated land to the peasants, collecting arms, sedentarizing the nomadic populations, settling the dispersed population in villages on the plains, destroying villages in inaccessible areas, suspending state employees local to the region from office, and constructing roads and railroads were the major proposals to buttress state authority.

In 1935, the government set up a separate legal and administrative system in Dersim to put its plans into force. As a result of the Tunceli Law, which the parliament passed in December, the former Dersim district was renamed the province of Tunceli. It was put under the authority of the newly created Fourth Inspectorate-General, which would be headed by a military commander with extraordinary powers, such as execution of death sentences and deportation of people. The Inspectorate-General coordinated attempts to disarm the population and started to build police stations, roads, bridges, and railway lines. These efforts presented a clear challenge to Dersim's de facto autonomy. A rebellion began in April 1937 under the leadership of an Alevi cleric, Seyit Rıza, when a group of Kurds destroyed a bridge and attacked a Turkish police station. Later, the revolting tribes issued an ultimatum to the government demanding that it reverse its increased interference in the region.[23] The rebels asked that they should be allowed to carry their guns, that the tribal leaders should be able to negotiate taxes with the government, and that no government institutions and gendarmerie posts should be established in Dersim. The mountainous terrain and poor conditions of transportation worked in favor of the rebels and the revolt took more than a year to crush with the mobilization of 25,000 soldiers (Çağaptay 2006, 111–112). Military operations continued until October 1938, after the execution of the chief rebel Seyit Rıza in November 1937.[24] The government undertook a massive campaign to detribalize and pacify the region by resettling families in different regions, to end banditry, and to collect arms from the population. Sporadic clashes between state and local forces continued throughout 1938 (Watts 2000). According to the recently declared official figures, 13,806 people were killed in military operations that included air strikes and the use of poison gas, and 11,683 people were deported from Dersim.[25] Not only people belonging

---

[23] Aygün (2011, 122) notes that only a small minority of tribes in Dersim revolted against the state.
[24] For an account of the capture and execution of Seyit Rıza, see Watts (2000, 23–25).
[25] These figures are based on official documents that Prime Minister Recep Tayyip Erdoğan revealed in the Turkish parliament in 2011 when he formally apologized for

the same tribe but also members of the same family were dispersed in different locations (Aygün 2011, 142–143). Military officers adopted girls from Dersim who were orphaned or had lost their families with the intention to assimilate them into Turkish culture.[26] The Dersim operation showed the state's perseverance and determination to extend its authority into remote peripheries and to stamp out the local centers of power with extreme use of violence.

Despite the state's suspicions about the tribal leaders, the relationship between the state and the tribes was an ambivalent one, shaped by the variable interests of both sides. While the Turkish state did not hesitate to ally with and use some of the Kurdish tribes for social control, especially during the times of rebellions, sectarian divisions and tribal conflicts led many tribal leaders to cooperate with the state against the revolting tribes. The Kurdish tribal leaders did not act uniformly during the times of rebellion. As Watts (2000, 8) states: "Many of Dersim's local Kurdish elites chose not to rebel but rather to cooperate with the government – a fact that should be viewed not as some kind of aberration or deviance from a Kurdish national norm but as evidence that Dersim's Kurds believed they might establish more than one kind of relationship with the new regime." Mutual interests led to negotiated settlements between Kurdish tribes and the state even during tranquil times. Negotiations and alliances would intensify when the RPP had to start competing with political opponents after the transition to the multi-party system in 1946. Political competition pushed the RPP to strengthen its thinly spread party organization in the Kurdish areas.[27] Nevertheless, during the single-party era such alliances were merely tactical and kept at a minimum. The slim representation of tribal leaders in the Turkish parliament starting with its second assembly in 1923 was one of the indicators that

---

the Dersim massacre. For more see, *Today's Zaman*, November 23, 2011, available at www.todayszaman.com/news-263658-pm-erdogan-apologizes-over-dersim-massacre-on-behalf-of-turkish-state.html (accessed August 10, 2013).

[26] In 2010 the story of these girls was made into a documentary, "İki Tutam Saç: Dersim'in Kayıp Kızları" (Two Locks of Hair: The Lost Girls of Dersim). For more information, see the website of the documentary, www.dersiminkayipkizlari.com (accessed August 10, 2013).

[27] As late as 1939, the RPP did not have branches in twelve predominantly Kurdish provinces, Ağrı, Bingöl, Bitlis, Diyarbakır, Elazığ, Hakkari, Mardin, Muş, Siirt, Tunceli, Urfa, and Van. Three of the previously opened branches (Van, Siirt, and Muş) were closed down because they did not work in conformity with the RPP's center. The party elite was skeptical about the participation of the Kurds within the RPP, particularly after the Sheikh Said rebellion (Turan 2011, 99–106).

the Kurdish–Kemalist strategic alliance, which formed during the War of Independence, had come to an end. Retired members of the military, the civilian bureaucracy, and professionals dominated the parliaments of the single-party period. Only six out of a total of 2,210 deputies serving in the parliaments between 1920 and 1957 were tribal leaders (Frey 1965, 80).

Increased state intrusion into the Kurdish areas and ambitious attempts to break the tribal structure did not necessarily lead to a successful transformation of the social structure of the region. The goal was too ambitious to be achieved in the short term before an economic transformation. As Belge (2011, 97) argues, kinship networks "have constituted an alternative reservoir of resistance to the state-building and nation-building projects of republican Turkey. Such resistance was not always motivated by Kurdish nationalism but sometimes by the instinct for survival in the face of an increasingly interventionist and repressive state and by an ethic of reciprocity that regulated social relations." The resettlement policies failed to impose a major transfer of land from Kurdish landowners and tribal leaders to the peasants due to its unanticipated results. In his report in 1934, the First Inspector-General Hilmi Ergeneli complained that the peasants to whom the lands were distributed were quite reticent in obtaining the deeds because they did not want to pay taxes for the land. The peasants were also financially dependent on the aghas for seeds and other equipment to cultivate the land and did not want to acquire land against the wishes of aghas (cited in Koca 1998, 419). Many landlords, whose lands were confiscated by the state, found a way to reacquire their property through their continuing authority over the peasants and their contacts in land registration offices (Belge 2011, 103). Having to compete with an opposition party forced the RPP to pass a comprehensive amnesty law in 1947, which allowed many of the deportees to return to their places of origin. Although these families found that their land had been confiscated and distributed, they reacquired them through different means. In some cases the state returned the land to those whom it perceived as harmless. Others received their lands back by paying small amounts to the current owners.[28] But most importantly, a large-scale land reform, which the state leaders frequently brought up, could not be initiated. The state did not want to undertake a destabilizing reform in the wake of World War II. Even though the parliament passed a land

---

[28] For more on the experiences of the deportees and how they reacquired their confiscated land upon their return, see Diken (2005, 219–221).

distribution law in 1945, very little land was actually distributed afterwards because the RPP had to take the opposition of the landowners seriously and appease them with the transition to multi-party politics in 1946 (Tezel 1982).

One consequence of the Kurdish revolts and the state's inability to achieve a structural transformation in the region was the heavy militarization of the area, which led to additional problems in its relations with the locals and hurt the efforts to elicit Kurdish allegiance to the regime. Dündar (1999, 103) notes that in provinces where Kurdish-speakers were found in great numbers, the number of army personnel was exceptionally high. According to the population census of 1927, 32,665 people declared that they were army members in Bitlis, Diyarbakır, Hakkari, Mardin, Van, Siirt, Beyazıt, and Kars.[29] Heavy reliance on military power in achieving social control intensified the arbitrary and abusive behavior of state officials and security forces. The reports of the RPP inspectors indicate that arbitrary, abusive, and unlawful acts by the gendarmerie were quite common. In addition, many reports pointed to the problem of gendarmerie members' private collection of wealth either through coercive practices or illicit partnerships with the locals. A parliamentary law of 1931 passed after the Ağrı rebellion prescribed that the state would not prosecute the security forces and state officials for operations aimed at suppressing the rebellion of 1930.[30] This shows that the state understood the severity of the violations and their illegality and yet chose to disregard them, which encouraged further, similarly arbitrary behavior.

Ali Reşat Göksidan, a parliamentarian from Hakkari, for instance, wrote in 1943 that people's complaints about the gendarmerie were a common problem in the Eastern provinces. "I have listened to many complaints about the gendarmerie from this vicinity's people who are very poor and whose benefit from land is only through vineyards. These complaints are about gendarmerie's practice of extorting produce from vineyards," he wrote. "Although people seem quiescent and compliant in their relations with the state, such compliance is based on fear rather than love (for the state)," he added.[31] Muzaffer Akpınar, an RPP parliamentarian from Balıkesir, who inspected the rural areas in the Erzincan district in 1939, wrote about the problem of bribery by state and military officials. He added that, although some soldiers who were involved

---

[29] Only the 1927 population census collected data on people's professions.
[30] The full text of the law can be found in Bucak (1991, 25–26).
[31] BCA 490.01-1001.866.2, Report on Mardin by Diyarbakır Inspector Ali Reşat Göksidan, December 13, 1943, pp. 8–10.

in corrupt activities were caught, the civilian courts refused to take their cases, claiming that it was a military matter. He stated that taxes were collected by extreme use of force, such as by whipping people. There were no investments in the region and that the places he visited suffered from extreme poverty and backwardness. "People shout 'the government is coming!' and they begin to flee when they see the gendarmerie and the tax-collector in the villages of Tortum," he wrote. "The people are quiescent and loyal. It is necessary to put an end to these situations. What a pity and shame!" he added.[32] Another RPP inspector who wrote a report on Hakkari stated that the gendarmerie constituted the main subject of complaints among the people. According to him, members of the gendarmerie acquired wealth through smuggling, obtained food supplies from poor peasants by force, and maltreated people:

In Hakkari Province today, there is a very serious problem of a corrupt gendarmerie organization that is in need of control. From the commanders to the privates, everyone has a strong desire to make money and their ill-treatment for this end pushes people away from the government, and leads them to make bitter and meaningful complaints like "the gendarmerie, instead of protecting us, steals from us like bandits."[33]

The inspector concluded that although people seemed quiescent, the chances of making them good citizens were slim as a result of the coercion of the gendarmerie and the influence of their kinfolk in Iraq. Similarly, Muhtar Ertan, a parliamentarian who visited Tunceli (Dersim), Bingöl, and Elazığ provinces in 1943 called attention to the frequent beatings by the gendarmerie. He wrote:

In order to make people approach the government and make them forget the painful memories of the past, the administrators should treat them with compassion. Our fellows should never forget that too much coercion and illegal treatment would create an undesired reaction from the people, who were indoctrinated by ignorance and harmful inculcation. Unfortunately, one runs frequently into the inappropriate behavior of some state officials and gendarmerie these days. People are very troubled by this.[34]

With the transition to the multi-party system, the RPP inspectors' and local party officials' concerns over the party's legitimacy in the region

---

[32] BCA 490.01-1206.229.1, Report on Erzincan region by Muzaffer Akpınar, February 19, 1939, p. 106.
[33] BCA 490.01-998.856.1, Report on Hakkari People's House by Bitlis Region Inspector Hasip A. Aytuna, November 10, 1942, p. 51.
[34] BCA 490.01-997.852.1, Report on Tunceli, Bingöl, and Elazığ by Elazığ Inspector Muhtar Ertan, October 18, 1943, p. 12.

increased. Their complaints about the security forces, particularly the gendarmerie, became more pronounced in the documents sent to the state's center. Militarization increased the level of the state's presence and intrusiveness in people's lives considerably, but to the detriment of Kurdish integration into the national domain. Although militarization eventually secured public order, it undermined efforts to build legitimacy for the new regime in the long term. The military repression and population deportations of the 1920s and 1930s are still strongly inscribed in the collective memory of the Kurds today and constitute the main stories of suffering and misery within the Kurdish nationalist narrative.[35]

FORGOTTEN TURKISHNESS: ASSIMILATION POLICIES IN THE EARLY REPUBLIC

The Turkish state's aim to centralize power and establish its sovereignty in the Kurdish region in opposition to the local centers of power gave it the autonomy to undertake a comprehensive nationalizing project. During the single-party era, the state carried out a series of ambitious policies to assimilate Kurds into a strictly defined understanding of Turkishness. The formulation and enforcement of these policies took place without much concern over the reactions of the tribal leaders and local religious authorities. Autonomy from local centers of power allowed the state to push for a highly comprehensive and intrusive nation-building process, which aimed at an "extreme makeover" of the Kurdish population. As a result, the Turkish state has interfered much more into the private sphere of Kurdish society than the Moroccan state did vis-à-vis the Berbers.

The Kemalist elite regarded the integration of non-Turkish-speaking Muslims into the Turkish national identity as possible because they thought that the minimum characteristics of a common culture were already present among the Muslim communities. Although the republic was founded as a strictly secular regime, it is a well-known paradox that Turkishness came to be determined primarily by Muslim identity in the eyes of the state elite as well as the general public. There has been a duality of Turkish citizenship as distinct from Turkishness. Not everyone who happened to be a Turkish citizen was considered a Turk. This was especially the case for non-Muslims. While non-Turkish Muslims, such as Kurds, could become Turks as long as they considered themselves to

---

[35] For some examples, see Arslan (2006), Bedirhan (1997), and Süphandağ (2001). On the development of the Kurdish historiographical discourse, see Bozarslan (2003).

be so and spoke Turkish, this was not so easy for the Greek, Armenian, and Jewish citizens of the Turkish Republic. They encountered different forms of discrimination at the official and social levels even when they embraced the Turkish national identity. Two reasons can be given to explain why Muslimhood was central to the definition of Turkishness. First, as Çağaptay (2006) argues, while the state elite excluded Islam as a religious faith from the public sphere, they conceived it as an important cultural element and a source of a similar lifestyle shared by the majority of the Anatolian population.[36] In addition, the social and economic transformations within the Ottoman Empire in the nineteenth century sharpened the differences between the Muslims and non-Muslims in terms of lifestyle and culture. Therefore the equation of Turkishness with Muslim identity had a strong appeal within the society at large. Second, non-Muslim citizens' loyalty to the Turkish state was suspect for the state elite. The collaboration of some Armenian groups with Russia during World War I and the Greek occupation of the Western coast during the War of Independence made non-Muslims potential enemy agents in their eyes.

The Kurdish revolts in the first two decades of the republic created doubts among many members of the state elite about the assimilability of Kurdish citizens into Turkishness. As Yeğen (2004, 65–66) argues, the assumed loyalty to the state could sometimes take precedence over religious identity in determining Turkishness. In general, however, the state elite perceived these revolts to be fomented by feudal elites, whose future loss of power would resolve the integration problem. Kurds were considered as potential Turks, like the other Muslim ethnic communities.[37]

Because of the secularist character of the regime, the state elite explicitly emphasized a common language, rather than religion, as the main element of the national identity in formation. The language policy encompassed a wide range of practices in the early Turkish Republic. Purifying Turkish of foreign vocabulary and grammar, changing the script from Arabic to Latin, collecting words that were used in everyday speech and old Turkish texts to create the new Turkish vocabulary, Turkifying personal and

---

[36] The disintegration of the Ottoman Empire changed the demographic composition of Anatolia to a great extent. Before World War I, one out of every five people living in present-day Turkey was non-Muslim. This number decreased to only one out of forty people after the war (Keyder 1987, 79). While the war homogenized the Anatolian population in religious terms, ethnically it was still highly mixed.

[37] Elsewhere I have written on the position of non-Muslims, particularly Jewish citizens, in the conception of Turkishness: Aslan (2007). Also see Çağaptay (2006) and Yeğen (2004, 2007) for lengthier discussions of how Turkish nationalism depicts non-Muslim and Muslim minorities.

geographical names, and spreading the use of Turkish among the population were the milestones of this large-scale linguistic engineering project.[38] The new Turkish language would symbolize the singular national and secular culture as opposed to the multi-ethnic and religious heritage of the Ottoman past. This new language would mean a radical rupture with the Ottoman past, which the state elites associated with backwardness. They also considered the pluralistic character of the Ottoman Empire as the main reason for its dissolution and perceived the spread of a common language as indispensable for political and cultural unity. As Şükrü Kaya, the Minister of the Interior, stated: "The biggest responsibility of a government is to assimilate all who live within its boundaries into its own community ... While many people did not assimilate [in the past], the Ottomans suffered from that" (quoted in Çağaptay 2006, 61).

Kurds, who constituted the largest non-Turkish-speaking Muslim minority, became the main targets of Turkification. According to the 1927 census, the population of Turkey was 13,629,488, of whom 1,184,446 people declared their mother tongue as Kurdish. In 1935, the number of Kurdish-speakers had increased to 1,430,246 out of 16,157,450 people. Around 70 percent of the Kurdish-speakers did not know Turkish and around 75 percent of the Kurdish-speakers were living in the Eastern and Southeastern provinces of Turkey during the early republican period. In eight provinces, namely, Diyarbakır, Elazığ, Bitlis, Beyazıt, Mardin, Siirt, Van, and Hakkari, the Kurdish-speakers constituted the majority.[39] A chairman of the People's Houses wrote in 1939 that 80 percent of the city dwellers of Hakkari did not speak Turkish.[40] Such a high number of non-Turkish-speakers created serious concern within the Turkish state elites, not only because they thought that national unity could be achieved solely through cultural and linguistic uniformity, but also because of the administrative problems that arose in the Kurdish areas.

The communication gap between state officials and local residents in the Eastern provinces was considerable. As state-centered analyses of nationalism (Hechter 2000; Laitin 1992; Tilly 1994) suggest, state elites' concerns over administrative efficiency have motivated their demands for linguistic homogenization. State centralization and the increasing direct

---

[38] For more on the language policy in the early republican period, see Çolak (2004, 67–91).
[39] For population figures, see Dündar (1999, 101–116).
[40] BCA 490.01-985.817.3, second bi-annual activity report of Hakkari People's House, Chairman of the Hakkari People's House to RPP General Secretariat, January 20, 1939, p. 2. Among its many activities, the People's Houses also collected census data.

contact with the citizens necessitated that the state's language be congruent with that of the citizens. In 1939, in a report sent from Hakkari, a city close to the Iraqi border and where the overwhelming majority of people spoke Kurdish, the chairman of the People's Houses wrote that people had difficulty in explaining themselves to the Turkish administrators and could communicate with them only through the help of their fellow townsmen. Especially in courts, he noted, unofficial and arbitrary translations could lead to wrongful decisions.[41] The Bingöl deputy wrote to the RPP General Secretariat that the Village Law, which specified certain standards for all villages to be met, could not be enforced because the villages were too small and poor and because the villagers did not speak Turkish.[42] Similarly, after his visit to the Eastern provinces, Secretary General of the RPP, Memduh Şevket Esendal, wrote that it would not be feasible to open party branches in these areas because very few people were literate and knew Turkish.[43] "In this regard, these provinces stand out as if they were patched on our country, not only seemingly but also in reality," he added.[44] He also complained of not being able to talk to the local residents in places he visited. His conversations took place mostly with high-level bureaucrats and professionals, who were sent to the region from the state's center.[45]

Esendal's complaint reflected a common problem for modern states; social control requires detailed information about the society but the language barrier hinders state officials' attempts to know more about the society in order to direct and control it. As James Scott (1998, 72) states: "The great cultural barrier imposed by a separate language is perhaps the most effective guarantee that a social world, easily accessible to insiders, will remain opaque to outsiders." The administrators of the region openly acknowledged this problem. In a long report that he wrote in 1943, the First Inspector-General, Avni Doğan, underlined the failure of the reform projects planned specifically for Turkey's Eastern regions and complained about the state's lack of basic information about Kurdish society. He wrote that the governors were

---

[41] Ibid.
[42] See Necmettin Sahir Sılan's report titled "Bingöl Vilayeti Genel Durumu (1939)," in Akekmekçi and Pervan (2010, 28).
[43] Even as late as 1938, the RPP did not have branches in the Kurdish provinces, although it was organized in other provinces of Turkey. See Çağaptay (2006, 113).
[44] BCA 490.01-571.2274.1, Report of Memduh Şevket Esendal, Secretary General of the RPP, regarding his visit to the Eastern provinces, June 14, 1945, p. 84.
[45] Ibid., p. 38.

unable to obtain even basic information such as the number of tribes in their regions, who the tribal leaders were, which of these tribal leaders participated in the rebellions against the state, and how many arms these tribes possessed. According to him, one of the most severe problems that the administrators encountered was the linguistic gap. He emphasized that the district governors were unable to understand the problems of the locals, whose language they did not speak. To ensure the success of the reform projects in the region, Doğan's suggestion was to form groups of experts who would analyze the conditions of life, opinions, values, economic activities, and social environment of the Kurdish masses in detail.[46] Such information, however, was still not available despite increased attempts at state expansion during the two decades of the Turkish Republic.

Linguistic uniformity was also essential to ensure state control over its own bureaucrats at the local level. Another concern of the administrators coming from the center was the formation of ties between lower-level bureaucrats and Kurdish citizens. If the bureaucrats knew Kurdish, they could easily communicate with the locals and disguise the content of this communication so that their superiors could not comprehend it. Such ties could pave the way to corruption and seizure of state institutions by local centers of power. As stated earlier, many reports written on the Kurdish regions advised against appointment of state employees who were native to the region.[47] "The Reform Plan for the East" (Şark Islahat Planı), which was prepared by the government immediately after the Sheikh Said rebellion in 1925, explicitly stated that Kurds should be kept away from the bureaucracy as well as the gendarmerie and the judiciary that operated in the East.[48] One practice to solve the problem of close relations between civil servants and locals was the frequent rotation of those who served in the Eastern provinces. A document written by the First Inspectorate-General in 1930, for instance, called the government's attention to the marriages between the members of the gendarmerie and local girls that led them to become involved in conflicts between families and tribes and to use their official positions to favor one side. This document asked the government to assign the members of the gendarmerie to different regions every three years.[49]

---

[46] See Avni Doğan's report in Bayrak (1994, 253, 268–269).
[47] For instance, see BCA 490.01-997.852.1, Report on Tunceli, Bingöl, and Elazığ by Elazığ Inspector Muhtar Ertan, October 18, 1943, pp. 12, 14.
[48] This report can be found in Bayrak (1994, 258–262).
[49] BCA 030.10-69.454.36, First Inspector-General to the Prime Ministry, January 4, 1930, p. 1.

The state elite saw the presence of Kurdish-speakers not only as a source of administrative problems but also considered the linguistic gap as an obstacle that curtailed the spread of the new state ideology and reforms in the Kurdish areas. The reports sent from the People's Houses operating in Eastern Turkey often called attention to the miscommunication problem with the local residents, especially in the rural areas where only a few men could speak Turkish. When the representatives of the "Village Development" sections went to the Kurdish villages, they needed the help of interpreters to talk to people. They noted that their inability to communicate with the villagers impeded real progress in their activities.[50] In her memoirs, Sıdıka Avar (2004, 127), the director of the Elazığ Girls' Institute, writes about how difficult it was to persuade the villagers to send their daughters to schools, given her lack of fluency in Kurdish. The problems she encountered would later force Avar to learn Kurdish, which helped her to form better relations with the villagers. She notes that addressing the villagers in Kurdish would sometimes be enough to immediately break the ice. The learning of Kurdish by bureaucrats and teachers, however, was firmly discouraged by the state.

There is nothing intrinsically surprising about why the state aimed to spread the Turkish language among non-Turkish-speakers. A more puzzling question is why the state tried to eradicate the Kurdish language completely and did not allow bilingualism. That is, the Turkish state not only demanded that its citizens use the Turkish language in the official and public domain, but also asked them to exclusively use it in the private domain. A provincial district governor in Yüksekova, Hakkari, stated:

> How bitter and ugly is the fact that we cannot understand the language spoken by part of this local community and that they cannot understand ours within our own geographical boundaries, in our indivisible territories, and among the great Turkish community. It is possible, however, to find the reasons for this bitter and ugly linguistic condition among the ills of the wrongful understanding of nation and state administration during the pre-Republican period. But the Republican administration ... and the citizens of the Republic have been fighting for and should fight for resolving this language issue and stamping the corrupt Kurdish language out of the homes and pushing it off the tongues. They should strive for replacing it with the language of the actual nation to which they [Kurds] belong.[51]

---

[50] BCA 490.01-985.817.3, second bi-annual activity report of Hakkari People's House, Chairman of the Hakkari People's House to RPP General Secretariat, January 20, 1939, p. 5; 490.01-998.856.1, Report on Hakkari People's House by Bitlis Region Inspector Hasip A. Aytuna, November 10, 1942, p. 48.

[51] This text was taken from a speech that the provincial district governor of Yüksekova gave in the People's Chamber on the occasion of the Annual Language Festival (Dil

The main reason why the state required the complete eradication of minority languages was the constant fear of territorial dissolution, separatism, and disloyalty to the state. For the state elite, a different language was the main proof of a different nation within the state's boundaries that might eventually ask for self-determination. Therefore, Kurdishness was considered as a serious challenge to the project of national unity and using the Kurdish language was perceived as a sign of disloyalty to the Turkish state.[52] In Atatürk's words, "One of the significant characteristics of the nation is language. One, who regards himself as a member of the Turkish nation, should first of all and in every case, speak Turkish. If, someone, who does not speak Turkish, claims membership to Turkish culture and community, it would not be right to believe in this" (quoted in Çağaptay 2004, 89).

Such mistrust of Kurdish-speakers was a result of a general feeling of insecurity among the state elite who had experienced the gradual dissolution of the Ottoman Empire, the formation of new nation-states within the old territories of the empire, and the long years of wars with the European states. The memory of the Treaty of Sèvres in 1920, which recognized an autonomous Kurdish region in Southeastern Anatolia, had already made the Kurdish-speaking citizens' loyalty suspect. Especially after the first revolts in the Kurdish areas in the early 1920s, Kurdish-speakers came to be perceived as a major threat. What the state elite mostly feared was the possibility of the rise of Kurdish nationalism and the Kurdish nationalists' alliance with an imperialist Western power in order to secede from Turkey.[53] Almost every report sent to Ankara from

---

Bayramı). BCA 490.01-1168.101.3, Chairman of Yüksekova People's Chamber to RPP General Secretariat, September 26, 1941, pp. 2–3.

[52] My contention is that the state elite considered a number of factors when assessing the extent of threat that an ethnic group presented to the state. A group's perceived loyalty to the state, its cultural proximity to the Turks, and its proportion of the general population were important factors. While there were other Muslim ethnic groups, such as Arabs and Circassians, within the territories of the Turkish Republic, the state elite did not consider them as big a threat as the Kurds, because their numbers were much smaller (1 percent and 0.7 percent respectively, according to the 1935 census). However, an archival document indicates that Turkish authorities still collected as much information as possible about all ethnic groups. A secret document sent from the RPP's General Secretariat to the provincial party office in Kars asked for information about non-Turkish racial groups that lived in the province. The head of the provincial office wrote that the majority of the population consisted of Turks, followed by the Kurds as the second largest group, and that there were very few Christians and Lazis. BCA 490.01-837.306.2, 1934, pp. 116–117.

[53] For a longer discussion of the Sèvres Treaty and the crystallization of the Turkish national identity as a result of international developments, see İçduygu and Kaygusuz (2004).

Policies of "extreme makeover" 63

the Kurdish areas addressed this fear and contained a few comments about the Kurdish-speakers' loyalty to the republic. "People of this province do not yet believe that they are part of the Turkish nation," wrote a parliamentarian who inspected Siirt, a city in Southeastern Turkey, in 1940. "They look at Ankara with awe and admiration but Ankara does not lie at all in their hearts. Therefore, during insecure times we should pay more attention to and act prudently about this province," he added. He also warned of the Kurdish provocation from Syria and Iraq and noted that it would be too early to believe in the complete loyalty of Kurdish-speaking citizens to the Turkish state.[54] In order to secure their loyalty, the state elite thought that it was necessary to transform how the Kurds perceived themselves by making them Turks.

As Soner Çağaptay (2004) argues, initially Turkishness did not refer to a biological community but was defined mainly through language. In other words, Turkishness could be achievable by Muslim non-Turks as long as they spoke the Turkish language, considered themselves as part of the Turkish nation, and were loyal to the state. In the 1930s, the rise of fascism and racist ideologies started to influence many Turkish intellectuals and the state elite. Thus, a search for an ethnic basis of Turkishness began. The Turkish History Thesis, which was formulated at the beginning of the 1930s, solved the problem of defining Turkish ethnicity without being exclusivist. According to the thesis, Turks were an ancient race whose roots went back to Central Asia, from where they dispersed around the world due to climatic changes. A section of them went to Anatolia and became the creators of the Hittite civilization. The most important implication of the thesis was that all of Anatolia's inhabitants were therefore racially Turks (Çağaptay 2004, 87–89). Thus, Kurds were another branch of Turks. The Turkish History Thesis served as the basis to deny the existence of a separate Kurdish ethnicity; a claim that lasted until the 1990s.

In many of the reports written about Southeast Turkey, Kurdish-speakers were referred to as "Turks who somehow forgot their mother tongue," "those who do not speak their native language," or "those who do not believe that they are a part of the Turkish nation." Similarly, the Kurdish language was depicted as "a mixture of Asian Turkish and Persian," rather than a separate language.[55] According to this viewpoint,

---

[54] BCA 490.01-1015.916.4, Maraş Deputy H. Reşit Tankut to RPP General Secretariat, October 16, 1940 pp. 3, 5.

[55] See BCA 490.01-989.830.2, 1935 Mardin People's House Activity Report, p. 14; 490.01-996.850.1, Lice People's House Activity Report, May 11, 1941, p. 65; 490.01-1015.916.4, Maraş Deputy H. Reşit Tankut to RPP General Secretariat, October 16, 1940, p. 3.

Kurds were "Mountain Turks" who forgot their Turkishness as a result of the multi-ethnic structure and the non-interventionist policies of the Ottoman state. While many of the administrators certainly believed (or wanted to believe) in the Turkish origins of the Kurdish-speakers and refrained from using the word "Kurd," paradoxically they also made a distinction between different ethnic groups. The reports written by inspectors who visited the Kurdish areas always contained separate information on the Kurds, such as their population figures, the numbers of people speaking different Kurdish dialects, the number of children going to school, people's main economic activities, political preferences, and their ties with neighboring countries. In contradiction to the official argument that denied Kurdish existence, the inspectors who wrote these reports explicitly pointed to a separate Kurdish ethnicity. In addition, there was no consensus at the official level on the idea that Kurds were in fact pure Turks or on the feasibility of this discourse. For instance, Memduh Şevket Esendal, Secretary General of the RPP, wrote in sarcastic fashion of how the Fourth Inspector-General, Hüseyin Abdullah Alpdoğan, believed that Kurdishness would disappear by repeatedly telling Kurds that they were Turks. "Maybe the general's allegations are correct. Or there might be some truth in it. However, one would clearly not believe that the people of Tunceli could be Turkified by having said these true words." Esendal was quite pessimistic about the assimilation of the Kurds into Turkishness. At the end of his report, he wrote that the Kurdish language was a Persian dialect and that it was only the Persians who could easily assimilate the Kurds. He suggested a population exchange between the Kurds in Turkey and the Turks in Iran to fundamentally resolve the problem.[56] Although there was not disagreement over the general aim of homogenizing the country among the state elite, how this should be achieved was a matter of continuous debate. Especially with regards to the methods to be used, the Kemalist state elite was not a monolithic bloc.

In Turkey, as in most other nation-states, compulsory mass education and military service were conceived as the two main institutions that would teach being Turkish and spread the national language among the population. However, especially in the first few decades of the republic, the state lacked the means to achieve high levels of schooling and enlist all eligible men to the army. The Kurdish areas were especially difficult to reach compared to the rest of the country. Poor roads, lack of easy

---

[56] BCA 490.01-571.2274.1, Report of the Secretary General of RPP regarding his visit to the Eastern provinces, June 14, 1945, pp. 5, 85.

transportation, and difficult geography and climate conditions could cut off certain rural areas from the outside world for months. In addition, the state lacked qualified, trained teachers and resources to build an adequate number of schools. In a report dated 1943, it was written that only those men who completed their military service knew Turkish in the villages around Mardin but almost 80 percent of the eligible men evaded conscription.[57] In the villages of Mardin only 0.4 percent of school-age children could go to schools in 1935.[58] Even as late as 1960, in cities where the majority were Kurdish-speakers, the rates of schooling were considerably lower when compared to the rest of the country. In Hakkari, Siirt, Bingöl, Mardin, and Diyarbakır the elementary school enrollment ratios in 1960 were 31 percent, 28 percent, 50 percent, 38 percent, and 37 percent, respectively, while the rate was above 90 percent in the cities of Western Turkey.[59] The People's Houses, along with the municipalities, worked hard to make up for this educational deficiency and came up with a wide range of practices to make people speak Turkish and think of themselves as Turks.

Because of the failure of the military and school system in the Kurdish areas, the local administrators used more coercive means, such as banning Kurdish on the streets, to ensure the faster acquisition of Turkish. During the early republican period, in Diyarbakır, for instance, the municipal police fined villagers or street vendors who shouted in Kurdish to advertise their produce (Ekinci 2010, 97; Miroğlu 2005, 66). According to Miroğlu these practices hurt the non-Turkish-speaking peasants economically because they then refrained from going to towns and city centers to sell their produce. There were, however, critics of the fine. In his speech in 1941, the chairman of the People's House in Yüksekova argued:

The language issue cannot be solved through laws, legal sanctions, fines, and threats. There are no pressures, threats, and punishments in the Turkish regime and republican principles. Therefore, we should love and respect each other and should work and fight altogether in order to learn to speak the Turkish language that is the only means of communication in this big community. In the markets, bazaars, stores, and state bureaus, we should not answer or help those who speak Kurdish and therefore force them to learn to speak Turkish.[60]

---

[57] BCA 490.01-1001.866.2, Report on Mardin by Diyarbakır Inspector Ali Reşat Göksidan, December 13, 1943, p. 7.
[58] BCA 490.01-989.830.2, 1935 Mardin People's House Activity Report, p. 21.
[59] BCA 030.01-91.570.4, pp. 1–4.
[60] BCA 490.01-1168.101.3, Chairman of Yüksekova People's Chamber to RPP General Secretariat, September 26, 1941, p. 3.

In a similar vein, the People's House in Mardin established "committees for the dissemination of Turkish," where teachers and youth in the countryside were mobilized to teach Turkish to non-speakers in language classes. The language used in the activity report from the Mardin People's House in 1936 reflects how Kemalist missionaries conceived of their tasks. The report referred to the teachers as "warriors utilized" (*kullanılan savaşçı*) and the students as "citizens whom we worked on" (*üzerinde uğraşılan yurttaş*) and listed the number of citizens who attended the classes for each month of 1935. The Mardin's People's House also organized conferences about the importance of the Turkish language and in one of these conferences the participants were asked to take an oath "not to speak in a foreign language again."[61] The same committee also aimed to control whether people spoke Turkish in their homes.[62] Many administrators tried to create positive inducements as well to motivate people to learn Turkish. For instance, the People's Chambers in the villages of Diyarbakır organized contests to test people's knowledge of Turkish, giving money to the winners. In Diyarbakır, Turkish-speaking peasants were recruited to teach Turkish to non-Turkish-speakers. In the end, the person who learned Turkish best and the best teacher won four oxen.[63]

These practices encountered Kurdish apathy and resentment. The administrators of the People's Houses complained about the lack of interest in the Turkish language classes. This was hardly surprising. Economic payoffs, which constituted the main incentive for assimilation, were slim for the Kurdish-speakers in the first decades of the republic. The majority of the Kurdish-speakers lived in rural areas,[64] and their prospects of using the Turkish language for social mobility were minuscule given the weak economic integration of the Kurdish regions with the rest of the country, low educational opportunities, and the dependence of the majority of the Kurdish peasants on tribal leaders and aghas.

In order to arouse people's interest in learning Turkish, the Kemalist missionaries had to invent new ways to motivate the Kurds. Correspondence from Mardin indicates that showing films was the most effective strategy to attract people to the People's Houses. Cinema was a new technology in

---

[61] BCA 490.01-989.830.2, 1935 Mardin People's House Activity Report, pp. 14–15.
[62] BCA 490.01-1005.880.3, Report on the inspection of Mardin People's House, August 28, 1935, p. 40.
[63] BCA 490.01-984.814.2, 1935 Diyarbakır People's House Activity Report, pp. 9, 13.
[64] According to the 1935 population census, only 1.5 percent of those whose mother tongue was Kurdish lived in areas with a population of more than ten thousand people. See Dündar (1999, 104).

Turkey and people were hardly familiar with it in those days. Because of its novelty and entertainment capacity, it could arouse interest.[65] In this correspondence, the chairman of the People's House in Mardin wrote to the regional inspector of Muş that the People's House searched for more appealing measures than coercive ones in order to make people learn Turkish and attract them to the literacy classes. He pointed out that conferences and theaters were highly ineffective in raising people's cultural level as the majority of them did not know Turkish. The only possible means for him was to make sure that people attended the literacy classes offered by the Houses. He stated that the most effective way that they could find to ensure people's attendance in these classes was to show films once a week for free and to give out gifts to those who got high grades. He added that the number of people who took Turkish classes decreased from 483 to 43 once they stopped showing movies.[66]

Radio was also used as a similar device to achieve linguistic uniformity. An inspector of the People's Houses asked for radios to be sent to the villages, stating that he heard children singing in Turkish in villages where there was a radio.[67] Radio, like cinema, being new then, could also attract considerable attention. A chairman of the People's House wrote in his report that the members of the People's House first gave their lecture to the peasants and then turned the radio on to ensure peasants' attendance at their activities.[68]

Such official struggles with Kurdish contributed to the politicization of the language issue and made the Turkish language increasingly an ethnic marker that distinguished and excluded. In fact, it can be argued that the state hurt its own aim of national integration through its policies. A common language plays an important role in economic and social integration and can be a tool for equal access to a political community (Deutsch, 1966; Gellner, 1983). As Csergo (2007, 12) points out, a common language can be seen as "an element of the social contract," which is important for political participation, the formation of shared civic

---

[65] Many of my Kurdish interviewees argued that the Turkish language spread dramatically among the Kurdish-speaking population only after the start of TV broadcasts in the 1970s.
[66] BCA 490.01-1001.866.2, Correspondence from Mardin People's House Chairman, Aziz Uras, to the People's House Inspector of Muş Region, Münir Soykam, December 26, 1940, pp. 123–125.
[67] BCA 490.01-1006.882.1, Report of Inspector Kemal Güngör on Hakkari People's House, May 9, 1942, p. 22.
[68] BCA 490.01-989.830.2, 1935 Mardin People's House Activity Report, p. 11.

FIGURE 1. A meeting in the People's House in Urfa, some time between 1935 and 1940. Note the military officer overseeing the meeting in the right-hand corner of the photograph. From the personal collection of Müslüm Akalın.

values, and equal citizenship. In Turkey, however, the heavy emphasis on the symbolic character of the Turkish language and intrusions into Kurdish citizens' private lives dissociated it from this functional value. The prohibition on the use of Kurdish led to the hardening of a boundary between Turkishness and Kurdishness, becoming one of the main sources of conflict between the Turkish state and the Kurds. Today, the Turkish state's coercive linguistic policy constitutes a central theme in the Kurdish nationalist historiography and the exclusive use and development of the Kurdish language is perceived as a way to restore Kurdish dignity.[69]

The state's aim of linguistic homogenization far exceeded the concerns over administrative efficiency and language rationalization in Turkish nation-building. Forcing people to speak the Turkish language in their

---

[69] Before the politicization of the language issue, the tendency of Kurdish families, especially those living in the cities, was to acquire Turkish. One of my interviewees, who came from a rich Kurdish family in Diyarbakır, recalled that his parents refused to speak Kurdish at home so that the children learned Turkish as soon as possible. He also added that Kurds living in the cities considered speaking Kurdish, which only peasants spoke, as uncultured and humiliating (interview with Canip Yıldırım, June 2006, Ankara). Official prohibition on the Kurdish language led to increased linguistic consciousness and sensitivity among the educated Kurds, creating an interest in learning, standardizing, and developing the Kurdish language. I will concentrate more on this in Chapter 4.

daily lives was one of the main pillars of the "extreme makeover" project. Speaking Turkish became a symbol of national identity and an indication of people's loyalty to the republic. While the laws of the state aimed at the use of Turkish as the only language of administration and the educational system, local state officials worked to ensure that people spoke Turkish in their daily lives through a wide range of practices, from coercive bans to imaginative inducements. The state's rigid conception of nation-building, shown in its uncompromising language policies, paradoxically undermined its efforts to build efficient state rule in the Kurdish areas. State officials' inability to communicate with the locals created administrative problems, hurt the efforts to collect information on the Kurdish society, and curtailed the spread of the state ideology and reforms in Kurdish areas.[70] The inflexibilities of the regime augmented challenges that state officials encountered in the region, in addition to increasing Kurdish resentment and opposition to the regime.

POLICIES OF WESTERNIZATION IN THE KURDISH AREAS

In Turkey, the attempts at establishing a homogeneous nation-state went beyond the creation of a common national identity through language. People's physical appearance, religious beliefs, moral values, family relations, and artistic tastes all became matters of the state's interest in imposing homogeneity on the population. The national subject should not only consider him/herself as a Turk and speak Turkish, but should also think, live, and act like a Westerner. As Mustafa Kemal declared:

> The people of the Turkish Republic, who claim to be civilized, must show and prove that they are civilized, by their ideas and their mentality, by their family life and their way of living. In a word, the truly civilized people of Turkey ... must prove in fact that they are civilized and advanced persons also in their outward aspect.
>
> (Quoted in Lewis 1968, 268–269)

According to the state elite, there was only one civilization that would lead to progress, and it was the Western civilization. If Turkey wanted to be a strong player in the international arena and avoid the humiliating decline of the Ottoman Empire, it was necessary to Westernize state

---

[70] For a lengthier discussion of how the ideological rigidities of the regime hurt its control over Kurdish areas, see Aslan (2011).

and society. While the Ottoman past reminded the state elite of backwardness, the domination of religion and superstitious beliefs, and chaos, the future of the Turkish Republic would be characterized by continuous development through science, reason, and an orderly society.

The founders of the Turkish Republic undertook a series of reforms that aimed not only at state centralization but also at a radical transformation of citizens' everyday lives. Within the first few years of the republic, the caliphate, special Sharia courts, and religious schools were abolished, and religious brotherhoods, dervish orders, and sacred tombs were closed down. These secularization reforms brought about the separation of state and religion and established firm state control over religious institutions and personnel. The educational system was unified and children were required to receive five years of elementary state education. The Swiss civil code, which was adopted in 1926, banned polygamy and religious marriage. In 1928, the Latin script was accepted and public use of the Arabic alphabet was prohibited. A dress code aimed at transforming how people look. It required all men to wear hats and banned the wearing of the fez and religious outfits by those not holding a recognized religious office. In the 1930s, women were given the right to vote and to be elected, members of the clergy were banned from wearing religious dress except in religious ceremonies, all measurements were standardized and conformed to European standards, and a law demanded that all citizens adopt a Turkish surname.[71]

The main challenge, however, was to put these reforms into practice. A key institution that undertook this civilizing mission was the People's Houses. Particularly in the Kurdish areas, where the RPP did not establish branches for a long time, the People's Houses were the main institutions through which the state propagated its ideology and collected ethnographic information on the population. The People's Houses operated under nine sections: 1. Language, History, and Literature; 2. Fine Arts; 3. Theater; 4. Sports; 5. Social Assistance; 6. Public Classes and Courses; 7. Library and Publishing; 8. Village Development; and 9. Museums and Exhibitions. These sections employed various means, such as films, theater plays, puppet shows, conferences, wall posters, village excursions, concerts, tea parties, and expositions, to spread their message to the masses.[72]

---

[71] For a detailed discussion of these reforms, see Lewis (1968), Zürcher (1998, 2004). Particularly with regard to the sartorial regulations, see Yılmaz (2013).

[72] For more on People's Houses, see Karpat (1963), Öztürkmen (1994), and Toksoy (2007).

Policies of "extreme makeover" 71

The People's Houses were under the direct control of the single party. While in other parts of Turkey, the provincial party organization chose the board of directors of the Houses, in the Kurdish areas, where there were no provincial party organizations, the Inspector-General of the region usually chose them (Toksoy 2007, 101). The board of the People's Houses was generally composed of state officials serving in the region as well as party members. The membership, however, was open to anyone. As Zürcher (2004, 107) points out, "The People's Houses' greatest success was probably in helping to build a dedicated middle class cadre for the Kemalists in the towns, rather than in gaining mass support of the reforms." The members of the Houses constituted the core group of Kemalist missionaries in peripheral areas. The majority of them were teachers, doctors, merchants, and other professionals who represented the relatively better-educated strata of their localities. The Kemalists perceived the low levels of education in the Kurdish regions to be the root cause of strong religious and tribal ties and patriarchal norms. The state expected the educated elites to be actively involved in teaching the masses how to be modern and Westernized. "People are ignorant and most of them do not even speak Turkish ... It is a duty of the educated Turks to train and enlighten these backward citizens of ours in these homes which are the essential centers for the establishment of our national culture and people's development," wrote an inspector, referring to the role of the People's Houses.[73]

Hundreds of activity reports and the photographs attached to them in the archives suggest that the People's Houses and Chambers carried out numerous activities to mold the Kurds into Westernized Turks. However, these reports also suggest that these activities were uneven and there was a wide variation in the level of activities depending on how dedicated the members were to the Kemalist project. These activities were not necessarily effective in transforming the Kurds, but mobilization of dedicated Kemalist missionaries in these institutions and their interpretation and recreation of state policies helped increase state intrusion, even in areas that were hard to reach and control. At the least these institutions and their representatives served to disseminate news about the state's ideology and policies that the local populations found hard to accept.

One of the main objectives of the state was transforming the way people look and Westernizing their outward appearance. "This grotesque

[73] BCA 490.01-1006.882.1, Report on Şirvan People's Chamber, November 11, 1940, p. 42.

FIGURE 2. The modest building in the middle that was painted white was the People's Chamber in Karakoçan, a village of Elazığ province. The photo shows Muhtar Ertan, Elazığ region inspector and Bitlis deputy, and his coterie with the villagers. Many inspectors' reports sent to the state center included photographs. BCA 490.01-997.852.1, April 10, 1941.

mixture of styles is neither national nor international," said Mustafa Kemal in a speech, referring to the traditional garments. "A civilized, international dress is worthy and appropriate for our nation, and we will wear it. Boots or shoes on our feet, trousers on our legs, shirt and tie, jacket and waistcoat – and of course, to complete these, a cover with a brim on our heads. I want to make this clear. This head-covering is called 'hat'" (quoted in Lewis 1968, 269). Following the Sheikh Said rebellion, the government passed a number of decrees and laws in 1925 to regulate people's outward appearance. First, a cabinet decree banned the wearing of religious garments by those who were not religious officers of the state. This was an attack on the religious establishment and created opposition from the religious dignitaries. In a directive sent to the governors and Inspector-Generals, the Ministry of the Interior wrote that there were still certain religious functionaries who wore religious garments and remained bare-headed. The Ministry emphasized that this was a criminal offense and that they would lose their government posts if they insisted on not abiding by the dress code.[74] After an order that required all state officials

---

[74] BCA 490.01-611.122.1, Directive of the Ministry of the Interior, July 4, 1935, pp. 1–2.

to wear hats and suits, the Law Concerning the Wearing of the Hat of November 1925 required all men to wear hats. The protests against the law in Kayseri, Maraş, and Erzurum were crushed with the declaration of martial law, executions, and imprisonments.[75]

Many local administrations and the People's Houses working in the Eastern and Southeastern provinces went beyond the law and worked hard on replacing people's traditional garments with modern clothes. Some municipalities banned the wearing of baggy trousers (*şalvar*), which were commonly worn in the East.[76] In a similar vein, some of the People's Houses and Chambers put up signs that warned people not to enter the building if they wore clothes that "represented backwardness."[77] In his memoirs, Tarık Ziya Ekinci (2010, 96) describes the gendarmerie pulling off and ripping the traditional headdress called *puşi* that was worn wrapped around men's heads in the rural areas. Different sartorial traditions were visual expressions of different ethnic identities in the country. Homogenization of clothing was considered necessary to create a unitary sense of national identity.

The Kemalists also worked for changing the appearance of women. Although veiling was never made illegal, the General Secretariat of the RPP sent a secret directive to the governors asking them to fight against it. Yılmaz (2013, 99–101) writes that the leaders of the RPP, including Atatürk, were concerned about a violent uprising if they banned veiling. Instead the state encouraged the administrators of the provinces to change women's appearance through propaganda and inculcation (Yılmaz 2013, 91). People's Houses organized conferences to encourage women to remove their veils and black chadors.[78] Some of the municipalities in the Southeast, including Siirt and Hakkari, passed decisions that banned veiling but it was not clear what measures they took to enforce the ban (Yılmaz 2013, 104–105). The result of the unveiling project, however, was highly disappointing for the Kemalists. An RPP inspector wrote from Muş that the reforms did not yet penetrate into the local population and that girls were not even being sent to school, let alone changing their dress habits. He added that girls who were sent to school

---

[75] For a detailed discussion of the hat law and its consequences, see Brockett (1998) and Yılmaz (2013).
[76] BCA 490.01-17.88.1, Correspondence from the Chairman of RPP Maraş Administrative Council to General Secretariat, November 5, 1935, pp. 4–6.
[77] BCA 490.01-844.340.2, Letter from a Bozova resident to the RPP General Secretariat, February 1946, p. 60.
[78] See, for instance, the 1935 Activity Report of Malatya People's House, BCA 490.01-989.829.2, p. 14.

wore their veils in the classrooms.[79] Memduh Şevket Esendal pointed out that, even though some women from prominent families removed their black chadors, they used umbrellas to cover themselves up in public.[80]

Another component of the Westernization project was training women and making them more visible in public life. This was a particularly difficult task in the Kurdish areas, which were predominantly rural and conservative. A common activity of the People's Houses was organizing conferences on subjects such as childcare, housework, protection from diseases, and hygiene. In the cities, they offered free classes to teach women reading and writing, sewing, needlework, and embroidery. Different strategies were used in order to make women participate more in public life. For example, the People's Houses encouraged women to perform in their theater plays. Finding women who would be willing to perform in theatrical pieces, however, was almost impossible. In a letter sent to the RPP's General Secretariat, the chairman of the People's Houses in Silvan asked the RPP to send plays in which all the characters were men. The answer coming from the secretariat was unyielding: "In principle, performances without women do not conform with the objectives of the People's Houses. For this reason, I hope that you will try to find women."[81] Similarly, the People's Houses tried to increase the numbers of its female members. Women were encouraged to become members and work side by side with men in the Houses. The lack of women who would work at the People's Houses in the Eastern provinces constituted a major problem for the Kemalists, who tried to close this gap by enlisting the spouses of state officials.[82] A pamphlet that was prepared to advertise the activities of the People's House to the population of Elazığ stated: "It is possible to have fun at nights without spending any money. However, the one condition to attend is to come to these family parties with your wives, mothers, sisters, female relatives, or friends' families."[83] These family parties were intended to create spaces where men and women got used to mingling socially.

---

[79] BCA 490.01-1206.229.1, p. 119.
[80] BCA 490.01-571.2274.1, Report of the Secretary General of RPP regarding his visit to the Eastern provinces, June 14, 1945, p. 76.
[81] BCA 490.01-920.583.2, Correspondence between the Chairman of Silvan People's House and RPP General Secretariat, January 1940, p. 20.
[82] BCA 490.01-1003.874.1, Hozat People's House Report, Muş Region Inspector Münir Soykam to RPP General Secretariat, April 21, 1941, p. 22.
[83] BCA 490.01-997.852.1, Pamphlet attached to reports from Elazığ People's House, p. 235.

Policies of "extreme makeover" 75

FIGURE 3. An official ceremony in Urfa, some time between 1935 and 1940. The spouses of state officials at the front represented models of the new Turkish woman. From the personal collection of Müslüm Akalın.

The other practices that the People's Houses undertook in order to "civilize" the population included educating the peasants about agriculture and public health, increasing literacy, stimulating interest in reading, familiarizing people with Western music, and promoting physical exercise. The People's House of Elazığ offered piano and violin classes, established a jazz orchestra, and organized dance parties every month.[84] The People's House in Hakkari worked to teach the national marches to the peasants and to improve their sense of rhythm by making them listen to music on the radio.[85] The report of the People's Houses in Malatya noted that its orchestra contained only Western instruments but occasionally it played one or two pieces of Oriental music.[86]

Because an ideal Turk was depicted as someone who was a good athlete and because physical exercise was seen as a way to bring discipline to people's lifestyles, the People's Houses worked hard to promote sports. Some of the Houses opened up fields where people could play soccer and volleyball, established teams, and organized sports contests. Many

---

[84] BCA 490.01-997.852.1, Report on Elazığ People's House, Muş Region Inspector Münir Soykam to RPP General Secretariat, February 1, 1941, p. 228.
[85] BCA 490.01-985.817.3, Bi-annual Report of Hakkari People's House, December 12, 1935, p. 7.
[86] BCA 490.01-989.829.2, 1935 Activity Report of Malatya People's House, p. 15.

FIGURE 4. A brass band in Siverek, playing in front of the hat-wearing town dwellers. BCA 490.01-1078.1122.3, 1943.

members saw the mountainous terrain and climate of Eastern Turkey as suitable for skiing, hunting, and scouting. In village excursions, the members of the sports section introduced these activities to the villagers. Most of the People's Houses established libraries, which contained over 1,000 books. In some cities, English, German, and French language classes were offered along with Turkish reading and writing.[87]

These practices, which aimed at civilizing the Kurds, yielded similar results to the language policies, however. Many of the reports included long complaints about the lack of popular interest in the activities of the People's Houses. An inspector who visited Hakkari wrote that the People's House looked as if it were the meeting place of only a few state officials.[88] Some People's Houses and Chambers existed only in name and did not undertake many activities.[89] Many of the classes were closed because of the lack of students. Usually it was the existence of a radio that attracted people to the Houses, and without the radio people hardly

[87] BCA 490.01-997.852.1, Report on Elazığ People's House, Muş Region Inspector Münir Soykam to RPP General Secretariat, February 1, 1941, p. 230.
[88] BCA 490.01-998.856.1, Report on the inspection of the People's House in Hakkari, Bitlis Region Inspector and Tokat Deputy Hasip Aytuna to RPP General Secretariat, November 10, 1942, p. 57.
[89] See, for instance, BCA 490.01-841.326.2, a letter sent to the RPP General Secretariat from a primary school teacher in Varto, complaining about the town's idle People's House, March 9, 1942.

FIGURE 5. A sports team going hiking in Elazığ. BCA 490.01-997.852.1, July 1941.

set foot in them. The practices that aimed at Westernizing the Kurds made the state seem an alien force that should be avoided as much as possible. In order to ensure people's participation, they were encouraged to use the Houses for ceremonies such as weddings. However, there were unintended consequences. Increased participation by the locals actually transformed the Houses into different spaces than what had been planned. There were complaints that some Houses turned into coffee houses where people played cards, domino, and backgammon.[90] In Ergani, a province of Diyarbakır, people performed their ritual prayer in the People's House, an act that was harshly condemned by the First Inspector-General Avni Doğan.[91] These activities merely hint at the attempts made by the locals to transform the institutions according to their own preferences.

The lack of popular interest in the republican modernization project was not solely a result of the deep conflict between the state's ideals and local values in the Kurdish areas. The bureaucrats' disdain and maltreatment of the locals was a common problem, which curtailed the integration of the Kurds into the new order. In his long and detailed report, the First

[90] BCA 490.01-844.340.2, Letter from a Bozova resident to the RPP General Secretariat, February 1946, p. 69.
[91] BCA 490.01-832.284.1, Correspondence from Avni Doğan to the RPP General Secretariat, October 27, 1943, p. 55 and directive from the RPP General Secretariat to Ergani People's House, November 24, 1943, p. 53.

Inspector-General in 1943, Avni Doğan, complained that the state officials were corrupt and that they intentionally created difficulties for the locals and treated them unfairly. Doğan was aware that the behavior of the state officials was hurting the state's efforts to establish its authority and legitimacy. He asked the government to appoint honest, experienced, and capable people to the Kurdish region and to improve the state officials' working conditions as well as their salaries in order to prevent corruption.[92] The state officials' dissatisfaction with living in a poor and difficult region, coupled with their preconceived views about Kurdish ignorance, backwardness, fanaticism, and opposition to the government, led to mistreatment of the local population and scapegoating of the Kurds. For instance, in her memoir, Sıdıka Avar (2004, 39, 65, 266) complained about the negligence of the teachers and their supercilious attitude towards the students. She recalled that the teachers and workers in the school called the Kurdish students "mountain bears" or "tailed Kurds," inflicted harsh punishments on them, and forced them to do the janitors' jobs, such as cleaning the toilets. She wrote that the teachers should be tolerant, accommodating, and enthusiastic in order to assimilate this group of students who were different in customs, manners, and ways of thinking, and to attach them to Turkishness. She asked the Ministry of Education to send teachers who were willing to serve in her school and who would work with the students intensely outside class hours. The Turkish state's civilizing attitude coupled with the state officials' denigration and contempt of the Kurds fomented further animosity towards the regime and contributed to the development and spread of Kurdish nationalist consciousness. Humiliation of Kurds by Turkish nationalism and restoration of Kurdish dignity with the emergence of Kurdish nationalism has been a recurrent theme in Kurdish activists' discourse.

CONCLUSION

During the early republican era Westernization reforms were imposed in other parts of the country as well. Feelings of resentment towards the Westernization project of the state were not unique to the Kurdish areas. In her work on the cultural reforms in the early republic, Hale Yılmaz (2013) discusses similar practices that the People's Houses, state schools, and Kemalist missionaries undertook to modernize people and how people showed their discontent at the reforms through various means, such as

---

[92] The report can be found in Bayrak (1994, 233–270).

foot-dragging, evasion, and false compliance. What was unique in the Kurdish areas, however, was the range of changes that the state demanded from society. Policies of Westernization simply added another layer to such demands. The state's practices to makeover the Kurds involved detribalizing, sedentarizing, and disarming the population, along with changing their mother tongue, identity, customs, norms, thinking, behavior, and identity. And the Kurdish population had more opportunities to show a stronger reaction than mere apathy to the Turkish state as the population was well armed and lived in a terrain that was hard to reach, and the local centers of power, such as religious figures and tribal leaders, had the capability to mobilize large-scale collective action. In the end they showed the most serious resistance against the republican project. Sixteen of the eighteen revolts that broke out during the single-party period involved the Kurds (Kirişci and Winrow 1997, 100). The violent Kurdish protest against the state's transformation project led the Kemalist elite to pay more attention to the area, bolstering their enthusiasm to makeover the Kurds, and the increasing militarization of the area starting with the Sheikh Said rebellion changed people's lives like never before. One of the oldest Kurdish activists, Tarık Ziya Ekinci (2010, 245), underlines in his memoirs that the people in the region came to associate the single party with the coercion of the gendarmerie and arbitrary rule.

The highly coercive and rigid nation-building policies paradoxically hurt the establishment of state authority in the Kurdish areas. The central authority's ideological rigidities and willingness to use coercive power to ensure compliance hindered negotiation and compromise and undercut necessary adaptations in state policies when new challenges on the ground arose. Many of the policies formulated at the state's center had unintended consequences. Extensive militarization of the region to bring law and order to the Kurdish areas itself became a major source of illegality, to the detriment of government wishes to legitimize the regime among the Kurds. The language barrier as well as the detachment of state officials from the locals exacerbated these unintended consequences and curtailed the state's social control. The diversity of state officials, in terms of their ideals, the way they perceived the locals, and their intentions, generated a cacophony of state practices. In the end the existence of a highly ambitious "makeover" project increased state intrusion into everyday life, and military force did not translate into high levels of state power. During the single-party era, the Turkish state mostly remained ineffective in the face of Kurdish resistance against its nationalizing, modernizing, and assimilationist project.

3

State-building and the politics of national identity in Morocco

Every year the ceremony of the renewal of allegiance to the king in Morocco gathers the ulema, members of the government, parliamentarians, high-level state administrators, and local notables from all over the country around a courtyard of one of the palaces. The guests, whose number reaches four to five thousand and who uniformly wear the traditional white hooded robes (*jellaba*), are arranged in rows facing each other and await the king's procession to show him their respect and loyalty. The king, who is also in traditional garb, perches on a thoroughbred, directed by the palace servants. The scene looks centuries old. As the king proceeds, the guests bend five times and call in unison for divine grace on the king. In the meantime, the palace servants scream to the crowd, "Our master blesses you and calls the divine glory upon you!"[1]

The allegiance (*bay'a*) ceremony can be considered as a symbolic expression of the state- and nation-building strategies of Morocco. This ceremony, which constitutes one of the most important symbolic practices of the regime, is intended to underline the religious basis of the king's absolute power, constructs a reimagined national past, and portrays the king as the symbol of Moroccan unity. More importantly, it reaffirms the support of the rural notables and dignitaries, many of whom are Berbers, for the monarchy and conveys their role as intermediaries between the people and the regime.

After achieving independence in 1956, the Moroccan state adopted a different course than the Turkish state in its efforts to build a national

---

[1] I took the description of the ceremony from Benchemsi (2006, 44–45). Also see Daadaoui (2011, 83–87) for a good discussion of the ceremony.

identity in an ethnically divided society. Its nation-building strategy was much less reformist and more open to accommodating the social pluralism than its Turkish counterpart. The power struggles in the early years of state-building and the way the king consolidated state control generated a different approach to nation-building. As in Turkey, during the first few years after independence, the Moroccan state encountered a similar problem of tribal dissidence in the Berber areas against the expansion of state authority. This tribal challenge, however, was resolved in a very different manner. Rather than trying to eliminate the authority of local power centers, the king used Berber notables and tribal leaders to consolidate his power, making them the backbone of his regime. He established the state's direct rule over the Berber society by integrating Berber notables into its political and administrative network.

The immediate aftermath of independence in Morocco was marred by a fierce power struggle between the king, Mohammed V, and the nationalists under the Istiqlal Party, who had different visions of the state to be established. Although Istiqlal embraced an Islamic discourse and advocated the symbolic power of the king, its vision of how state authority should be built was similar to that of the Turkish nationalists. It endorsed policies of detribalization and imposing direct rule in the countryside. Unlike in Turkey, however, the Istiqlal leadership could neither marginalize the monarch nor establish control over the tribal countryside to achieve the monopoly of rule. While the first Kurdish rebellion gave the Republican People's Party (RPP) the chance to silence all opposition and establish its monopoly of rule in Turkey,[2] the Istiqlal Party in Morocco was weakened by tribal dissidence against its centralizing policies and lost power to the king.

Why did the Istiqlal Party fail to consolidate power at the expense of the king? The Istiqlal leadership did not emerge out of the nationalist struggle with the same level of strong legitimacy that Atatürk and his cadres enjoyed after the War of Independence in Turkey. First, the anti-colonial movement in Morocco was composed of different factions that were independent of each other and it was not as coordinated and unified as the Turkish nationalist movement. Istiqlal was the most prominent organization but it was hardly in control of the whole anti-colonial struggle (Lawrence 2007, 232–233). The French crackdown on the Istiqlal

---

[2] As explained in the second chapter, the government passed the Law on the Maintenance of Order in 1926, which was used to suppress not only the Kurds but also other opposition to the government. The law gave the government the authority to ban any organization and publication that were considered to cause disturbance to law and order.

Party in 1952 drove many of its members underground or abroad, hurting the party's institutionalization and ties with its constituency. Istiqlal's leaders were either in prison or abroad during the most violent episode of the struggle against the French between 1952 and 1956. The rural insurgency under the Liberation Army, which was composed largely of Berber tribal bands,[3] operated independently in the countryside. The Istiqlal Party's links with the rural resistance were weak and largely symbolic (Waterbury 1970, 54). Second, the nationalist resistance did not take the form of a full-fledged war as in Turkey. The nationalist violence that started in 1952 against French rule was a low-intensity conflict and did not lead to a large-scale mobilization of society.[4] Vinogradov and Waterbury (1971, 54) argue that Moroccan independence was won by default without any major battles being fought. Dealing with the Algerian war at the time, the French did not want to get involved in another armed conflict. This meant that none of the actors involved in the anti-colonial struggle emerged out of it with mass support. Istiqlal neither enjoyed mass legitimacy nor had the armed forces under its command that would help it establish a hegemony of rule.

The swiftness with which the Kemalists in Turkey abolished the sultanate in 1922 contrasts sharply with the power struggle between the king and Istiqlal. At first sight the success of the Kemalists can be explained by Sultan Vahdeddin's highly diminished prestige as a result of his anti-nationalist stance and cooperation with the Entente powers during the war. In Morocco, Sultan Mohammed Ben Youssef first collaborated with the French but supported the nationalists after World War II. Particularly after his exile by the French in 1953, he gained prestige, emerging as the symbol of Moroccan nationalism, which the Istiqlal Party also utilized to appeal to the masses. Yet, attributing the different regime outcomes solely to the variation in the monarchs' prestige would be an incomplete and easy answer. In 1922, the Turkish nationalists were hardly a monolithic unit, as many in the Turkish parliament were loyal to the dynasty, if not to Sultan Vahdeddin. The abolition of the sultanate was not an uncontroversial matter (Zürcher 2010, 142). Neither was the consolidation of power by the monarchy in Morocco certain. Many in Istiqlal were republicans

---

[3] It is important to note that the Liberation Army did not represent a specific Berber identity and there were Arab commanders within its ranks (Maddy-Weitzman 2011, 85).
[4] Anti-colonial violence started in 1952 in the form of riots, assassination attempts, arson, and sabotage in the urban areas. The Liberation Army began to carry out attacks against French military posts and Moroccan collaborators with the colonial regime as late as 1955 (Lawrence 2007, 229).

and believed that the sultan should either be discarded or have a solely ceremonial role after independence (Vinogradov and Waterbury 1971). The success of the Kemalists in abolishing the monarchy cannot be fully understood without taking into consideration Mustafa Kemal's political skills and unrivalled prestige as a war hero. Mustafa Kemal's takeover of power, however, was gradual and uncertain; in particular, he used the threat of the sultan's displacement of the nationalists in the peace negotiations as a convincing reason to rally support for abolishing the sultanate. In Morocco, the absence of a large-scale war made the continuity of the old regime more likely, particularly given the context that the nationalists were quite fragmented and the anti-monarchists within Istiqlal did not enjoy the same authority and prestige as Kemal and his close circle.

The social structure of Morocco was also different. At the time of independence, a great majority of the population in Morocco was living in rural areas, where tribal authority and kinship networks were strong. Unlike in Anatolian society, in Moroccan society kinship was a predominant mode of social organization. The strength of tribal loyalties was partly a heritage of the pre-colonial period, which was characterized by a constant struggle between a weak central authority and an autonomous countryside. French colonial rule brought modern state institutions to Morocco and led to years of a long pacification campaign to bring rural tribes under state control. The military and bureaucratic structure that the French brought eliminated the previous levels of autonomy that tribes enjoyed. Nevertheless, the French policies did not necessarily hurt the tribal structure of the countryside. By manipulating tribal divisions, coopting tribal authorities, and incorporating the tribal armed forces into the colonial army, French rule preserved and empowered tribes, especially the Berber-speaking ones, in order to control the countryside (Wyrtzen 2011). After independence, the tribal structure of the society limited the unilateral expansion of state authority. In the first three years after independence, tribal resistance against the incursions of pro-Istiqlal administrative cadres into the countryside allowed the monarchy to ally with tribal leaders against Istiqlal. The rural areas, where the majority of the Berber-speaking population lived, became the backbone of the monarchical regime in Morocco.

The result of such alliance was low levels of state intrusion in the countryside. The Moroccan state's interference in the Berber areas was minimal and gradual because of its dependence on rural elites for support. Furthermore, contrary to the Turkish "makeover" project, the Moroccan monarchy emphasized traditional norms and symbols, and most importantly Islam along with the king's religious authority, to create a sense of national belonging. Despite the popularity of Arab nationalism during this period, the monarchy sustained a careful balance between Arabs and Berbers in its attempts at national integration. The policy was to refrain from making a clear-cut, thick definition of Moroccanness but rather to define it in ambiguous and flexible terms, which later would allow for negotiation, compromise, and change in state policies. The official policies and discourse during the early years of state-building simply neglected Berber identity and culture rather than attempting to transform them. This neglect hindered the politicization of Berber identity and delayed its mobilization.

The following section introduces the main political actors of Morocco in the immediate post-colonial era and gives an overview of their political agendas on the questions of what type of state should be built and how to achieve national integration. A discussion of the Berber tribal uprisings in the first three years of Moroccan independence and how they affected state formation will come next. In the third section, I analyze the formation of an alliance between rural notables and the monarchy and how this power structure influenced the state's manipulation of symbols and "invention of traditions" to create its nation. The chapter concludes with a discussion on the definition of Moroccanness, the policy of Arabization, and the birth of Berber activism.

POLITICAL ACTORS OF THE POST-INDEPENDENCE PERIOD

After forty-four years of French colonial rule, Morocco became independent in 1956. The nationalist pact, composed of the Istiqlal Party, the sultan, and the Liberation Army, proved to be fragile as each faction had major disagreements about how power should be exercised in a society that was fragmented along ethnic as well as tribal lines. According to Charrad's estimate (2001, 152), between 51 and 77 percent of the total population belonged to a tribe. While French colonial rule largely subdued the tribal areas and established modern state institutions, the French administration in the countryside was weak and highly dependent on alliances with tribes (Waterbury 1970, 33–58). Rather than instituting direct rule, the French controlled the rural areas through a limited number of tribal leaders. One result of such a policy was the preservation and strengthening of tribal institutions and identity. The linguistic division of the country between Berber- and Arabic-speakers added another layer of heterogeneity to this social picture. Although no definite figures exist and bilingualism was common, it was estimated that 40 percent of the population spoke one of the three Berber dialects and the rest were Arabic-speakers (Hart 1972, 26; Waterbury 1970, 11).[5]

At independence there were three main actors on the political scene: the Istiqlal Party, the king, and a rural establishment, composed largely of Berber-speaking tribal and religious dignitaries. The Istiqlal Party, which was officially founded in 1944, led the anti-colonial nationalist movement throughout the 1940s and 1950s. It drew most of its leadership from the urban, commercial class, particularly from Fez, as well as religious scholars in the cities. By 1951, the number of Istiqlal Party members reached one hundred thousand, composed of urban laborers and the unemployed (Waterbury 1970, 51). It was the largest and strongest political party in the country. According to Ashford's calculations (1961, 246), its membership reached 1.6 million by 1958. In the first five years of independence the Istiqlal Party held the most important ministries in the cabinets, although it could not form homogeneous governments and had to share government posts with a minor party and independents.[6]

Istiqlal shared a number of similarities with the RPP in its vision of state–society relations. The party aimed at rapid Arabization, which meant not only the substitution of French with the exclusive use of Modern Standard Arabic in education, administration, and the courts, but also banning the Berber dialects. Its founders considered Berberness as an artificially created identity by French colonialism and aimed at unifying the population under an Arab-Islamic identity. According to Allal al-Fassi, the leader of Istiqlal, the educational system would play a crucial role in making Morocco a nation that would be based on Arabic civilization

---

[5] David Hart notes that urban–rural divergence roughly corresponds to the ethnic fragmentation in Morocco. He states: "All the cities were and are Arabic-speaking, but the tribes were roughly half and half, with Arabic-speaking groups tending to be nearer the urban centers, and Berber-speaking tribes tending to be further removed from urban influences. With certain exceptions, the generalization of 'Arabs in the Plains; Berbers in the Mountains' still holds good today" (Hart 1972, 27). That is why Arab–Berber divergence also corresponds to the conceptual categorization of traditional Morocco into government land (*bilad al-makhzen*) and lands of dissidence (*bilad al-siba*). During the pre-colonial era, all the urban centers and the predominantly Arab tribal lands surrounding them were entirely under government control and therefore constituted the *bilad al-makhzen*. "Siba" areas, which were outside of the central government's control because its inhabitants did not recognize the *makhzen*'s authority, however, were entirely tribal and predominantly Berber. It was the French administration that brought the *siba* areas under the control of the central state for the first time.

[6] For a complete list of the members of the first five cabinets, see Ashford (1961, 98–99).

and Islamic culture. He argued that the preservation of local dialects by a large number of tribes presented a danger to political and social unity because language, as a medium for the transmission of ideas, had a great influence on people's mentality. That is why Arabization, especially at the elementary level in education, was necessary to create a homogeneous Moroccan identity (cited in Mezran 2007, 37). Similar to the attempts to prove the Turkish origins of the Kurds, the school textbooks written by the Istiqlal-controlled Ministry of Education emphasized the Arab origins of the Berbers. According to this thesis, Berbers were originally from Yemen, the heart of the Arab land, before they arrived in Morocco via Ethiopia. The textbooks were selective in recounting the history of Morocco and did not mention the pre-Arab and pre-Islamic period of the country (el-Khatir 2005, 323–325).

The party also aimed at establishing a highly centralized state by destroying tribal authority and any local particularism. It planned to replace all local administrators, who were mostly tribal leaders or landed notables during the Protectorate period, by officials who had no local ties and were directly appointed by the state's center. The Ministry of Justice, under the control of Istiqlal, abolished customary tribal law, unified the judicial system, and appointed non-local judges to the tribal areas (Ashford 1961, 111–116).[7] One of the projects of the party was to sedentarize the nomadic Berbers, transforming them into farmers who use modern agricultural techniques (Marais 1972, 280). The leaders of Istiqlal "wished to replace ties of solidarity based on kinship with new forms of association based on social and economic interests such as markets, schools, hospitals, and networks of agricultural production" (Charrad 2001, 154). Istiqlal's ultimate political aim was to establish a constitutional monarchy, where the monarch would reign but not rule, acting as a symbolic power. The party leaders wanted to establish a single-party system, which would dominate all state institutions and transfer complete state control to the party. Marais (1973, 190) suggests that Istiqlal looked at the first years of independence as a transitional stage, when they had to act as if they accepted the king's supreme power: "As the party could not control the political levers because of the king's influence, they placed their men

---

[7] Immediately after the promulgation of independence, the Berber Dahir was abolished in September 4, 1956 and the judicial system was unified under Islamic law. See the September 7, 1956 issue of *Al-Istiqlal*. The Dahir continued to be embedded in collective memory and was frequently brought up by Moroccan politicians after independence. Particularly the Arab nationalists used it to highlight that the distinction between Arabs and Berbers was an artificial construct, promoted by French colonialists.

in posts of responsibility in the administration, so as to be fully prepared to get control of the machinery of the state should a crisis break out."

The main point of departure between the Kemalists and the Istiqlalis, however, concerned the role of religion in society and politics. The Istiqlal Party leaders did not envision a complete rupture between state and religion.[8] On the contrary, they thought of Islam as the main element for unifying the society. Since the very early days of the anti-colonial struggle in Morocco, religion and nationalism were in fact intertwined. The Istiqlal Party's ideology had its origins in Salafism, an Islamic reform movement that called for a return to the traditions of religion practiced during the time of Muhammad and the early Muslim generation. Many of the early Istiqlal leaders were the old ulema from Qarawiyin University in Fez, which is reputed to be one of the oldest centers of Islamic education. As Waterbury (1970, 45) suggests, the ideals of purification of the Muslim community and the expulsion of colonialists were the twin objectives of the nationalists, and reference to religion provided them with increased domestic as well as international support from the rest of the Arab world. Consequently, an important part of the Istiqlali leadership sought to establish a state based on Islamic principles. Although Istiqlal's and the RPP's attitudes towards state–religion relations were different,[9] their belief in social engineering and social homogenization was similar. The founding cadres of the Istiqlal Party sought to homogenize Moroccan society not only linguistically but also religiously. The party's

---

[8] Gellner makes an interesting point about the connection between ideological modernization and state tradition in Muslim countries. He argues that there are two variants of ideological modernization in the Muslim world. In the Ottoman variant, where the state controls a higher proportion of the countryside and creates a political elite through the devshirme system, the secularist trend is stronger. In the Ibn Khaldun type, however, where the central state is weak and tribes are strong, ideological modernization comes in the reformist type: "Where the old state was strong, the old clerisy is too well-heeled and well-entrenched to toy with Reformism, and hence those who wish for change take to secular banners and political means. Where the state was weak, on the other hand, local politico-religious centers, namely living-saint-cults, which are repugnant to puritan Islam and to the modern spirit alike are correspondingly strong; hence those who strive for change can do so in opposition to such heterodoxy and in the name of the purification of religion, rather than of opposition to it" (Gellner 1981, 175).

[9] The nationalist cadres also used Islamic discourse and rituals to mobilize the masses during the War of Independence in Turkey. The war was done in the name of uniting the Ottoman Muslims. However, as Mustafa Kemal and his close circle of friends consolidated power, they pursued policies of secularization. As Zürcher (2010, 107) underlines, the early republican top governing elite comprised a total of thirty-six people including Mustafa Kemal. They were largely former military officers and all received their education in the secular schools of the late Ottoman Empire.

aspirations to makeover Moroccan society started during the colonial period when the party declared its aim to eradicate the religious pluralism and unorthodox practices that existed in the countryside, represented by various brotherhoods and marabouts.[10] As Mohammed Tozy (1993, 103) states: "The drive of the Istiqlal party to promote a single interpretation of Islam carried it into a witch-hunt against the brotherhoods and marabouts." The party sought to abolish any practice that did not conform to its vision of Islam. For example, the market days, which brought together different tribes once a week for commercial exchange, could be held any day of the week. During the days of anti-colonial struggle, Istiqlal proscribed the Friday markets, as this would be contrary to the Islamic principle that Friday is the day of rest (Hart 1972, 34).

Rural notables, who were predominantly Berber, represented the second group of political elites in Morocco. Waterbury (1970) argues that rural notables could be considered partly a creation of the French administration because the French used them as intermediaries between the central administration and the local communities in order to rule over the countryside. Such policy led to the strengthening of rural notables' power. Ben Kaddour (1972, 259) concurs with Waterbury and claims that some of the tribal leaders were merely creations of colonialism. Although during the pre-Protectorate period there were local chiefs who enjoyed strong authority over parts of the land and the people, their authority was intermittent. By giving them official titles and augmenting their property holdings, the French administration brought permanence to notables' authority. The attempts of the French to create a loyal, indigenous ruling class out of the children of Berber notables constituted another policy that would have a tremendous impact on how the elite struggles after independence would turn out. The Collége of Azrou was a secondary school that was established in 1924 to educate the Berber youth for administrative positions. The idea was to send the graduates to their places of origin and employ them as petty bureaucrats such as school teachers, telephone operators, and interpreters (Waterbury 1970, 110–113). Partly due to the "divide and rule" strategy and partly due to ideological convictions about Berber assimilability to French culture, the Berber notables' children were given preferential treatment not only in the administration but

---

[10] Marabouts are holy men, or the "saints of Islam," in Gellner's words. They traced their descent from the Prophet, are considered to possess *baraka*, or holiness, and are believed to have magical powers. Belief in marabouts is prevalent especially in mountainous Berber areas because of the weak influence of official, literate Islam and a central government in those regions. For more, see Gellner (1972b).

also in the military. The French colonial army recruited heavily from the rural Berber areas. The French perceived the Berbers as a martial race that could be utilized in the army, balancing against the Arab population. At the time of independence, 90 percent of the soldiers in the Moroccan army were Berber and had a rural origin (Coram 1972, 272). As a result of these policies, the rural Berber notables welcomed independence with enhanced authority and wealth in the countryside and more bargaining power at the national political arena.

It was the Popular Movement (*Mouvement Populaire*, MP) that represented the interests of the Berber notables during the post-colonial period. The MP was founded unofficially in 1957 by Mahjoub Aherdane, an ex-officer of the French army and the former governor of Rabat (following the typical career path that the French colonial regime opened up for the Berbers), and Abdelkrim Khatib, who was a Liberation Army leader in the Rif. The party was established in direct opposition to Istiqlal and voiced the resentments of the tribal leaders and notables about Istiqlal's attempts to penetrate into their areas of authority. As I will discuss in the following pages, the Istiqlal Party began to replace the old administrative cadres with supporters of the party. Waterbury (1970, 235) writes:

> Istiqlali personnel, hostile and scornful towards the rural notables, were rapidly infiltrating the blad as interior, police, justice, education, and public works employees, as well as party organizers. The intruders impinged upon the alliances carefully constructed under the protectorate, upset local patronage systems, and, in a more general way, often revealed a lack of understanding of rural politics.

At the press conference in which the leaders declared the inauguration of the MP, they did not refrain from making explicit their opposition to Istiqlal. "We did not achieve independence in order to lose freedom," became the slogan of the party (Coram 1972, 271). This was a direct reference to the role of the Liberation Army in achieving independence and was a hint that the tribes, which were still armed, would not accept Istiqlal's rule. Some units of the Liberation Army did not immediately give in to the state's forces. They did not accept laying down their arms or giving up collecting taxes and exercising police functions (Lawrence 2007, 276). Integrating them into the state's army was a difficult process.

The MP's program explicitly defended the interests of the local notables and tribes under the motto of "Islamic socialism." The party leaders defined themselves as socialists. They defined their socialism as based on Moroccan realities, characterized by Berber traditions. They advocated that communal lands be administered by communal traditions and demanded the distribution of the lands that the state confiscated from the French after independence to tribes and local collectivities. The party also openly asked for recognition of tribal customary law and setting up a school system where Berber dialects would be taught. The party leader, Mahjoub Aherdane, was adamant in defending the development of the Berber areas, strengthening Berber traditions, and preserving the Berber way of life and culture (Palazzoli 1974, 172–184). The party members were largely Berbers and the party's support was strongest among the rich peasants and large landowners. Zartman (1964, 99) writes that the party was the most active political organization within the ranks of the Royal Armed Forces. Right after its establishment, the Istiqlal Party accused the MP of being representatives of French colonialism (Sedon 1981, 174). The palace supported the formation of the MP behind the scenes to curtail the possible rise of the Istiqlal Party as a single-party regime. As Ben Kaddour (1972, 263) underlines, a Berber-based party would also increase Berbers' sense of political representation in a way that could be controlled by the palace.

In sum, the projects of the Istiqlal Party and the Popular Movement were almost diametrically opposed to one another. The Istiqlal Party represented urban interests and stood for establishing an authoritarian single-party regime that would push for state centralization, detribalization, suppression of particularism, and modernization of the society. The MP, by contrast, represented the interests of the rural power centers and advocated the preservation of particularistic (tribal and Berber) identities, communal law, and values in the countryside and supported the continuation of the monarchy as the highest authority in the system. The projects of the Istiqlal Party encountered strong resistance from the rural areas, which gave way to the emergence and rise of the MP. In addition to the opposition of the countryside, the Istiqlal Party also had to compete with another rival: the king.

The king, Mohammed V, belonged to the Alawite dynasty, which came to power in 1666. Since the eighth century, Moroccan monarchs have legitimated their right to rule by their claimed descent from the Prophet. During the pre-Protectorate period, such legitimation clearly was not enough for the establishment of a strong state in the region. As Mounira Charrad (2001, 103–109) argues, there was a weak state and a weak dynasty with no stable bureaucracy that would ensure the continuity of state power. The tribes of Morocco had control over their regions with almost no state interference. The power of the sultan was highly variable depending on the strength of alliances between the palace and tribal areas: "Although which tribes were in active opposition to the sultan fluctuated over time, about half of the territory constituting Morocco was in a near permanent state of dissidence in the precolonial period. Dissident tribes were an ever present threat to central authority, a source of potential dynastic rivals" (Charrad 2001, 104).

It was during the Protectorate period that the king's legitimacy was strengthened and he became the symbol of Moroccan nationalism. This growth in the monarchy's symbolic value was largely an unintended consequence of French policies and the strategies that the nationalists pursued in opposition to the French. In the 1930s, when the nationalist movement began to gain ground in the cities, the sultan (his title became the king after independence) was a passive figure, who did not show much opposition to French decisions and whom many Moroccans hardly knew much about. By the mid-1930s the sultan and the nationalists began to cooperate since such an alliance served both sides' interests. The sultan found in such cooperation the possibility to increase his legitimacy and his visibility in the public eye, and the nationalists found in the sultan a symbol that had the potential to generate mass support that the party could not generate on its own, especially in the rural areas. The figure of the sultan gave nationalists an opportunity to invent new traditions and rituals, such as the Feast of the Throne (*la Fête du Trône*), to mobilize people for demonstrations and to use (and also to build on) his religious legitimacy.[11] The sultan's charisma and legitimacy were further strengthened after the French sent him into exile in 1953 because of his cooperation with the nationalists. During his exile, legends were circulated about his spiritual power and miracles in the countryside. People claimed that his face appeared on the moon and began to imagine him as a godlike figure. Through these myths about the king, the nationalists presented the restoration of the monarchy as a religious duty (el-Khatir 2005, 315–317). The exile of the sultan in 1953 led to the organization of armed bands in the countryside (which would later become the loosely connected Liberation Army), where rural fighters demanded the return of Mohammed V and an end to the Protectorate regime. Istiqlal's emphasis on the sultan's religious significance also contributed to the development of the sultan's cult. This emphasis would later put the party in a difficult situation, as the king would be its main rival and an obstacle to the realization of the Istiqlali agenda after independence. As Waterbury (1970,

[11] The Feast of the Throne became the first nationwide celebration in Morocco. A detailed description of how the nationalists created and organized the Feast of the Throne and the conflicts that the celebrations caused with the French administration in the 1930s can be found in Rachik (2003).

47) argues: "The Istiqlal has, since independence, found itself the victim of its own success during the period before 1956." The king returned from the exile as a national hero with his prestige and power strengthened to a great extent at the expense of the Istiqlal Party.

The first few years of the post-Protectorate period were marked by a power struggle between the king and Istiqlal, out of which the king emerged victorious. In the next section, I will analyze the tribal Berber uprisings as a reaction against state expansion immediately after independence and discuss how the king's management of the uprisings gave him the upper hand in the political arena. The developments during this period led to a long-lasting alliance between the monarchy and the power centers of the countryside.

TRIBES AGAINST STATE EXPANSION: REBELLIONS IN POST-COLONIAL MOROCCO

A series of tribal uprisings made their mark on the immediate post-colonial period in Morocco. All these uprisings took place in Berber-speaking regions and were directed at repelling the incursions of the bureaucracy dominated by the Istiqlal Party into the countryside. The king's attitude in this confrontation played a very important role in building his long-lasting alliances with the rural power centers and marginalizing the Istiqlal Party (and the ideology it represented) in the emerging political arena. The result was a deviation from a centralist, homogenizing, and transformative nation-building project into one that produced relatively peaceful Berber–state relations in independent Morocco.

The first serious signs of a conflict between the Istiqlal Party and tribes took place during the attempts to create a unitary army on the eve of independence. The Liberation Army, which was formed by tribal military power in the countryside, did not lay its arms down as readily as the Istiqlalis expected. Although the number is not precise, Ashford (1959, 16) estimates that there were around 10,000 tribesmen who joined the Liberation Army. The tribal warriors had minimal contact with the Istiqlal representatives during the anti-colonial struggle and recognized the king as their leader. In addition, Istiqlal's political vision created annoyance and confusion among the tribesmen. During the negotiations to incorporate the Liberation Army forces into the new Royal Army, the Istiqlal representatives failed to attain the tribes' loyalty to the government. The king was quick to take advantage of the situation, inviting leading members of the army chiefs to the palace. Coram (1972, 270) notes that during this secret meeting no Istiqlal member was present, and Aherdane, who would later become the leader of the Popular Movement, and Lahcean Lyoussi, who was Morocco's first minister of the interior and who would later try to organize the tribal resistance against Istiqlal, attended the meeting. In this meeting, the army chiefs agreed to give up their arms or to merge with the Royal Army. The assassination of the chief of staff of the Liberation Army, allegedly ordered by Istiqlal's Mehdi Ben Barka, once more increased the hostility to the party. After an open rebellion that lasted for one month in the Middle Atlas, the pacification of the Liberation Army was made possible only by the king's visit to the Berber areas. Eventually it was to Mohammed V that the army chiefs surrendered their arms (Ashford 1959, 19–20; Coram 1972, 270–271). In his speech, the king emphasized the brotherhood of Arabs and Berbers under Islam and the importance of national solidarity (Wyrtzen 2009, 368).

If one of the reasons why the army chiefs recognized the king as the supreme power was the king's religious significance, the other reason was his careful political stance. During the turbulent years of the post-colonial era, he refrained from identifying himself openly with any political faction and started to build an image as the "supreme arbiter." Such a role ensured that he would hold the monopoly of violence in his hands, as a unified army and police force loyal to the monarchy came into being and helped him to emerge as the supreme authority in the country. During the tribal uprisings, his response to the rebellions and his willingness to negotiate with the dissident tribes consolidated his position as the "father of the nation" and gave the first signs of an alliance between the monarchy and the rural establishment.

The first rebellion took place in 1957 in the Tafilalt region, in Southeastern Morocco, and was instigated by Addi ou Bihi, who was a governor and an influential notable of the Berber Ait Izdig tribe. Addi ou Bihi was resentful of Istiqlal's attempts to control his area and his hostility against the party increased when Lyoussi, a Berber tribal leader who was the minister of the interior, resigned from his post and a high-ranking Istiqlal member replaced him. Afterwards Lyoussi returned to his native area in the Middle Atlas, began to openly criticize Istiqlal's style of government, and contacted several Berber leaders to unite against the party, but in support of the king. Lyoussi's main attack was against the centralizing policies of Istiqlal. He stated: "It is contrary to the interests of the people to confer all political, social, and economic responsibility to some men who ignore all the tribes and the countryside" (quoted in Ashford 1961, 200). His calls did not fall on deaf ears. Addi ou Bihi declared that he did not accept any intermediaries between himself and King Mohammed V and that he refused to recognize the authority of any officials appointed by the government. He distributed 7,000 rifles to his tribesmen and arrested the judge and the police chief of his area. Hart (1999, 87) writes that he even planned to arrest the minister of the interior and the minister of justice when they came to his area for an inspection. The rebellion came to an end without bloodshed after Prince Hassan, who was in charge of the army, offered amnesty to the rebels. Addi ou Bihi was taken to Rabat (Hart 1999, 88). The palace treated those who were involved in the revolt leniently. Waterbury (1970, 237) notes that ou Bihi stayed in the palace for six months after his arrest and Lyoussi was kept as one of the three members of the Crown Council until his flight to Spain in 1959. Two years after the rebellion both men were put on trial and given death sentences. Addi ou Bihi died in prison in 1961 due to illness. Lyoussi, who escaped to Malaga during the trial, returned to Morocco a year later as a result of a royal pardon.[12] The king's conciliatory manner to resolve this contention signified his willingness to accept a political alliance with the rural centers of power against Istiqlal's projects of state-building.

Rural unrest continued, culminating in another uprising in the autumn of 1958. It took place in the northern zone of Morocco, a former Spanish territory known as the Rif region. It was political and administrative marginalization coupled with economic problems that caused the rebellion. The Aith Waryaghar tribe was resentful that none of its tribe members was appointed to the new local and provincial administrations as all these posts were filled by pro-Istiqlalis who were not native to the area. The language gap between the new administrators and the locals constituted a problem. The bureaucrats were French-speaking Arabs while the majority of the latter spoke Spanish and their Berber dialect. Another source of resentment was the closure of the Algerian border. The region's economy was largely dependent on earnings from migrant labor to Algeria. With independence, the Rifians were cut off from their major source of revenue and unemployment became a major problem in the region (Hart 1999,

---

[12] The use of royal pardon has a symbolic meaning, strengthening the image of the monarch as the father of the nation and the dispenser of justice. An order or declaration of the king has the force of law even without being published in the Official Bulletin. The royal pardon, which the kings usually declare on national holidays, is also a strategy to co-opt political opponents. Through the royal pardon the king creates "links of obligation with various groups, rendering as many people as possible beholden and grateful to his generosity. Criminals, political or others, are more often pardoned than amnestied; their sins are not expunged, just magnanimously overlooked by the sovereign" (Waterbury 1970, 150).

89–90). The government was well aware of the local dissatisfaction and the possibility of an outbreak of violence. Thus, before the rebellion, it passed a series of regulations that banned the illegal possession of arms (Ashford 1961, 212).

The rebellion started when a local Istiqlal Party office was stormed by a group of tribesmen. Later roads were blocked, other Istiqlal offices were looted, and demonstrations were held. As in the first revolt, the tribesmen did not challenge the monarchy but were upset by the attempts of Istiqlal to expand its power in the countryside. The king indicated his willingness to negotiate. Three weeks after the first incident, he accepted a delegation composed of Rifian tribesmen to listen to their complaints. The delegation submitted an eighteen-point list of its resentments and demands. These included recruitment of local administrators from among those who were native to the area, appointment of Rifian judges, appointment of a Rifian to a high-level post in the Moroccan government, tax reductions, initiation of an agricultural development program, creation of scholarships for Rifian students, rapid Arabization of education all over Morocco,[13] and the creation of more rural schools in the region (Hart 1999, 91–93). Mohammed V, in conformity with the fatherly image that he was constructing, responded: "All the injustices that have been reported will be repaired. All legitimate rights will be satisfied. Return to your tribes in tranquility and without fear. Transmit to your brothers our paternal solicitude. Transmit to them equally our order: that each return to his village since we have given our instructions that no one should be troubled" (quoted in Ashford 1961, 214). The assurances of Mohammed V were not adequate to put an end to the rebellion, however. A second round of unrest broke out when the Rifian tribes learned that the new cabinet was dominated by Istiqlal's left-wing members (Zartman 1964, 89). This time tribal demands for regional autonomy led to a serious, repressive military operation by the Royal Armed Forces. Rif was a particularly sensitive region for the state due to its previous history of separatism. Between 1921 and 1926, a revolt took place against Spanish rule led by a *qadi* from a leading Berber tribe, Abdelkrim al-Khattabi. This revolt led to the establishment of the Rif Republic in 1923 until the French forces defeated al-Khattabi in 1926. This history of proto state-building in the region as well as Rifian tribes' continuation of dissidence after contacting the king was met by a harsh state response that led to significant violence

---

[13] Hart explains their demands for Arabization by the Rifians' hatred of the administrative use of French by civil servants sent to the Rif, which was formerly a Spanish zone.

by state forces. The state continued to perceive the region with distrust in the following years. King Hassan II, who commanded the army as the crown prince during the revolt, avoided visiting the region during his rule and Rif remained one of the most underdeveloped and poorest regions of the country (Maddy-Weitzman 2011, 86).

Despite the violent suppression of the revolt, the palace continued to build its alliance with the rural and tribal power centers. Gellner (1981) notes the monarchy's lenient treatment of the leaders and participants in the rural rebellions. While the main leader of the uprising escaped to Spain, the warriors of Aith Waryaghar were jailed but were released a year-and-a-half later in an amnesty granted by Mohammed V on the occasion of the Feast of the Throne. Two years later, all those who escaped to Spain were allowed to return (Hart 1999, 95). This period coincided with the consolidation of the power of the king at the expense of the Istiqlal Party. In accordance with an official investigation report, which emphasized that local administrators should be familiar with local Berber dialect and customs, efforts were made to appoint local men to official positions (Seddon 1981, 179). A new government was formed in which a Rifian was appointed as the minister of posts, telephone, and telegraph, and the Popular Movement was legally recognized as a political party.[14] After Mohammed V's death, the first government of Hassan II included both leaders of the MP, the party that became the spokesman of the rural Berber areas (Waterbury 1970, 241, 246).

This alliance gained more strength by the split in the Istiqlal Party in January 1959 as the more radical and leftist faction broke up to form the National Union of Popular Forces (*Union Nationale des Forces Populaires*, UNFP). One reason why this split occurred was the disagreement between the moderates and the radicals over how to approach the palace and how to control the monarch's desire to withhold power. While the younger and the radical group was highly critical of the king's insistence on appointing the ministers of the interior and defense and worried about his control of the army, the moderates emphasized a more gradual and accommodationist approach to tame the political desires of the palace. Waterbury (1970, 144) writes that Mohammed V promoted this division by encouraging disputes among Istiqlal's leaders while supporting the formation of rival groups, such as the MP, and rural discontent, to counter the power of Istiqlal. Charrad (2001, 157) underlines that

---

[14] Waterbury (1970, 238) notes that Istiqlali officials delayed granting legal recognition to the MP for two years on the pretext of legal technicalities.

although ideological convictions played a role in people's decisions about which side to take during this process of political fragmentation, patronage networks and alliances shaped political alignments even more.

After the split of the Istiqlal Party, all governmental activity was gradually subordinated to the palace (Waterbury 1970, 195). The king could keep power by allying with the rural notables (a majority of which were Berber speaking) through an extensive system of patronage, relinquishing any large-scale, top-down reform for the sake of the conservation of the status quo. Unlike in Turkey, the state, which came under the domination of the palace, did not aim at the disintegration of the tribal system and modernization of the countryside. This meant minimal interference in the rural areas to keep them as stable as possible. As Charrad (2001, 153) states,

> The threat of reactivation of tribal ties was ever present in the Moroccan countryside in the aftermath of independence. Although manipulation of tribal alliances was played with more restraint than in the precolonial and colonial periods, it remained nevertheless central to the functioning of the Moroccan political system in the period when a sovereign national state took shape.

In the next section, I will explore how tribes and local notables were incorporated into the state administration and how this incorporation influenced the formation of official policies, symbols, and discourses for national integration.

RURAL LEADERS AS ALLIES AND THE RETRADITIONALIZATION OF SYMBOLIC SPACE

Four years after independence, the palace ensured its complete control over politics by encouraging intergroup rivalry among political actors and contributing to their fragmentation. The continuity of the monarch's monopoly of power was largely dependent on his alliance with and cooptation of the tribal notables in the countryside. This did not denote a return to the pre-colonial political system. On the contrary, the rural areas increasingly came under the central state's jurisdiction. This alliance meant that the rural areas became the backbone of the political system in Morocco and the guardians of the monarchy. The king's strategy to govern the countryside overlaps with what Boone (2003, 32) calls "powersharing." In this political arrangement, "a dense network of state institutions in the rural areas provides political infrastructure for de facto or de jure devolution of authority to indigenous elites." Boone (2003, 332) predicts that the powersharing strategy impedes projects of rural transformation or modernization because these projects can destabilize the existing power structure. The Moroccan case confirms Boone's hypothesis. The allegiance of the rural elites to the regime was achieved not only through an extensive network of patronage that led to their integration into the state administration but also through minimal state interference in rural life and the use of traditional symbols and loyalties for national integration.

After Mohammed V's death in 1961, Hassan II acceded to the throne and soon achieved complete control over the governmental apparatus. Waterbury (1970, 275) calls the years between 1955 and 1960 the "period of defense," in which the monarch had to negotiate with Istiqlal on the appointment of the ministers and had to consent to the ministers' choices of high-ranking bureaucrats within their jurisdiction. The post-1960 era became the "period of offense" for the monarchy. The king emerged as the most powerful figure in the political arena and came to decide on all governmental posts of any importance along with the ministries. In March 1961, Hassan II not only assumed the throne but also declared himself the prime minister, the minister of defense, the minister of the interior, and the minister of agriculture.

With the king's firm grip on executive power, the project of detribalization, which the Istiqlal-dominated government planned to initiate in the first years after independence, was reversed. Unlike in Turkey, where the state elite saw detribalization as an indispensable component of state-building, in Morocco tribes were officially recognized and registered for administrative purposes. The disintegration of tribal solidarities was not to the advantage of the monarchy as this could have led to the erosion of state control in the countryside and political instability. One indicator of the state's reluctance to detribalize the rural areas was the civil registry practices. Until the mid-1990s, the tribal affiliation of citizens was marked on national identity cards (Hoffman 2000). The monarchy used the tribal leaders' ability to control their societies by making them state officials and by institutionalizing tribal divisions within the local state apparatus. The way that rural communes were established, for instance, indicates how tribal leaders were incorporated into the Ministry of the Interior. The progressives of the Istiqlal Party aimed at transforming the traditional *jemaa*, which were tribal councils in the predominantly Berber areas formed by the elders of the community, into modern rural communes that would cut across tribal lines and be organized solely with economic and geographic considerations.[15]

---

[15] For more on the earlier projects of rural administration and the Istiqlal Party's intentions to form rural communes, see Lewis (1960) and Ashford (1961, 355–362).

Istiqlalis wanted to create these institutions as the basis of rural administration that would regulate rural modernization programs. They also saw them as tools to facilitate the erosion of tribal loyalties by breaking the tribes into different rural communes. Seddon (1981, 277–282) writes that by 1959 this project started to die. Local administrators created rural communes that followed tribal lines and tribal notables were integrated into the new administrative framework. This policy was an important tool for the monarchy to coopt the Berber-speaking tribal leaders. Consequently, the majority of the rural commune councils were composed of supporters of the Popular Movement and many councilors were former members of the *jemaas* of the Berber tribes. According to Ben Kaddour's (1972, 265) calculations from the official results published by the Ministry of the Interior, by 1963 the MP filled 10,000 out of 11,200 seats in the commune councils, 201 out of 281 seats in the Chambers of Commerce, 292 out of 312 seats in the Chambers of Agriculture, and 147 out of 225 seats in the provincial assemblies. As a result of the MP's domination of local institutions, their members and supporters had easy access to rural loans and benefited from economic transactions performed by the municipal and rural councils. According to Hatt (1996, 134), "The communes also serve as electoral districts for representatives to the National Parliament (majlis), a body which has, through several incarnations, not developed much beyond an advisory role in the operation of government, although the representatives do serve as useful patrons for tribesmen having business with the national government." Rather than being an institution of legislative authority, the Moroccan parliament has primarily acted as an arena for patronage distribution.[16] The patron–client relationship was firmly built between the palace and rural notables at different levels of the state. In line with an already existing tradition, Hassan II married two Berber women from powerful tribes that underlined his regime's alliance with Berber centers of power (Maddy-Weitzman 2011, 88).

Other positions that created venues for integration of the local elites into the administrative framework were those of the *shaykhs* and *moqaddems*. While the former were responsible for administering tribes, the latter administered villages or conglomerations of villages. Governors usually appointed local notables for these positions. *Shaykhs* and *moqaddems* were the administrators who had direct contact with the local populations and acted as the agents of the central state. They

[16] For a detailed analysis of how parliaments work for patronage distribution, see Lust-Okar (2006).

were, however, strictly controlled by the governors and the *qaids*, who were the administrators at the rural district level. Both governors and *qaids* were appointed by the state's center from among career officials and were usually not natives of the areas they ruled. However, Venema and Mguild (2002) write that in certain areas provincial governors were recruited from the local population until the 1970s. The monarchy was also careful about the ethnic composition of the high-level state administrators while recruiting for the professional civil service. Marais (1972, 281) writes that from 1960 onwards, Berbers increasingly became *qaids*, and that they constituted a majority at the École de Kenitra where future local officials were trained. Ben Kaddour (1972, 261) confirms Marais' claim and states that in the early 1960s, 250 out of 320 *qaids* of the Ministry of the Interior were Azrou graduates, who were predominantly Berbers. Venema and Mguild (2002) argue that while the authority of the central government expanded in the post-independence period, the growing government bureaucracy did not undermine the legitimacy of the village councils (*jemaa*). The governors usually appointed those who were proposed by the village councils as *shaykhs* and *moqaddems*. Venema and Mguild point out that *shaykhs* and *moqaddems* should not be seen necessarily as figures who were controlled and manipulated by the regional government bureaucracy. Rather, they should be considered as intermediaries who represented the interests of the local population. In addition, Venema and Mguild argue that even today the village councils are still vital institutions in regulating the social and religious life of the rural areas although the provincial governors are no longer recruited from among the local population and the central government enjoys a higher influence in the Middle Atlas.

One important consequence of the alliance between the monarchy and the rural notables was socio-economic stasis in the countryside. The monarchy was cautious about initiating any reform programs that could antagonize the rural elites. Land reform that would weaken the feudal relationships in the countryside and distribute land to poor peasants was out of the question. Such land reform was one of the projects of the Istiqlal Party and was abandoned after the party lost its power in the government. The state recognized the collective ownership of tribal lands. At the end of the 1990s tribal lands constituted around 14 percent of land tenure in Morocco (United Nations Economic Commission for Africa 2010, 102). As part of the monarchy's policy of ensuring allegiance in the rural areas through patronage, the lands that belonged to the French administration and some colonists' lands were distributed largely to the members of the MP (Ben Kaddour 1972, 266). The rural notables, with the encouragement of the palace, established the Moroccan Union of Agriculture, which became one of the strongest lobby groups in the country. Hammoudi (1997, 30) writes that through such institutions the notables reactivated clientele networks, established close relations with the palace, acquired formerly colonized land, and marginalized groups that advocated agrarian reform. The monarchy actively supported the preservation of the status quo in the countryside. For instance, a decree stipulated that land recipients should hire relatives in agricultural production and refrain from wage labor. This was a clear attempt to maintain a kin-based social structure and slow down the development of capitalistic relations (Charrad 2001, 156). Similarly, Hammoudi (1997, 37) writes about the lack of innovation in the rural areas which was seen as threatening the traditional relationship between the local notables and the peasants. He also points to the noncapitalistic management style of the notables, who spent the fruits of production on "maintaining a clientele through generosity and the cycle of gifts and countergifts." The cost of the protection of the status quo in the countryside was the very slow rate of socio-economic development.[17] Micaud (1972, 437) writes that the monarchy did not undertake any programs to modernize the countryside and improve the living conditions of the peasants. The rural masses kept quiescent largely as a result of the patronage system of the rural notables.

The king sustained a large patronage network to build a loyal clientele for the palace largely by manipulating his own wealth and keeping a strict control over bureaucratic posts. Although investigating the private finances and affairs of the king and the extended royal family is forbidden by law, the king is known to be Morocco's largest landowner as well as the controller of the Maghreb's largest holding company, Omnium Nord-Africain (ONA). Hassan II used his control over private economic activities in order to extend his patronage network: "No Moroccan businessman has been able to occupy an important place in the private sector since independence without the personal agreement of the king," wrote Leveau (quoted in Zartman 1987, 29). In addition, at times of crisis he allocated land to build political support under the pretext of "agrarian

---

[17] A classic study that discusses the alliance between the monarchy and the rural notables and how this led to political stability but low economic performance is Leveau (1976).

reform." The king also controlled the high-level posts in the bureaucracy, which is a major means of personal aggrandizement. Waltz (1995, 118) writes:

> Palace favorites may be rewarded with control of public enterprises, and public office has facilitated access to such benefits as real estate, import licenses, commercial licenses, and noncompetitive contracts. Even the contractual particulars in the lower echelons are subject to royal intervention and manipulation, so that the entire corpus of government lies open, and vulnerable, to the king's pleasure.

She adds that the political parties have also made use of financial support from the palace (1995, 118). These patronage networks have been critical for the stability of the monarchy, consolidating the king's role as the supreme arbiter and decision maker in the country.

The nationalist discourse, practices, and symbols developed and used by the monarchy were concomitant with its alliance with the rural power centers. In other words, the way the monarch imagined its nation, legitimized its rule, and promoted a sense of belonging to a common national culture mirrored the dominant power structure in Morocco. The balance of power achieved through the help of the countryside, which was fragmented along tribal and ethnic lines, did not allow for an explicit condemnation of diversity in cultural practices, identities, and traditions in the rural areas. The loyalty of the population in the countryside was sought not only by satisfying the demands of local notables through political cooptation and patron–client relationships, but also by constructing national symbols that invoked tradition, historical continuity, and Moroccan authenticity.

Moroccan nationalism promoted by the monarchy emphasizes the role of Islam as the bond that unifies the Arabs and the Berbers and defines Moroccanness, first and foremost, by Muslim identity. Islam is the official religion of the country and the monarch portrays himself as not only the head of state but also the religious leader of the religious community. Since the eighth century when the first Islamic dynasty was established, the rulers of Morocco have claimed descent from the Prophet Mohammed. The post-colonial kings of Morocco, who belong to the Alawite dynasty founded in the mid-1600s, developed and used this idea of sharifism and referred to themselves as the "Commander of the Faithful" (*Amir al-Mu'minin*). According to the notion of the religious foundations of the state, the king, as the descendant of the Prophet, carriers *baraka*, which can be defined as a divine force that brings prosperity and good fortune on the community of believers. *Baraka* is believed to be transmitted from father to son and, therefore, legitimizes the succession to the throne (Bourqia 1999, 246–248). The saintliness of the monarch also justifies his right to make decisions without any regard to constitutional restraints. Attacking the monarch in Morocco is not only a crime but also a sacrilege (Hammoudi 1997, 13).

The authority of the king as the spiritual leader of the nation was in fact neither unchallenged nor deep-rooted. Gellner (1972a, 363) points out that there have been many others within Moroccan society who have claimed descent from the Prophet and thus the title has never been unique to the king. In addition, the religious sanctity of the rulers did not preclude large-scale tribal resistance to the dictates of the central power during the pre-colonial period. According to Hammoudi (1997, 15), the religious foundation of the monarchy was largely a modern construct that was developed during the anti-colonial struggle. The nationalist movement's attack on local religious figures, who chose to collaborate with the colonial powers, hurt the prestige of the religious brotherhoods and helped raise the king to the status of a national hero, who fought for the protection of Muslim honor against Christian denigration. As Hammoudi (1997, 18) states: "In the first years of independence, following his return from exile, Mohammed V captivated the masses: he was in everyone's eyes the Prophet's descendant and the hero of independence ... His actions persuaded Moroccans that only he possessed the active and forceful prophetic charisma that was needed at that moment."

Unlike the earlier periods, the palace had at its disposal powerful tools after independence, such as the media and the school system, to promote an image of the monarch as the national unifier. Lisa Wedeen (1999) underlines how cults of state leaders help to create a sense of national belonging by producing symbols and rhetoric that are meaningful only to the people who belong to that particular nation-state. Pointing to the case of Syria, she writes: "Cults may also contribute to nation-state building by helping to territorialize official politics ... National membership is expressed through people's facility with the vocabulary and the regime's ability to reproduce the symbolism of Asad's rule. The nation-state, in this sense, extends as far as the cult does" (1999, 157). Both in Turkey and Morocco, the states resorted to symbolic politics extensively in order to cultivate a sense of national belonging and developed their leaders' cults to present a role model to the nation. However, the content of the cults are dissimilar, indicating the differences in the ideological formulations of nation-building and the respective states' intentions about their society. Unlike in Turkey, where Atatürk's images symbolize radical transformation and modernization, the Moroccan regime's iconography heavily draws on religious symbols, old state ceremonies and rituals, and popular customs.[18] As I wrote earlier, it was the Istiqlal Party that started to build a cult around Mohammed V, by promoting him as a divine figure who carried God's blessing. This image was further developed by Hassan II, who was careful in invoking culturally resonant symbols for the society to emphasize the historical continuity of the Moroccan dynasty and its Islamic roots.

The monarch's imagery as the indisputable leader and the unifier of the country is regularly invoked in national ceremonies and official rituals. For instance, the *bay'a* ceremonies, in which tribe leaders, rural notables, state officials, politicians, and religious leaders offer their allegiance to the king, have constituted an important part of the monarchy's symbolic performance. *Bay'a* refers to an Islamic principle that means recognition of a ruler's authority by those who promise him obedience. The *bay'a* ceremony reinforces the king's sacred imagery and the long durability of Moroccan state traditions. Hammoudi (1997, 42–43) calls attention to how the media contributes to the reproduction and display of monarchical power by disseminating images of humility and submission in the king's presence: "This vital and dramatized representation of obedience is at the heart of the exercise of authoritarian power; in ritual and ceremony it takes the concrete form of prostration and hand kissing, which every notable must perform at regular intervals. Such images, enhanced by the court etiquette, enter every household through the media." During Ramadan, he appears as the religious head of the country when he presides over the religious meetings of the ulema every day. The ritual is televised live and watched by a wide audience.

It is not only the emphasis on Islam but also the emphasis on culturally resonant images that sets the Moroccan state ceremonies and leader cult apart from its Turkish counterpart. Unlike in Turkey, where the state elite considered traditional outfits as relics of a backward past that should disappear from public life as soon as possible, in Morocco, clothes that are worn in everyday life are politically utilized to mark cultural difference and national identity. During the colonial struggle, traditional garments such as the turban, fez, and *jellaba* emerged as national symbols at a time when the nationalists called for a boycott of French products.[19] Especially

---

[18] A good analysis of the king's cult in Morocco can be found in Benchemsi (2006, 40–54).

[19] *Jellaba* is a hooded outer garment that stretches almost to the ground. It is made of cotton or wool.

in demonstrations against the French, people wore clothes that indicated their Moroccanness.[20] In the post-colonial era, Moroccans still commonly wear traditional outfits, particularly the *jellaba*, in everyday life, regardless of their ethnic identity. The monarchy regularly invokes it as the national symbol, and the king and state officials wear it in ceremonies. Hassan II preferred to be photographed in traditional clothes more often than in European ones. In 1979, the wearing of the white *jellaba* by parliamentarians during the opening ceremony of parliament became compulsory (Claisse 1987, 42). Such public visibility accorded to Moroccan traditional symbols by the state also corresponds to what Hammoudi (1997, 35) calls "refashioned tradition in daily life." The revival of certain old social practices that Hammoudi refers to, such as the appearance of old wedding rituals in new forms and the use of antiquated family titles such as Moulay, a honorific title borne by the Moroccan sultans, parallels the retraditionalization of state practices in the post-colonial era.

Although the monarchy appropriated Islam as the state religion and resorted to Islamic symbols to build its legitimacy, it was careful not to promote only one interpretation of Islam and ask the society to conform to it. The Moroccan kings, starting from Mohammed V, knew that their support largely depended on the countryside, where there was a plethora of religious practices and organizations. Thus, the monarchy did not attempt to challenge the popular conceptions and practices of Islam. These popular practices developed over a long period in a predominantly illiterate society that found it hard to incorporate the Qur'anic teachings and dogma preached by the ulema of the cities. The population's difficulty in reading religious texts gave rise to holy men (marabouts), who were believed to possess divine grace and, therefore, the ability to approach God directly. Mohammed V regularly made references to the cult of saints dominant in the countryside and he did it with respect. The descendants of the saints were officially recognized and venerated through royal decrees, gifts were sent to the main marabouts from the palace every year, and ministers attended the celebrations of annual festivals for the saints (Tozy 1993, 107). Eickelman (1987, 88) argues that such popular beliefs about marabouts were not challenged by the monarchy because the relationship between saints and people replicated the patron–client ties that the monarchy promotes in its relations with the population. The monarchy's stance vis-à-vis popular Islam was also consistent with the lack of official interference in social life in order to regulate and

---

[20] For more on the discussion of national costumes, see Rachik (2003, 89–95).

transform it. As Leveau (1976, 206) points out, since independence the state has intervened minimally in the social life and relations of individuals, except during Ramadan.[21] The lack of a state-led transformative project in Morocco has kept daily life free of official interference, especially in the countryside.

MOROCCANNESS AND BERBER IDENTITY

The monarchy's attitude with regard to the ethnic diversity of the country was an ambivalent one. On the one hand, the 1960s and 1970s were the heyday of Arab nationalism in the Middle East and the Arabist discourse was quite popular not only within the political elite (except those who were in the cadres of the Popular Movement) but also with the educated, urban Moroccans. On the other hand, the monarchy's power rested on a delicate alliance with the rural areas, largely dominated by Berber-speakers. Therefore, an ardent insistence on homogenization of the population through Arabization, by attacking the local Berber dialects and cultural practices, would be a risky project that could disrupt the alliance between the monarchy and the rural centers of power. The tribal resistance to Istiqlal's projects of intruding into the countryside was a crucial warning for the monarchy. In addition, largely as a colonial legacy, the majority of the army, the *makhzen* militia, and the gendarmerie were composed of people of Berber origin (Marais 1972, 281). The palace achieved complete control over these institutions after independence but the security forces' loyalty to the king could have been weakened if the monarch had taken an uncompromising pro-Arabist attitude, which carried the risk of politicizing the Berber-speakers. As a result, while there were some fierce debates and conflicts about the definition of Moroccanness among politicians and intellectuals, the palace, as the ultimate decision maker, refrained from becoming overly involved in this debate, at least until the 1980s when Berber activism started to grow. It did not support, let alone officially recognize, Berber identity and culture but neither did it impose prohibitions on the expressions of Berberness, such as language, dress, and music, in daily life as long as these expressions were cultural.

Both for Mohammed V and Hassan II, Islam, rather than Arab identity, constituted the basis of Moroccan national identity. When Mohammed

---

[21] Leveau must be referring to the official ban on eating and drinking in public during Ramadan.

V went to the areas of rebellion in the Rif, on a trip he called "the voyage of unity," he emphasized Muslimhood as the unifier of Arabs and Berbers. "Our people, who are situated in the shadow of Islam, who do not accept any discrimination between Arabs and Berbers, and who have only their love for fatherland as their ideal, is an example of solidarity and fraternity," said the king in a speech addressing the tribal resentment of Istiqlal's policies (quoted in Mezran 2002, 57). Hassan II resorted to a similar Islamic discourse when referring to matters of national unity and Moroccan identity. For instance, when he organized the Green March in 1975 to claim Morocco's sovereignty over Western Sahara, he used Qur'anic vocabulary to mobilize people. He presented the march as a jihad against the Spanish occupation and himself as the "imam" of the community. While thousands of people were walking to cross into the Western Sahara, they were asked to carry the Qur'an and to recite the *sura al-Fatiha*, the first chapter of the holy book (Rollinde 2003, 141).

The king's endorsement of Islam as the basis of Moroccan national identity did not mean that the Moroccan state established its institutions as ethnically blind. As Kymlicka (1995, 3–4) argues, states that do not oppose the freedom of people to express their particular ethnic identity should not necessarily be regarded as ethnically blind, because through their policies of language, immigration, and education they support one ethnic identity and culture to the disadvantage of the others. After independence Arabic became the official language. The program of Arabization, which aimed to replace French with Modern Standard Arabic to be used as the sole national language in schools, administration, and courts, put Berber-speakers in a disadvantaged position. Coupled with the popularity of Arab nationalism in the 1960s and 1970s, Berber-speakers, especially those who lived in the urban areas and who competed with Arabic-speakers for jobs, felt marginalized. The Ministry of Education has largely been dominated by administrators who were ardent Arab nationalists. In some cases, teachers punished Berber students when they spoke in their own dialect. The arrival of Arabic-speaking teachers, who were influenced by the ideas of Pan-Arabism, from the Middle East due to a shortage of teachers in Morocco deepened the feeling of marginalization among Berber-speaking students. Denigration of the Berber dialects and culture became a common phenomenon in schools (Lehtinen 2003, 143). Like the Kurds in Turkey, students whose mother tongue was Berber encountered many difficulties in comprehending their teachers. History textbooks acknowledged the Berbers' existence in Morocco and presented them as the original inhabitants of the country. Nevertheless, the Berber image that was depicted in these textbooks was pejorative. Berbers were presented as a primitive race that used to live in caves, eating plants, before the arrival of the Arabs, who brought Islamic civilization to the Maghreb and enlightened the Berbers (el-Qadéry 1995, 7).

In general, the political parties, such as Istiqlal and the UNFP, were also adamant about Arabization and the general opinion in these parties' circles was that Morocco was an Arab country and that it was necessary to eradicate the Berber language and culture. A condescending attitude to Berber-speakers as being ignorant, uneducated, and rural was common within the Arabist circles as well as among the urban population. According to the socialist leader Mehdi Ben Barka, the Berber problem was a remnant of colonial cultural policy. He stated that a Berber was simply a man who has not been to school (el-Khatir 2005, 324). These parties were highly critical of incomplete Arabization and prepared report after report on the issue in the 1960s and 1970s.[22] A member of the USFP (the Party of the Socialist Union of Popular Forces),[23] Abd al-Jabiri, advocated that Arabization should not only be considered as a struggle against the status of the French language, but should also have the objective of eliminating the Arab and Berber local dialects. He asked for an official ban on the use of any language other than Modern Standard Arabic and stressed the importance of expanding education, especially in the mountainous areas (el-Khatir 2005, 336–337).

The position of the monarchy with regard to Arabization, however, was different. As Grandguillaume (1983, 94) points out, the monarchy saw Arabization as analogous to Islamization. The Arabic language not only referred to Arab ethnicity but also had a highly symbolic religious significance as the language of the Qur'an. The kings emphasized the sacredness of Arabic, rather than using it as an ethnic marker. Moroccans were expected to learn it as was every other Muslim. That is why Hassan II initiated Qur'anic education as a requirement for children at the pre-school level. Berber-speaking children without prior knowledge of Arabic

---

[22] Arabization of the educational system in Morocco proceeded slowly, partly due to a shortage of skilled teachers and partly because of a lack of ideological commitment. After the demise of the Istiqlal Party, the moderates, who advocated Arab–French bilingualism to consolidate Morocco's economic relations with the francophone world, dominated the Ministry of Education. King Hassan II publicly supported bilingualism. As a result, French was kept as the second language in the school system and is still widely used in the administration, except in the courts, along with Arabic. For more on Arabization, see Grandguillaume (1983), Sirles (1999), Yacine (1993).

[23] The USFP is a continuation of the UNFP.

would have to learn it in Qur'anic schools for two years before they entered elementary school (Wagner and Lotfi 1980).

Both Mohammed V and Hassan II rarely spoke directly about the Berbers as a distinct group in the country until the 1990s. Once, in an interview with the French newspaper *Le Monde*, Mohammed V stated that the Moroccans were not Arabs but Arabized Berbers. He added that the Moroccans belonged to the Arab-Islamic culture not through blood ties but through cultural ties (Mezran 2002, 48). This was a carefully balanced position, which neither presented an attack against Berber presence nor discredited the project of Arabization. Other than the Basic Law of 1961, no Moroccan constitution defined Morocco as exclusively an Arab state. Lehtinen (2003, 127) writes that although Allal al-Fassi, then the minister of Islamic affairs, proposed the phrase "Arab kingdom" to be added in the 1962 constitution, the king declined this proposition. In the 1962 constitution Morocco was characterized as a Muslim kingdom. In the following constitutions, while the status of Arabic as the official language remained the same, Morocco was characterized either as part of the "Great Maghreb" (1970 and 1972 constitutions) or "Great Arab Maghreb" (1992 and 1996 constitutions), as well as an "African state."[24] This language in the Moroccan constitutions suggests the reticence of the monarchy to equate national identity solely with Arab identity.

Hassan II, who came to power in March 1961 after his father's death, was more vocal about the necessity of Arabization, and from time to time underlined that Morocco was an Arab country in its traditions and language. Nevertheless, in terms of state policies there was no systematic sanctioning against the expressions of Berber language and culture. The Berber population did not encounter any bans on Berber music, dress, or festivals. Newspapers, including the newspaper that is the mouthpiece of the palace, publicized Berber art festivals. The state radio channel continued to broadcast in three Berber dialects as it had in the times of the French protectorate. Berber music was played and dances were performed in official ceremonies and the kings occasionally wore Berber clothes in public. As Aomar Boum (2007) underlines, elements of Berber culture, such as jewelry and pottery, were advertised by the state as touristic objects. Tolerance for public visibility of apolitical expressions of Berberness, however, did not necessarily signify an inclusionary understanding of national identity. The state folklorized Berberness and used it

---

[24] For the full text of all Moroccan constitutions until 2011, see Hattabi (2005). In 2011, the definition of Moroccan identity changed once more, as I will discuss in Chapter 5.

as a showcase for exoticism. As such it implied the backwardness of the Berber culture. Nevertheless, while the issue of Berber identity remained a sensitive topic in Morocco, it never became a taboo subject.

The sensitivity of the Berber issue during Hassan II's reign showed itself in three challenges to the regime in the early 1970s. While none of these incidents had an explicit Berberist agenda, the monarchy's responses underlined its anxiety over possible ethnic-based unrest among the Berbers. There were two military coup attempts, in 1971 and 1972, after which King Hassan II assumed direct command of the armed forces and the Defense Ministry. Although the coup attempts were not motivated by Berber identity claims, the fact that most of the officers involved were Berbers troubled the monarchy. After the coup attempts the composition of the officer corps progressively changed, giving rise to a less Berber-dominated army, though no systematic data on the extent of purges are available (Claisse 1987, 49). In 1973, a rebellion that was organized by the revolutionary leftists of the UNFP and supported by Libya arose in the Middle Atlas and involved Berber militants of the ex-Liberation Army. The rebellion was severely repressed but Hassan II undertook measures to improve relations with the Berbers where the unrest occurred. He appointed a Berber native of the region as the chief administrator, ordered the government and the minister of agriculture to deal with the problems of the region, and met with the veterans of the Liberation Army, promising to improve their economic well-being.[25] As I will address in Chapter 5 in more detail, the monarchy has dealt with challenges that came from Berber circles through a fine balance of selective rewards and punishments. While the monarchy severely repressed disloyalty, it attempted to build loyalty through cooptation and patronage.

CONCLUSION

The Moroccan state- and nation-building processes in the first two decades after its independence followed a different trajectory than the Turkish case. The monarchy's incorporation of Berber rural centers of power into an extensive patronage network precluded a nation-building project that was similar to the Turkish experience. The king's preservation

---

[25] See Wikileaks, "Senior Berber Officer Named Administrator in Morocco's Middle Atlas," March 23, 1973, www.wikileaks.org/plusd/cables/1973RABAT01286_b.html and "King and Prime Minister Address Veterans of Independence Movement," March 28, 1973, www.wikileaks.org/plusd/cables/1973RABAT01372_b.html (accessed September 3, 2013).

of authority was dependent on his alliance with the rural centers of power. A state-led process of homogenization and modernization that could have destabilized the countryside was out of the question. The monarchy favored social fragmentation that reinforced the monarch's role as an arbitrator (Gellner 1969, 66). Consequently, the Moroccan state's interference in the Berber areas was minimal and gradual. The definition of Moroccan national identity has been loose and flexible. The monarchy defined Moroccanness primarily by Muslim identity and left room for the expression of the Berber identity in private and in public, as long as such expression did not imply a political project.

The Berbers' involvement in Moroccan politics in the 1960s and 1970s and their participation in discussions over national identity were far from monolithic. Many educated Berbers were in fact attracted to the leftist message of the UNFP, rather than the Berber-based Mouvement Populaire, which attracted support from the Berbers of the rural areas (Coram 1972, 275). Many young Berber students even supported Nasserism and Arabism, which they saw as progressive and revolutionary, as opposed to a Berberist discourse, which they perceived as traditional and reactionary (Aït Mous 2006, 136). The MP was the advocate of the Berberist discourse. MP members advocated the protection of Berber identity and culture, but they were also loyal to the monarchy and quite moderate in terms of their specific demands for the Berbers. The MP asked for the teaching of Berber dialects in schools but did not challenge the efforts to make Arabic the common language of the population (Grandguillaume 1983, 87).

However, Morocco was not an ethnically neutral and inclusivist state. Arabic language and culture occupied a superior position in official and social domains. The Arabist ideology was quite popular among Moroccan society as well as within the bureaucratic cadres and the political parties. The social process that led to the formation of Berber activism was similar to the experience of Kurdish mobilization in Turkey, as I will elaborate in the next chapter. Young Berbers, who were privileged to pursue their education in the big cities, began to develop a consciousness of being different as they saw the gap between rural Berber areas and the cities and as they were belittled because of their different Arabic accent or Berber dialect. They attended student meetings where they felt marginalized as they encountered staunch Arabists. Most of today's activists were involved in the leftist National Student Union (UNEM) as student revolutionaries during the 1960s.[26] However, they felt increasingly alienated

---

[26] For more on the initial emergence of the Berber movement, see Aït Mous (2006).

from the leftist circles that did not show any sensitivity to the problems of Berber society.

The first Berber organization that aimed to do research on Berber language and culture was the Moroccan Association for Research and Cultural Exchange (*L'Association Marocaine de Recherche et d'Échange Culturel*), or AMREC. It was founded in 1967 by a group of teachers and university professors in Rabat. The members of AMREC were fearful of declaring their particularistic aim because of the sensitivity of the Berber issue and kept the organization low-profile. The only public signifier that hinted at the association's identity was its logo, which was a picture of a Berber pendant; however, it did not create any problems for AMREC. Discussing Berber identity politically, however, held many risks at the time. The regime was becoming increasingly more repressive, particularly towards the left and the student movements, and was thus quite intimidating for Berber intellectuals.[27] In the 1970s, AMREC was specifically involved in cultural activities. It collected Berber oral poems and stories, made documentaries on Berber culture, organized literacy classes for illiterate Berber-speakers, and helped the formation of a Berber music band, Ousman (Aït Mous 2006, 141). In 1978, a Berber organization that is still important today, Tamaynut, came into being. Like AMREC, it was initially formed under the name New Association for Culture and Popular Arts (*Association Nouvelle Pour la Culture et Les Arts Populaires*, ANCAP), which gave no hints about its Berberness.[28] The Berber activists increasingly refused to use the word "Berber" because of its pejorative roots, coming from the word "barbarian." Instead, they began to refer to themselves as "Amazigh," meaning "free men".[29] Over time AMREC and ANCAP became the two biggest Amazigh organizations nationwide. A few other small organizations were also formed in cities other than Rabat by the end of the 1970s. These organizations avoided antagonizing the

---

[27] For a general discussion of the political atmosphere in the 1960s and 1970s and the dark period of state repression, known as *les années de plomb*, or "the years of lead," see Miller (2013).

[28] ANCAP Berberized its name and became Tamaynut in 1996. It is worth noting that many Amazigh activists emphasize the distinction between the popular culture, which they claim to be based on Berber culture, and the elite culture, which is Arab and which is not indigenous to Morocco. The choice of these names aimed not only to hide the real intention behind the formation of these associations but also to make a subtle claim that the Berbers are the real bearers of the original culture of Morocco.

[29] While referring to Berber activism, I will use the term "Amazigh." Nevertheless, I will continue using "Berber" in referring to the larger ethnic group. This will help differentiate between the ethnic movement and the larger ethnic group.

regime by functioning solely in the cultural arena. It was in the 1980s that Berber activism began to assume a more political character and put pressure on the state with explicit demands for cultural and linguistic rights. The Moroccan state strategy to deal with this new Amazigh challenge was again quite different than the Turkish state's attitude towards Kurdish activism.

4

The making of an armed conflict
State–Kurdish relations in the post-1950 period

In 1950, Hüsamettin Tugaç, a parliamentarian of the Republican People's Party (RPP) from Kars, sent a letter to the party's General Secretariat after inspecting Urfa province. He underlined that the majority of the population in Urfa either belonged to tribes or were under the authority of village aghas. According to Tugaç, establishing strong party branches in the province required a change in the party's attitude towards local notables. It was necessary to safeguard the status and reputation of tribal leaders and village aghas in order to attract them to the RPP's side. With the formation of the Democratic Party (DP) in 1946, the RPP came under increasing pressure to compete with opposition for social support. Tugaç's efforts in Urfa addressed the need to expand the party organization in the Eastern provinces. Since no tribal leader wanted to submit to the domination of another tribal leader, he recommended establishing party branches that would correspond to each tribe. He was concerned that if tribes were neglected, they would be open to the DP's influence.[1]

The Turkish state's policies towards Kurds have not remained constant in the history of the Turkish Republic. The multi-party era pushed the RPP to accommodate tribal interests and soften its policies towards the Kurds. The victory of the DP in Turkey's first democratic elections led to a major change in state–Kurdish relations. The political actors who took

---

[1] BCA 490.01-490.1975.1, Mardin Region Inspector, Hüsamettin Tugaç to RPP Secretariat, February 7, 1950, pp. 15–16. Quotations from Turkish state documents throughout the chapter have been translated by the present author.

state power through competitive elections abandoned the comprehensive transformative policies of the single-party period and reduced the level of state intrusion into the Kurdish areas. This period also brought the integration of the traditional Kurdish power centers into political parties and the parliament. The abandonment of the "makeover" project and the state's withdrawal from regulating Kurdish daily life led to a period of relative quietude among the Kurdish masses until the military coup of 1980.

This chapter analyzes the evolution of state–Kurdish relations in the post-1950 period. It traces the emergence of a modern, Kurdish ethnic mobilization in a new political and social context in Turkey, which gradually gave way to the formation of a new Kurdish elite that separated itself from traditional centers of power, such as tribal leaders and religious sheikhs. This urban-centered and well-educated Kurdish elite became, in Laitin's (1998, 31) term, the "identity entrepreneurs" of Kurdish society and succeeded in developing a lasting ethnic movement, unlike the rebellions of the early republican period. The main aim of this chapter is to explain how and why this ethnic movement gradually radicalized, found appeal with the Kurdish masses, and became a major threat to the Turkish Republic. As Laitin (1998, 30) suggests, the identity entrepreneurs who hope to revive languages and reverse the tide of assimilation will always be ready in every society. The main question is when these cultural elites' projects will be endorsed and recreated by the masses.

The first half of this chapter discusses state–Kurdish relations between 1950 and 1980, a period when the state's interference into Kurdish daily life was minimal. Kurdish activism was limited to an urban-based intellectual elite. This was the period when the Kurdish movement looked very similar to the Berber movement in Morocco in terms of its demands and structure. In the 1950s and 1960s, Kurdish activism was a part of the Turkish left and its demands largely revolved around cultural rights and democratization. It was also fragmented in its organizational structure. In the 1970s, Kurdish activists increasingly separated themselves from the Turkish leftist organizations, which they accused of not being sensitive enough to the Kurdish problems. The Kurdish movement in the 1970s went through a process of radicalization as the state excluded the entire Kurdish opposition from the legal sphere of contention. Unlike in Morocco, the Turkish state's attitude towards ethnic activists relied on indiscriminate repression.

The second half of this chapter analyzes state policies after the military coup of 1980, which was a breaking point in state–Kurdish relations. After the coup the Turkish state began to enjoy an overpowering presence in Kurdish everyday life. The Kurdish areas became subject to another set of policies of "extreme makeover," but this time with increased state intrusion accompanied with high repression. The policies to wipe out the cultural expressions of Kurdishness, in dress, speech, music, and the like, led to an outcome that was contrary to what the government and the military intended. The revival of comprehensive and intrusive policies pursued by the military government was critical in giving shape to the grievances of the Kurdish masses and raising their political consciousness. These policies not only changed and politicized the meaning of the cultural representations of Kurdishness but also contributed to the gradual growth of support for the insurgency by the Kurdistan Workers' Party (PKK) within Kurdish society. The PKK emerged as the savior of Kurdish identity and the defender of Kurdish honor. The armed conflict between the PKK and the state security forces created its own dynamic of a vicious circle, which radicalized and polarized both sides of the conflict. By the 1990s, cultural practices that denote Kurdishness, such as giving Kurdish names to children and singing Kurdish songs, turned into intractable controversies between Turkish state authorities and the Kurds. The armed conflict between the PKK and the state security forces turned the Kurdish regions into war zones where unidentified murders, disappearances, and torture had become ordinary facts of daily life in the 1990s. According to the official figures, around 40,000 people have died as a result of the conflict since 1984, when the PKK first started its operations against the state (Çalışlar 2009).

This chapter also underlines the heterogeneity of state responses as the intensity of the conflict increased in the 1990s. State actors at different levels of the state showed contradictory responses in dealing with the Kurdish problem because they were influenced by the conflict in different ways and to varying degrees. Such differentiated state responses hurt the credibility of any policy reform initiated by the parliament, undercut their implementation, and failed to reduce the tension by easing the restrictions on Kurdish linguistic and cultural practices. A detailed analysis of the contestation over Kurdish names and music suggests that local state officials had been as influential in shaping state policy as the state's center. The resistance of local state officials working in the conflict-ridden Kurdish areas to policy changes was critical in the failure of policy reforms and the instigation of further conflict.

1950–1970: STATE–KURDISH RELATIONS IN TRANSITION

In 1945, the RPP leaders allowed the formation of opposition parties and initiated the democratic process in Turkey. Two factors were influential in leading to such a drastic change in Turkish politics. First, the party leaders were aware of the RPP's increasing unpopularity among the masses and the years of economic hardship during World War II aggravated this general dissatisfaction, even among bureaucratic circles. In addition to the domestic pressures for change, international conditions played a crucial role in bringing about a transition to multi-party politics. The state elite's decision to move towards the United States and Western Europe in the immediate post-war period and their hope of benefiting from American economic and military aid forced the RPP leadership to allow opposition parties to form and run in elections.[2] Eventually, the beginning of political competition changed the nature of state–Kurdish relations profoundly. Until the 1980s, except during short periods following the military coups of 1960 and 1970, the governments abandoned the makeover policies of the single-party period and refrained from interfering in the fine details of the private lives of its Kurdish citizens.

The abandonment of the social-engineering project opened a "period of relaxation," in the words of some Kurdish activists, in the East. The political parties competing for votes tried to coopt the Kurdish local centers of power in exchange for support. While the government sought to rule the Kurdish countryside through these intermediaries, the tribal leaders and landowners used their political connections to bring state resources to their areas of influence. No Kurdish revolts occurred in this period and the Kurdish regions were relatively tranquil. This did not mean, however, that there was no Kurdish challenge to the state. Ironically, a new form of Kurdish activism began to form among those Kurds on whom the makeover policies had been the most successful. This was an unanticipated outcome of the Kemalist modernization project. Leading this new Kurdish activism was a group of young, Turkish-speaking, Westernized, and privileged Kurds, largely sons of provincial elites of the East, who went to the big cities of Western Turkey in the 1950s to take advantage of the expanded educational opportunities offered by the state. These Kurdish university students, along with Kurdish professionals living in

---

[2] For more on the Turkish transition to democracy, see Zürcher (1998) and Ahmad (1993).

the West, began to think about "Kurdishness" and the problems of the Eastern region and formulated political solutions to address Kurdish grievances. It was through their efforts that Kurdish protest evolved into a well-developed ethnic movement by the 1970s. Their activism, however, still had limited appeal within the Kurdish masses until after the military coup of 1980. While the abandonment of makeover policies and low state intervention in the countryside impeded mass Kurdish mobilization in the rural areas, the demands and activities of the politicized Kurds in the urban centers gradually radicalized as the state showed no tolerance towards any expression of a separate Kurdish identity.

The establishment of the Democratic Party (DP) in 1946 led to a major revision of the RPP's policies in the Kurdish areas. In its quest for power, the DP played on the Kurdish feelings of resentment towards the RPP's policies and soon became the center of attraction for many dissident Kurds. A letter sent to the RPP's General Secretariat in 1948 by the RPP Inspectorate in Diyarbakır drew attention to the large-scale participation of Kurdish sheikhs and notables in the DP. They were those who had recently returned to their native regions from where they had been forcefully resettled in the 1930s. "In all the districts and subdistricts of this province that I visited, the people who founded the Democratic Party's organization are those who are not happy with the government and who were punished in various occasions," wrote an RPP deputy who went to Diyarbakır as the party's inspector. He reported that a sheikh, who had been imprisoned because of his involvement in the Sheikh Said rebellion, became the chairman of a provincial DP office in Hani. The sheikhs and local notables could express their opposition to the government more explicitly within the local organizations of the DP and hurt the prestige of the RPP in the region, he complained.[3] Unlike the RPP, the Democrats tried to establish close ties with the religious orders, tribal leaders, and extended families. It included many prominent Kurdish families in its ranks, including some of the members of the Sheikh Said family. As Hamit Bozarslan (1996, 141) argues, "The integration of the traditional Kurdish actors, namely in the case of the family of Sheikh Said, symbolizing two banned ideologies from the republic – Kurdish nationalism and religious opposition – signified a real enlargement of the political space."

The RPP leadership was well aware of the threat posed by the DP and in the second half of the 1940s began to revise some of its policies that

---

[3] BCA 490.01-470.1924.1, RPP Diyarbakır Region Inspector, Dr. H. Fırat, to RPP Secretariat, September 15, 1948, pp. 96–99.

caused resentment. It allowed religious instruction in schools and established a limited number of vocational religious high schools (*İmam Hatip Liseleri*) (McDowall 1996, 396). Political clientelism became the main strategy pursued by the political parties in the Kurdish areas after the transition to a democratic system. The efforts of the DP to appeal to the sheikhs, tribal leaders, and large landowners in the Kurdish areas pushed the RPP to do the same. Wide inequality in land ownership, the high proportion of landless peasants, and the strength of tribal groups and religious orders in the Kurdish areas made a perfect ground for the development of patron–client relationships between political parties and local power centers. Local patrons could mobilize large numbers of votes and in turn gain additional prestige and wealth through party ties (Romano 2006, 40; Sayarı 1977, 107).[4] In the second half of the 1940s, political competition pushed the RPP to reverse its policy of detribalization. In 1947, the government allowed 2,000 exiled tribal leaders and aghas and their families to return to their native region (McDowall 1996, 397). These exiled notables were also allowed to have their land back.[5] Many of the dissident notables joined the DP ranks and constituted the majority of the DP parliamentarians from the Eastern provinces (McDowall 1996, 397). During the election campaign, the DP representatives brought up the RPP's past atrocities in the region and advocated more religious freedoms. Both parties picked largely local candidates to run in elections, as a result of which 71.6 percent of the parliamentarians elected in 1950 from the Southeastern and Eastern provinces were natives of those provinces. This was a serious shift from the previous composition of parliaments. In the 1943–1946 parliament, only 26.6 percent of the parliamentarians from the region were locals (Demirel 2011, 94).

---

[4] For more on patron–client relationships in the Southeast, see Kudat (1975) and Beşikçi (1992). Lale Yalçın-Heckmann (1990) questions the classic arguments that underline the ability of the tribal chiefs and rich landowners to secure peasant votes en bloc and calls attention to the bargaining power of the tribesmen and peasants that is ignored in the literature. She argues that tribal leadership does not automatically bring political leadership and that tribal leaders who enter politics have to take the interests of their tribesmen into account in order to get their support. She portrays the tribal leaders and tribesmen (or aghas and peasants) relationship more as an interdependent one, rather than a relationship that is marked by the dependency of the latter on the former.
[5] Some of the RPP administrators returned the lands of the exiles on the condition that they withdrew their support from the DP. See Diken (2005, 219). This book is an interesting collection of interviews conducted with the family members of those who were exiled and provides invaluable information on their encounters with the authorities and the peasants after they returned to their villages.

The DP's victory in the 1950 elections caused a great deal of excitement in the East, where the DP won in most of the Kurdish provinces (Aktürk 2012, 135). Many believed that the DP government would reverse the RPP's modernization reforms. Sıdıka Avar (2004, 306), director of the Elazığ Girls' Institute, for instance, recalled how passengers on a bus taunted her on the day the DP's victory was announced by saying that girls' schools would be closed, that women would not work in state bureaus any more, and that men would be able to marry up to four women. The DP leadership was careful not to question the basic principles of the republican state, but revised state policies in a way to appeal more to the conservative rural constituency. The Democrats promised to ease the cultural restrictions in the Kurdish areas and reduce the oppressive practices of the gendarmerie (Barkey and Fuller 1997). As soon as it came to power, the DP government also began to ease the state's control over religion. For instance, it lifted the ban on the call to prayer in Arabic and the ban on radio broadcasting of religious programs. In addition, it introduced compulsory religious education in schools. Although the DP government did not attempt to change the fundamentals of the republican regime, it considerably reduced state intervention into the daily lives of citizens in the Kurdish areas. In 1951, it closed down one of the main institutions of the single party's makeover project, the People's Houses. During the 1950s, Kurds could speak their language and wear their traditional dress in public without encountering any official harassment. In a move to address Kurdish complaints about the military, the DP also brought to the parliament the issue of the killing of thirty-three Kurdish villagers by a group of soldiers in the RPP period. The villagers were shot without trial on the orders of General Muğlalı for smuggling from Iran in 1943. The discussion of the affair in parliament led to the trial of General Muğlalı, who was sentenced to twenty years in prison in 1951.[6]

The DP government's economic policies accelerated the integration of the Kurdish areas with the rest of the country. Greater mechanization of agriculture in the East empowered many landowners and deepened land inequalities. This process also pulled many small farmers and peasants to the cities, which, over the long term, accelerated the erosion of the traditional structures in the Kurdish areas. Migration to the cities led to the emergence of a new generation of Kurdish intellectuals, students, and workers, who would constitute the core of Kurdish activism in the 1960s and 1970s (Romano 2006, 42). During the DP period, those Kurds who

---

[6] For more on the affair, see Özgen (2003).

had recently moved to the big cities of Istanbul and Ankara began to organize meetings among themselves and established small associations carrying the name of their hometown. It was in these circles that Kurdish university students, many of whom came from prominent, well-off families of the East, started to discuss the economic and social problems of their regions as well as the previous RPP policies concerning the Kurds. Their activities, however, were still much more cultural than political. They did not encounter any official attempts to curtail these activities. In get-togethers called "Eastern Nights" (*Doğu Geceleri*), which student associations organized collectively, people from the East could perform Kurdish folkloric dances and sing Kurdish songs without any interference.[7] They also had contacts with the DP parliamentarians from the East, who initially supported these student organizations and participated in their activities.

In the second half of the 1950s, the Democrats began to encounter serious economic problems and increasing opposition to their government. Having to cope with such opposition led them to gradually resort to authoritarian measures. They restricted academic and press freedoms, tried to establish political control over the judiciary, and prohibited political meetings except during election campaigns (Zürcher 1998, 240–242). The relations between the party and Kurdish intellectuals, students, and professionals started to turn sour as a result of this growing authoritarianism. Some of these Kurds who would become the prominent activists of the 1960s, such as Tarık Ziya Ekinci and Canip Yıldırım, chose to join the ranks of the RPP in the last years of the 1950s, taking into account the changing political atmosphere (Ekinci 2010, 358).

This period also coincided with the growing politicization of Kurdish intellectuals and students, who were influenced by the return of Mustafa Barzani to Iraq after the 1958 military coup and the growing Kurdish nationalism there. The developments in Iraq created a public debate in the Turkish press about "Kurdism" (*Kürtçülük*) and its spillover effects. In 1959, when Musa Anter published a poem in Kurdish, titled "*Kımıl*," in Diyarbakır's local newspaper *İleri Yurt*, it immediately attracted a significant amount of attention and criticism from the Turkish press.[8]

---

[7] Some of the earlier generation of Kurdish activists, such as Naci Kutlay (1998, 41–42) and Canip Yıldırım (Miroğlu 2005, 122), gave information about the "Eastern Nights" in their memoirs.

[8] Musa Anter included Kurdish sentences in his Turkish articles that he wrote for the newspaper even before this incident in 1959. At that time there was no law that banned writing in Kurdish but his use of Kurdish attracted the immediate attention of the local

Consequently, Musa Anter, as well as the newspaper's editorial chief, Canip Yıldırım, and its owner, A. Efhem Dolak, were arrested on charges of "making publications that could harm the political esteem of the state and could damage the trust and confidence of the people towards the state and lead to the destruction of the wellbeing and tranquility of people and the public" (Gündoğan 2005, 85–86). The Democrats exploited the growing sense of threat from "Kurdism" and communism as they encountered more opposition from the public and the military. As Yeğen (2007, 130) maintains, the perception that foreign incitement was largely responsible for creating the Kurdish problem had been quite common among Turkish nationalists, especially the military. Constitutional recognition of national rights for the Kurdish population in Iraq after Barzani's return worried the Turkish state elite about its possible repercussions for Turkey's Kurds. In 1959, fifty-two Kurdish activists were arrested and taken to court on a charge of trying to form a separate Kurdish state with the help of foreign powers.[9] They were imprisoned in Harbiye Military Prison and their trials, which lasted for years, began after the military coup of 1960. The DP government's use of political oppression against Kurdish intellectuals was an attempt to regain its political support by using the ethnic card. As Anthony Marx (2002) argues, rulers try to manipulate and reinforce ethnic difference and use exclusive strategies against an ethnic minority in order to unify a core constituency and create a coalition in support of their rule. Faced with a politically fragmented constituency, rulers are tempted to resort to exclusive nationalism. The DP government's policy towards the Kurds in the late 1950s supports Marx's thesis.

The DP government's political oppression of Kurdish activism, nevertheless, was a minor concession to the military-bureaucratic elite, who became more and more dissatisfied over the years as the DP threatened their economic and political power in favor of the rural, provincial elite. The military-bureaucratic elite was a hangover from the RPP. Even

---

prosecutors, who took him to court several times based on different accusations such as promoting dissent among citizens by raising old political events or advocating separatism. In his memoirs he writes that he was acquitted in these court cases. His poem in Kurdish became a nationwide issue by coincidence, when it attracted the attention of a reporter in a national newspaper. For more, see Anter (1999).

[9] These Kurdish activists were students and professionals living in Ankara and Istanbul and those who established regional associations and organized the "Eastern nights." Because their number was later decreased to forty-nine, the incident is referred as the "Incident of 49s." Naci Kutlay, who was among the arrested Kurds, published a detailed book that includes several primary documents on the case: (1994).

though the RPP had been voted out of office, it still maintained a power base within the military-bureaucratic establishment, which claimed to be the guardians of Kemalism. The discontent of the military-bureaucratic elite coupled with the DP's growing authoritarianism eventually led to the coup of May 27, 1960.[10]

Military rule, which lasted eighteen months, led to the enactment of certain policies that were reminiscent of the RPP's "makeover" attempts. The National Unity Committee (*Milli Birlik Komitesi*) that exercised power in the name of those military officers who undertook the coup was concerned about the empowerment of tribal leaders, sheikhs, and landowners in the East during the DP period at the expense of state power. Only a few days after the coup, 485 Kurds, who were landowners, intellectuals, and local politicians supporting the DP, were taken to a camp in Sivas for six months without trial (Gündoğan 2005, 58). Fifty-five of them were not allowed to return to their hometowns and were sent to live in exile in several cities in Western Turkey.[11] The National Unity Committee accelerated the Turkification of place names. The majority of the village names in the Kurdish areas were Turkified during this period (Bora 1986, 26).[12] The Committee also planned to establish boarding schools in the East with the specific aim of spreading the Turkish language and culture. During military rule, state intervention in the private lives of citizens resumed. For instance, a local newspaper in Urfa, *Demokrat Türkiye*, reported that some people were taken to the police station for breaking the "Hat Law," by wearing *poşu*, traditional headgear worn by men in the Southeast (*Demokrat Türkiye* 1961a, 1961b).

Nevertheless, these daily interventions did not extend beyond the period of military rule. Parliamentary elections were held in October 1961, and a civilian government was formed in November. The new constitution was more liberal than the old one as it expanded press freedoms, guaranteed academic autonomy, introduced new checks and balances on the executive power, and increased civil liberties. This constitution encouraged educated, urbanized Kurds to participate in politics, to voice their complaints and demands in several platforms, and to publish

---

[10] For more on DP rule and the military coup, see Kasaba (1993).
[11] These fifty-five people were landlords and sheiks. In his memoirs, Kutlay (1998, 105–106) writes that the majority of these individuals did not go to their places of exile and stayed in hotels or with their relatives in Ankara. A few years later they were allowed to return to their native lands but the parliament passed a law that allowed the state's confiscation of their lands. These lands were later returned back to them.
[12] See Öktem (2008) for an analysis of toponymical engineering in republican Turkey.

many pro-Kurdish journals. In the Kurdish countryside, tribal leaders and sheikhs continued to be the major authorities (Bozarslan 2008). The political parties founded after the military coup used the tribal leaders and sheikhs to build their clientele in the Kurdish provinces. Daily life in the Kurdish provinces was largely free from state intervention. Necmi Onur (1979, 257–260), a journalist who went to the East at the beginning of the 1960s, complained about the state's indifference to the extensive use of Kurdish in the East. During this period, Yusuf Azizoğlu, a Kurdish agha and the health minister between 1962 and 1963, could give speeches in Kurdish when addressing his electorate.[13] By 1964, a columnist writing in Urfa's local newspaper complained about people wearing their traditional clothes and called on the governor to resume the dress controls (Okutan 1964).

Urbanization of the Kurdish population gained momentum in the 1960s, as in other parts of Turkey. High population growth and deepening land inequality pushed the peasants to the urban centers, first to the Eastern cities, then to Western Turkey. Between 1950 and 1965 the urban population grew from 18.5 percent to 34.4 percent of the national population (Gündoğan 2005, 38). The population of Diyarbakır, for instance, more than doubled, from 65,000 in 1956 to 140,000 in 1970 (McDowall 1996, 401). Urbanization created a Kurdish stratum, which had new grievances and consequently new demands of the state. These demands emanated out of many Kurds' sharpened awareness about the socio-economic gap between the Western and Eastern provinces and the problems that they encountered in the cities. In contrast to the Kurdish dissidents during the single-party era, they wanted the state to intervene to develop the Eastern provinces and to bring more state services, but with more sensitivity to cultural differences, most notably, the Kurdish language. With urbanization, the low proficiency in Turkish of Kurdish migrants became an important problem as their contact with Turkish-speakers increased. As Gellner (1983, 61–62) emphasizes, ethnic consciousness is born out of the real experiences of rural migrants in the cities, who increasingly encounter bureaucrats and fellow-citizens speaking a language that is foreign to them. The reason behind the emergence of an urban-based

[13] In the early 1960s, Azizoğlu's New Turkey Party was the most popular in the Kurdish provinces. The party leadership had strong ties to local notables and tribes in the Kurdish provinces and pushed for bringing economic development and social services to the region. The party was not a pro-Kurdish one, however. It did not advocate recognition of ethno-cultural rights for the Kurds. For more, see Watts (2010, 37–38) and Aktürk (2012, 143–149).

Kurdish mobilization in that sense was quite similar to the process of the development of a Berber identity in Morocco by the late 1960s.

The migration from rural to urban areas also led to an increase in the number of Kurdish university students, who expanded the core group of Kurdish activists that emerged in the 1950s. More Kurds from modest socio-economic backgrounds could find the chance to receive higher education. They became familiar with the ideas of socialism and anti-imperialism, began to discuss the underdevelopment of the East and the oppressive state practices of the past, and were inspired by Mustafa Barzani's armed rebellion against the Iraqi government in the 1960s. There was an increase in associations formed in the large Western cities by fellow townsmen and students from the East. These associations and Kurdish intellectuals began to publish several journals, which discussed the socio-economic inequalities between the Eastern and Western provinces, language problems, the exploitation of the peasants by the aghas, and the state's neglect of the East.[14] Some of these journals, such as *Dicle-Fırat* (1962, Istanbul), *Deng* (1963, Istanbul), and *Yeni Akış* (1966, Ankara), were vocal about the ethnic dimension of the problems in the Eastern provinces. Their demands largely revolved around cultural and linguistic rights, such as the official recognition of Kurdish existence and permission for Kurdish education and radio broadcasting. Many of these publications used the Kurdish language very cautiously in order not to attract attention, despite the lack of a law that explicitly banned the use of the Kurdish language in publications.[15]

In the 1960s, the majority of the politicized Kurds were attracted to the Turkish Labor Party (TLP, *Türkiye İşçi Partisi*), a socialist party founded in 1961. The party's anti-imperialist stance, its interest in the underdevelopment of the East, and its critique of land inequality appealed to Kurds. Many prominent Kurdish activists, such as Tarık Ziya Ekinci, Kemal Burkay, Naci Kutlay, Canip Yıldırım, and Mehdi Zana, were actively involved in the organization of the party in the East and formed the so-called group of "Easterners" within the party ranks. In the 1965 election, the TLP got

[14] For instance, *Keko* (1963, Ankara) was published by the Association of University Students from Siverek. *Çıkış* (1967, Ankara) was published by the Association for Bitlis' Development and Publicity. For a complete list of Kurdish newspapers and journals in this period, see Lewendî and Lewendî (1989). Many of these publications are available at the National Library in Ankara.

[15] The parliament passed a law in 1967 that banned the distribution of materials, such as publications and tapes, in the Kurdish language from foreign countries (McDowall 1996, 408). This was an attempt to prevent the diffusion of Kurdish nationalism from abroad, especially from Iraq.

3 percent of the vote and entered parliament with fifteen deputies, four of whom were Kurdish. These deputies brought the Eastern question before parliament and tried to attract the government's attention to its particular problems. Under the leadership of the TLP's Kurdish members, mass rallies, which were called the "Eastern Meetings," were organized in the Kurdish provinces in 1967. These meetings represented the first serious attempt of the urban-based Kurdish activists to reach out to the Kurdish masses in the East. They succeeded in bringing together thousands of protestors, who listened to the speeches about the backwardness of the East and the state's unequal treatment of it (Gündoğan 2005).[16]

The Turkish state authorities did not show much tolerance towards this new Kurdish activism. The majority of the newspapers and journals that the Kurdish activists published were banned on a charge of separatism after only a few issues. The Turkish state's main containment policy was denial of the Kurdish issue and silencing any form of Kurdish activism. Local authorities tried to prevent rallies, and civil police always kept a close eye on them. Many speakers and participants were taken to the police station for interrogation after each meeting. Kemal Burkay (2001, 208–209), a leading Kurdish intellectual and activist in the 1960s and 1970s, wrote in his memoirs that increased state suspicions as a result of the "Eastern Meetings" led to commando operations in the Kurdish rural areas in 1968 under the pretext of finding smugglers and other criminals. According to Burkay, the main objective of the repressive commando operations was to demonstrate state power and to intimidate the villagers about their potential support for Kurdism. By the end of the 1960s, the Turkish state became more intolerant of any Kurdish activity, even cultural ones. Mehmet Emin Bozarslan, who wrote a textbook for teaching Kurdish and who translated the Kurdish epic *Mem-u-Zin* into Turkish, was arrested and charged. In 1970, many Kurdish activists, most of whom were TLP members and formed the "Revolutionary Eastern Cultural Hearths" in 1969, were arrested and taken to court (McDowall 1996, 408). These organizations represented a major step on the part of the Kurdish activists to separate themselves from the Turkish leftist movement and to form a platform that would work solely for Kurdish cultural and political rights. By the 1970s it was clear that any opposition based on the Kurdish question was illegitimate for the Turkish state. As

---

[16] Some of the slogans shouted during these mass rallies were: "Stop the Agha, Sheikh, and Comprador Trio," "We do not want police stations, but schools," "Respect our language," "The West is the hometown, what about the East?" (Gündoğan 2005, 146).

Lust-Okar (2005, 79) suggests, when a state excludes an entire spectrum of opposition, the opponents progressively radicalize because they will gain little by making moderate demands. The Turkish state's continued oppression of any form of Kurdish activity progressively politicized the movement and made the state into its main target.

1970–1980: RADICALIZATION OF KURDISH ACTIVISM

On March 12, 1971, the military once again intervened in politics and issued an ultimatum that demanded the formation of a government that would end the anarchy and carry out Kemalist reforms. This ultimatum came as the violent clashes between leftists and rightists, bombings, and kidnappings in the cities got out of hand after 1969 and the government remained powerless to curb the growing urban violence. Kurdish separatism was given as one of the justifications for military intervention. Many leading intellectuals, students, labor union leaders, and Kurdish activists were arrested. The Labor Party was closed down on the charges of communism and Kurdish separatism. Many Kurdish activists stayed in prison until 1974, when Prime Minister Bülent Ecevit passed an amnesty law that freed the political prisoners. The imprisonments and subsequent trials caused many activists to lose hope about working within the system and led them to discuss more fundamental political changes such as national liberation, self-determination, and federalism. The trials of the "Revolutionary Eastern Cultural Hearths" became political platforms, where the prosecutors and Kurdish activists confronted each other with regard to the existence of Kurds in Turkey. The prosecutors tried to prove the Turkish origins of the Kurds and nonexistence of the Kurdish language. They accused the prisoners of forming an organization with the aim of weakening national sentiments and "making part of the Turkish citizens who live in the Eastern provinces believe that they belonged to the Kurdish race." In opposition to these claims, the Kurdish activists' defense was centered on Kurdish history, language, and culture to prove Kurdish existence (*Devrimci Doğu Kültür Ocakları* 1975).

The 1970s were the years when the Kurdish activists separated themselves from the Turkish left and their demands became more particularistic, radical, and political. The demands that revolved around cultural rights in the 1960s gave way to demands for major changes in the political system, such as federalism, in the 1970s. As Nicole Watts (2010, 44) points out, increasing numbers of Kurdish activists and politicians started to discuss the problems of the Eastern regions in ethnic terms, rather than within the discursive frames of socialism and underdevelopment. The movement's structure was highly pluralistic. Several small Kurdish groups and organizations, most of which were in conflict with one another, represented the movement. The process that led to the radicalization of the Kurdish movement was also a part of the general polarization of Turkish politics. Weak coalition governments, economic crises, and the growing divide between the right and the left characterized the 1970s. During the second half of the decade, political violence between extreme leftist and rightist urban guerrilla groups started to become a real problem. The state apparatus was also affected by the growing political polarization. The police and the security forces came under the influence of the radical nationalists and their partisanship played an important role in restricting the Kurdish political space further.

Özgürlük Yolu (1977a), a monthly pro-Kurdish journal published in Turkish, complained about illegal confiscations of its issues by the police and police threats to the owners of its printing houses in different cities. The journal represented moderate Kurdish demands and advocated socialism and alliance with Turkish leftists to end oppressive policies. It was one of the very few Kurdish publications that survived for more than a few issues due to its moderate stance but could not escape raids, searches, and interrogations of its editors by the security forces.[17] Other Kurdish journals suffered the same fate. The governor's office in Ankara did not allow the publication of *Roja Welat*, a bilingual newspaper published in Kurdish and Turkish, on the grounds that Turkish is the official language. The owner of the newspaper, Mustafa Aydın, who began to publish it in Istanbul, stated that there was no law that prohibited publishing in foreign languages, and that the police confiscations were made without a court decision. Another important Kurdish periodical of the 1970s, *Rızgari*, could not receive a publication license from the governor's office, which justified its decision based on a law that regulated the publication activities of foreigners (non-Turkish citizens) (*Özgürlük Yolu* 1977b, 73–79). Despite the absence of a law that banned publications in Kurdish, the pro-Kurdish journals and newspapers encountered arbitrary bans by the security forces and administrators.

---

[17] *Özgürlük Yolu* published forty-four issues from June 1975 to January 1979. It was the informal journal of the clandestine Socialist Party of Kurdistan, which was founded by Kemal Burkay in 1974. For more on Kurdish publications, see Yücel (1998).

In 1978, when the PKK (Kurdistan Workers' Party) was founded, it was a small, marginal organization, which embraced Marxist discourse and aimed at establishing an independent and united Kurdistan through armed struggle. It first attracted attention with its attacks on certain tribal leaders who had close connections with the government, particularly the Bucak family in Siverek, which the PKK branded a regime collaborator.[18] The extent of the support it received from the Kurds in the areas in which it operated is hard to gauge. According to Marcus (2007, 37–38), the PKK leader Abdullah Öcalan's clear and simple message, his aggressiveness, and endorsement of violent action attracted many young Kurdish men, who came from poor rural backgrounds and were university or teacher's school students or dropouts. Van Bruinessen (1984, 11) writes that some peasants looked on the PKK favorably because of its struggle against oppressive landlords, but its violence also terrorized the residents of these areas and led it to lose much of the initial sympathy it had garnered. In any case, the PKK was only one of several radical organizations at the time and was a latecomer within the Kurdish movement. Until the military coup of 1980, the mainstream Kurdish activists of the 1960s and 1970s did not advocate violence, although many lost faith in the political system and favored illegal strategies for their objectives.

It was largely the policies that the military regime pursued in the Kurdish areas at the beginning of the 1980s that turned the tide of the Kurdish movement gradually towards violence and the PKK. Increased state intrusion and violence in everyday life to makeover the Kurds attracted many Kurds to the message of the PKK. This study does not ignore other factors, such as the PKK's use of violence within Kurdish society to suppress any opposition, regional conflicts and instability that benefited the PKK, the on-and-off support it received from countries like Syria, Iran, and Iraq, its successful organization in Europe, its effective construction of nationalist symbols and myths, and the leadership cult of Öcalan in helping the PKK's growth and domination of Kurdish mobilization.[19] Nevertheless, the contention of this book is that the PKK would not have enjoyed widespread support from the Kurdish population if the effects of the highly comprehensive and intrusive state policies were not felt so strongly in Kurdish everyday life. The state's interventions into Kurdish cultural practices also directly influenced the formation of the

---

[18] For more on the formation of the PKK, see Marcus (2007), chapter 2.
[19] Aliza Marcus's (2007) account of the PKK's history examines these factors in detail. Also see Bozarslan (2008, 351–352) for a discussion of how Turkish nationalist symbols were Kurdified, and Güneş (2012) for the PKK's use of myths and symbolism.

symbolic and cultural capital of Kurdish nationalism. As Watts (2010, 56) points out, the PKK "significantly changed Kurdish political consciousness, offering new reference points for Kurdish nationalism and an alternative historical narrative that offered a Kurdified mirror image of Turkish nationalism." The PKK's and Kurdish political actors' policies of Kurdification in the 1990s and 2000s were generally modeled after the Turkification practices of the state.[20]

POST-1980: THE RETURN OF THE TRANSFORMATIVE STATE AND THE RISE OF THE PKK

The military coup of September 12, 1980 came as a response to the political chaos and violence that intensified in the last years of the 1970s. The military swiftly restored public order through the use of harsh measures. It banned all political activity; closed down political parties, labor unions, and civil societal associations; prohibited public discussion of political matters; dismissed mayors and municipal councils; and concentrated all state power in the National Security Council, composed of only military officers. The military, through its regional and local commanders, took control of all state institutions over the next three years. Immediately after the coup, mass arrests began. According to Zürcher's figures (1998, 294), 11,500 people were arrested immediately after the coup, and this number increased to 30,000 by the end of 1980. When compared to the previous military interventions, the coup of 1980 was the most comprehensive and repressive with regard to its leaders' objectives and policies. As Cizre Sakallıoğlu (1997, 162) states:

> The military autonomy of the period since 1980 represents a considerable shift in the military's influence, rather than a pattern of continuity. The pattern of politics established by the coup makers after 1980 was more authoritarian than ever before ... The military's claim that the 1980 coup saved Turkey's political democracy from civil war also bolstered its increased power. This claim was made in a military culture and a society that legitimized the military's historical mission and institutional political role as the guardian of the state, and it supported a new pattern of increased military influence.

The coup marked a turning point in state–Kurdish relations. While all political groups were adversely affected by the military takeover, it hit the Kurdish activists, along with the Kurdish masses in the East, the hardest. The emergence of Kurdish groups that advocated self-determination and

---
[20] For more on Kurdification practices, see Watts (2010), chapter 6.

the formation of the PKK convinced the military that separatism was an imminent and a serious threat that should be prevented at any cost. In 1983, out of 15,000 detainees who were charged with being members of left-wing terrorist organizations, 3,177 were accused of separatism, and the PKK suspects numbered 1,790 (Gunter 1990, 67–68). Many of the leaders of the PKK, including Abdullah Öcalan, had already escaped to Syria before the coup.

While the military leaders sought to restructure the political institutions and state–society relations in radical ways, they aimed at re-engineering Kurdish society by reviving the policies of the single-party period. Signs saying "Citizen! Speak Turkish" reappeared in public places in the Southeast. Banners and murals that displayed Atatürk's sayings, such as "From Diyarbakır to Istanbul, from Thrace to Van, there are only Turks" and "Happy is the one who calls himself a Turk," emerged in Kurdish cities and reminded the Kurds of their alleged Turkish origins. The military gave a clear signal that it did not recognize a separate Kurdish entity within Turkey's borders. The military court imprisoned Şerafettin Elçi, a former RPP parliamentarian and a minister in the government in the late 1970s, for having said in an interview that there were Kurds in Turkey and that he himself was a Kurd (Kirişci and Winrow 1997, 111). Unlike the first few decades of the republic, the state's intrusion into the daily life of the Kurdish areas could now be more forceful because more Kurds lived in the easily accessible urban areas and the state's infrastructural capacity was higher, which allowed the military to reach the far corners of the countryside. Any manifestation of Kurdishness, from speaking the Kurdish language to listening to Kurdish music, was interpreted as a challenge to the integrity of the state and was not tolerated. While in the earlier years of the republic, Kurdish cultural expressions were largely seen as undesirable practices that could be changed, in the post-1980 period they came to be perceived as major threats to the regime and the state's Kemalist project. One of my interviewees, who lived in Siverek during military rule, stated that soldiers' arbitrary brutality and verbal insults made daily life unbearable for the town's residents. People wearing traditional outfits were harassed and sometimes detained by the security forces patrolling the streets. Speaking Kurdish in public became almost impossible.[21] The military rule also initiated a large-scale literacy campaign with a specific focus on the Southeast as a way to disseminate the Turkish language. The government announced that those who attended literacy classes would be given priority in the distribution of state credits (*Urfa İçin Hizmet* 1982a).

[21] Interview with Mehmet Kuyurtar, May 29, 2006, Izmir.

Military repression on a daily basis accompanied the mass arrests of those who were suspected of supporting Kurdism, along with the systematic use of torture in prisons. Military operations in the countryside terrorized the villagers: "The army and police acted with unprecedented brutality in order to intimidate the population ... Persons suspected of contacts with Kurdish organizations were detained practically indefinitely" (Van Bruinessen 1984, 12). Because Kurdism was perceived mostly as a movement of foreign origin, the villages close to the borders were heavily militarized and controlled. Diyarbakır Military Prison became one of the centers of extreme brutality that the Kurdish prisoners encountered. By 1984, around 2,500 prisoners were kept in Diyarbakır prison on charges of separatism (*Le Monde* 1984).[22] The families of detainees also faced a severe interrogation process and periodic harassment by security forces. Harsh torture and brutal treatment of prisoners during this period became one of the main narratives of the Kurdish collective memory. The PKK was highly successful in expanding its support base in the large and crowded dormitories of the Diyarbakır prison and among prisoners' relatives (Marcus 2007, 112–113). Several PKK militants indicated that the torture of their relatives in the Diyarbakır prison motivated them to join the PKK.[23] As Bozarslan (2008, 351) points out:

A young generation of teenagers, who had been raised with the accounts of the sufferings of their elder brothers and sisters in prisons, welcomed guerrilla action as an honour-restoring means of revenge and as an end to their silent and largely introverted socialization. The guerrilla war offered them the possibility of gaining collective prestige and, at the same time, a venue for individual commitment and emancipation.

One other important change that the military coup brought was a new emphasis on Islam in state discourse and practice. Known as the "Turkish–Islamic Synthesis," this new approach underlined Islam as the major source of Turkish national culture and highlighted the Islamic past of the nation. The military endorsed this discourse as a tool to counter the impact of leftist ideas and to combat separatism through an emphasis on Sunni Islam as a unifying identity. Ideologically, such an emphasis set the post-1980 period apart from the single-party era, when the official discourse emphasized the pre-Islamic roots of Turkishness and tried

---

[22] The article can be found in the 5th Bulletin of the Kurdish Institute of Paris, *Bulletin de Liaison et d'Information*, No. 5, March–April 1984, p. 51. Available at www.institutkurde.org/publications/bulletins/list.php.

[23] See the interviews with the PKK guerillas done by Bejan Matur (2011).

to create a highly secular national culture. The Kurdish areas became the critical centers, where policies in conformity with this new approach of Turkish–Islamic Synthesis were implemented. In 1982, a local newspaper in Urfa announced that in boarding schools, the majority of which were in Eastern Turkey, students were required to say, "Praise be to God, long live our nation!" before meals (*Urfa İçin Hizmet* 1982b). The Directorate of Religious Affairs sent religious scholars (*müftü*) to the Eastern provinces to give talks on religious unity and warn people about separatist ideas (*Yeni Gündem* 1986b). New mosques were built while new Qur'anic schools and vocational religious high schools were opened in the region. In 1986, *Yeni Gündem*, a weekly news magazine, criticized the governor of Tunceli,[24] Kenan Güven, for ordering the construction of four mosques in two years in a predominantly Alevi Kurdish city where hardly anyone went to mosques for worship. Kenan Güven was a retired general who was appointed to Tunceli in 1982. His policies in Tunceli provide another example of renewed state efforts to transform the Kurds through intrusive daily practices. In an interview, Güven stated that he organized city-sponsored jogging sessions and put pressure on city residents to attend them in order to distract their attention away from politics. He also interfered in people's religious practices to make them compatible with Sunni Islam, asked men to cut their mustache and beards, and wanted those whom he suspected of Kurdism to make a written declaration that they were Turks. He was also known by his opposition to state employees who were natives to the area. He exiled a large majority of Kurdish state employees to other parts of the country.[25] Far from strengthening national unity, the military's redefinition and transformation of Kemalism to incorporate Sunni Islam under the Turkish–Islamic Synthesis alienated the Alevi population, both Kurdish and Turkish, from the regime (Bozarslan 1996, 138).

Military rule also played a significant role in politicizing the use of the Kurdish language and bringing the language issue to the core of cultural contestation. In the eyes of the military, speaking the Kurdish language symbolized Kurds' challenge to the very foundations of the Turkish Republic and could not be tolerated. The ban on the use of the Kurdish language began in prisons. Prisoners were not allowed to speak Kurdish

---

[24] Tunceli was known as Dersim before it was renamed in 1936. According to the religious traditions of Alevis, worshipping does not take place in mosques, but in meeting houses called *cemevi*.
[25] For two interesting interviews conducted with him, see *Yeni Gündem* (1986a) and *Nokta* (1986). Also see *Yeni Gündem* (1988).

with each other and with their visitors. The harsh treatment by prison authorities of those who spoke Kurdish turned the language into a tool for collective mobilization. Many Kurdish detainees refused to speak Turkish during court hearings in the 1980s. Mehdi Zana, the former mayor of Diyarbakır, became famous for defending himself in Kurdish in court as a way to demonstrate the existence of the Kurdish ethnic identity. In schools, speaking Kurdish could be a serious offense that resulted in corporal punishment. Teachers used students as informants to determine who spoke Kurdish at home with their families (Matur 2011, 44, 52).

The main instigator of the language conflict was the infamous Law 2932, which came into effect towards the end of the military rule in 1983. This law banned the use of the Kurdish language in public and private, and was reminiscent of the measures of the single-party era, except this time the state had more coercive power to implement the ban.[26] The law never mentioned the word "Kurdish," as it would mean the official acknowledgment of the existence of the Kurdish language, but it was carefully formulated to make Kurdish its sole target. The second article of the law stated: "No language can be used for the explication, dissemination, and publication of ideas other than the first official language of countries recognized by the Turkish state." The law also prohibited the spread of any language other than Turkish as the mother tongue. Until its repeal in 1991, the law was used to justify several interrogations, trials, and convictions of those who spoke, sang, or published in Kurdish.[27] A folk singer who sang at weddings in the Southeast was imprisoned for sixteen days for singing a Kurdish folk song at the time of the military rule in the 1980s. The police interrogated the members of a folk music group, *Grup Yorum*, in 1989, for singing a Kurdish song at its concert. An old woman who did not speak Turkish was sentenced to a year in prison for speaking in Kurdish at a political party meeting.[28] A PKK member who was a university student in the 1980s recalls how his

---

[26] For the full text of the law, see *Resmi Gazete* (1983, 27–28).

[27] According to official statistics, between 1986 and 1991, 115 court cases were opened and 189 people were tried for the violation of Law 2932. These data are compiled from the website of the General Directorate of Criminal Registration and Statistics of the Ministry of Justice: www.adli-sicil.gov.tr/istatist.htm. However, many more people were detained and interrogated but not prosecuted for violating Law of 2932. There are no statistical data about their numbers. In addition, in many cases the authorities considered speaking in Kurdish as a violation of the Turkish Penal Code's Article 142, which banned advocating separatism and propagating ideas that weaken national sentiments.

[28] For more examples, see *Cumhuriyet* (1991a, 1991b).

telephone conversation with his mother was cut off in his dormitory for speaking a banned language (Matur 2011, 89). Criticizing the law could also create legal problems. For instance, in 1990, the public prosecutor opened an investigation about the parliamentarian Halim Aras for having said that speaking in Kurdish should become legal (*Hürriyet* 1990b). Daily state intrusions against speaking Kurdish turned it into a symbol of cultural and political opposition in the following years. As one Kurdish intellectual stated, the law revealed the meaning of linguistic freedom for ordinary Kurds who had not felt the need to think about their language before.[29]

The new constitution, which was adopted in 1982, reflected the military's aspirations to discipline and reorder the society with more emphasis on the "Turkishness" of Turkey, public order, and national unity. It brought in extensive provisions to safeguard the territorial integrity of the country and limited freedoms of speech and association, which had been expanded by the 1960 constitution. The military's authority in decision making increased through the National Security Council.[30] As Cizre Sakallıoğlu (1997, 153–154) suggests, the constitution "entrenched the military's veto power in the political system to such an extent that it has made crude military intervention into politics redundant." The constitution established the State Security Courts to deal with offenses against the integrity of the state. Article 14 stated that those who abuse individual freedoms "with the aim of violating the indivisible integrity of the State with its territory and nation, of endangering the existence of the Turkish state and Republic" would be subject to punitive measures. Such ambiguous and broad clauses, further strengthened by other clauses in the Turkish Penal Code and the Anti-Terror Law of 1991, played an important role in turning any subject that related to the Kurdish population into a taboo in the post-1980 period (Muller 1996). Any idea or practice that could imply the existence of Kurds in Turkey could result in legal prosecution. In 1986, for instance, the administrators of the State Institute of Statistics were taken to the State Security Court for including the option of "Kurdish" under the question "Do you speak any languages other than Turkish?" in manuals prepared for state officials for

---

[29] Interview with Ümit Fırat, August 2006, Istanbul.
[30] The National Security Council (NSC) was initially established by the 1960 constitution to create a platform for the military to voice its opinion on issues of national security. The 1982 constitution increased the number and weight of senior commanders in the NSC and stipulated that its recommendations be given priority by the Council of Ministers. For more, see Cizre Sakallıoğlu (1997, 157–158).

the 1985 population census. They were accused of advocating separatism (*Hürriyet* 1986a).

In short, military rule between 1980 and 1983 was highly critical in furthering conflict in state–Kurdish relations, as the military increased the level of state intrusion in the Kurdish areas. It also revived many of the policies of the single-party period that pushed for a "makeover" of the Kurdish population with the expectation of creating a sense of belonging to the Turkish nation. The PKK, which was one of the smallest Kurdish organizations at the end of the 1970s and which many Kurds did not take too seriously, as one prominent Kurdish activist put it,[31] gradually succeeded in winning the support of the Kurdish masses in the 1980s and 1990s. It resumed its armed operations against state forces in 1984, which resulted in the further militarization of the region, aggravating the reciprocal relationship between Kurdish radicalization and the state's repressive intrusion. Daily life in the region did not normalize after the coup because of the start of the armed conflict. The state steadily increased the number of troops, which greatly deepened its intrusion into the region. Tunceli, which had a population of 19,000, had 55,000 soldiers deployed in it in 1986 (*Yeni Gündem* 1986a). By 1995, 300,000 members of the security forces served in the region (Kirişci and Winrow 1997, 130). Human rights violations committed by both sides transformed daily life in the Southeast.

In 1987, the parliament declared a state of emergency in ten provinces in the Southeast. A governor-general was appointed with extensive powers, such as curtailing press freedoms and evacuating villages when deemed necessary. Human rights organizations increasingly publicized village evacuations,[32] forced migrations, mass arrests, torture, unidentified murders, and the extrajudicial acts of the special counter-insurgency teams in the region. The PKK also did not refrain from using force against civilians and massacred many, justifying it either as unintended consequences of the war or as acts against "collaborators." Its practices of forced recruitment and taxation contributed to the transformation of everyday life in the Kurdish areas (Bozarslan 2001, 51–52; Marcus 2007, 117). One of the most important consequences of the war was massive migration, some of which was in the form of forced resettlements, from the conflict-ridden rural areas to the urban centers. Between 1990

---

[31] This Kurdish activist is Canip Yıldırım. See Miroğlu (2005, 240).

[32] According to the official records, during emergency rule between 1987 and 2001 692 villages and 2,000 hamlets were evacuated (Cemal 2003, 550).

and 1994, the population of Diyarbakır grew from 380,000 to 950,000 (Kirişci and Winrow 1997, 134). According to estimates, the number of internally displaced was around 1.5 million people (Watts 2010, 56).

Although the PKK's repressive attitude towards other Kurdish groups and individuals who sought to have an independent voice within the movement or who were critical of the PKK's demands and strategies partly explains its hegemonic status within the movement, it does not explain the PKK's high level of popularity among the Kurdish masses in the post-1980 era. The PKK resorted to forced conscription to increase its number of fighters in the 1980s but by 1990 it was popular enough that it suspended the measure. In 1992, the PKK commanded around 10,000 fighters and around 50,000 of a militia force (Marcus 2007, 119, 179; Watts 2010, 56). PKK fighters enjoyed the support and respect of the villagers and did not have much difficulty in getting necessary supplies and food from them (Güneş 2012, 257). The funerals of PKK rebels could incite thousands of people to demonstrate on the streets and the PKK could shut down a whole city like Diyarbakır to protest military operations. By the 1990s the PKK was not only an armed movement but also a political force with direct and indirect links to rights organizations, publishing houses, cultural institutions, and a series of political parties (Marcus 2007, 175, 217). One of the main factors that accounts for such support was the failure of the state authorities on the ground to distinguish between PKK supporters and ordinary Kurds who wanted to stay out of the conflict. The military-bureaucratic apparatus's increasingly harsh attitude towards the population and their treatment of every Kurd as a potential suspect played an important role in creating popular sympathy for the PKK's cause and turning it into a mass movement. "Especially in extraordinary circumstances, the authorities used to insult the people a lot. This signaled the way they perceived the Kurds," said one of my interviewees who lived in the Southeast in the 1980s.[33] As Romano (2006, 160) underlines, the PKK was successful at overcoming the sense of helplessness among the Kurds against the Turkish state and instilling in them a sense of pride in being Kurdish.

The fight against the growing influence of the PKK pushed the state to negotiate with tribal authorities in the region, which would result in one of the most serious unintended consequences of the state–Kurdish conflict: the empowerment of certain tribal authorities. Starting from 1985, the government began to recruit "village guards" from the rural

[33] Interview with Mehmet Kuyurtar, May 29, 2006, Izmir.

population to serve as local militia forces that would help the state forces in military operations against the PKK. Recruitment of peasants largely took place through negotiations with tribal leaders, who could mobilize large numbers of men into state service. The state not only provided arms and salaries to village guards, but also turned a blind eye to the tribes' past and future crimes, such as rape, homicide, and fraud, as long as they took part in the village guard system. According to official figures, there were around 60,000 village guards on the government payroll in 2003. The state's tolerance of their illegal activities allowed tribal leaders to enrich themselves through drug and arms smuggling and to reinforce their authority in their localities. The state also ignored human rights violations committed by the village guards (Balta 2004). In the end, the village guard system became more of a liability to the state than an asset. As Belge (2011) suggests, village guards acted in ways that undermined state authority in the region. Many village guards collaborated with the PKK while they were paid by the state: "Enlistment in the village guards could serve as a cover for enterprising strongmen, who moved in and out of contradictory alliances while amassing local power" (Belge 2011, 108).

The state's cooperation with tribes in the region did not shift its broader goal of transforming the Kurds culturally. This is because such cooperation did not create the level of interdependence that exists in Morocco between rural authorities and the state. In Turkey, those tribes that refused to cooperate with the state were subject to its coercive power. The state authorities considered those that did not want to be a part of the village guard system as active supporters or sympathizers of the PKK and subjected their villages to forced evacuations and destruction (Balta 2004). The village guard system was a security-related arrangement in the state's fight against the PKK. The state's determination to use violence against villages that wanted to remain neutral indicates that it was not interested in pursuing a broader alliance with rural authorities as in Morocco.

Far from eroding the transformative nation-building project of the state, the armed conflict contributed to the escalation of cultural and symbolic contestation between the state and the Kurds. Particularly in the conflict-ridden areas, the local security forces and bureaucracy grew less tolerant of any expressions of Kurdishness and resorted to indiscriminate repression of cultural practices. The armed conflict created a mutually reinforcing dynamic of increased state interference in Kurdish cultural practices and their increasing politicization through the 1990s.

THE FRAGMENTED STATE: CONTENTION OVER EXPRESSIONS OF KURDISHNESS

Towards the end of the 1980s, a debate started among politicians, members of civil society organizations, and intellectuals about how to solve the Kurdish problem through non-military means. The press also began increasingly to publicize the human rights violations in the Southeast. In 1986, the Social Democratic Populist Party (SHP) prepared a report criticizing the government for not taking seriously the suffering of the people living in the East. The report called attention to the state of fear that was prevalent among the people, state officials' mistreatment of those who did not speak Turkish, and corruption among state security forces. The report called on the government to establish democratic rights and freedoms and to prepare an urgent development plan for the region (*Hürriyet* 1986b). A year later, Turgut Atalay, a member of the central board of the SHP, stated that the ban on the Kurdish language should be lifted and that parents should be free to give Kurdish names to their children (*Nokta* 1987b, 28–29). Similar remarks were made by an SHP deputy, Ali Eren, who asserted that the Kurds were a national minority whose situation could be compared to the Turks in Bulgaria and Greece (Kirişci and Winrow 1997, 112–113). At the beginning of the 1990s, the government gave signs of relaxing the limitations on expressions of Kurdish culture. The infamous Law 2932, which banned the use of the Kurdish language in public and private, was lifted in April 1991 as a result of a general consensus among major political parties.[34] The following December, Deputy Prime Minister Erdal İnönü argued that Kurdish citizens should enjoy their cultural identity in full. On March 1991, the minister of culture issued a directive allowing for the celebration of Newroz, the Kurdish New Year, all over the country. The following year Prime Minister Süleyman Demirel announced that he recognized the existence of Kurdish ethnicity (Kirişci and Winrow 1997, 113). President Turgut Özal, especially, took important steps in an attempt to solve the problem through non-military means. In January 1990, he approved the compulsory jurisdiction of the European Court of Human Rights, which since then has become a crucial appeal mechanism for

---

[34] For more on the debates, see *Nokta* (1990, 17–22). Many politicians who supported the abolition of the Kurdish ban openly declared that they still did not recognize the existence of a separate Kurdish ethnicity. When asked about the draft law that would lift the ban on Kurdish, Oltan Sungurlu, the minister of justice, replied, "What language is that? I don't know such a language" (*Nokta* 1991, 27).

Kurdish activists. He also announced that he was partly Kurdish, argued for Kurdish broadcasting on state television, tried to form informal contacts with the Kurdish leaders, stated that a federal system could solve the Kurdish problem, and advocated the preparation of an amnesty law for the PKK fighters (Torunlu 1993, 39).[35] The mainstream newspapers, which had avoided writing about the Kurds in previous periods, started to refer to the Kurdish issue more frequently. As Murat Somer (2004, 246) states: "Beginning in 1991, not only did the number of articles escalate drastically, but also a large percentage of the articles began to use 'Kurd,' indicating that the discursive categories that the journalists were using in describing similar events were in transition." In a country where the official discourse could not even utter the word "Kurd" and identified the issue as a problem of regional backwardness or terrorism, these were drastic changes. As Yeğen (2007, 137) notes, Kurdish resistance pushed Turkish nationalists to publicly recognize the existence of a separate Kurdish identity, which they had denied for decades.

Several domestic and international developments resulted in a search for political solutions to the Kurdish problem. The Gulf War in 1991, the resulting massive influx of Iraqi Kurdish refugees into Turkey, and the power vacuum in the Kurdish region in Northern Iraq worried the Turkish state authorities that the developments in Iraq would fuel nationalist aspirations among Turkey's Kurds. At a more general level, the end of the Cold War and the rise of identity politics and the human rights discourse attracted not only the Kurds but also many Turkish politicians, who increasingly advocated the necessity of finding a non-military solution to the Kurdish problem. At the domestic level, the increase in the level of violence in the Southeast and the rise of PKK recruitment also alarmed the state authorities and bolstered the sense among many politicians that a military approach would not be adequate to deal with the PKK (Robins 1993, 665).

The Kurdish movement also gave signals of a possible transformation with the establishment of the pro-Kurdish People's Labor Party (HEP) in June 1990. The expression of Kurdish demands from a legal political platform increased hopes for a decline in armed conflict. In the 1991 elections, the HEP had an electoral pact with the SHP and entered parliament with twenty-two deputies under SHP's umbrella. The pro-Kurdish party members were influential in attracting public attention to Kurdish

---

[35] Özal died in 1993 of a sudden heart attack. Many believe that if he had not died, he would have led a major transformation in Turkey's ethnic policy. See Ataman (2002).

grievances and publicizing the state forces' human rights abuses from their parliamentary platform. The participation of a pro-Kurdish party in the political arena, nevertheless, has been a highly contentious process. The HEP and its successors encountered significant pressure from public prosecutors, police, military, and various political parties. Since its foundation, the HEP was under close scrutiny and was closed by the Constitutional Court in 1993 on charges of separatism. Its successor, the Democracy Party (DEP), which was founded prior to the HEP's closure, suffered the same fate in 1994. The parliamentary immunity of its deputies was lifted and seven of them received jail terms. Another party, the People's Democracy Party (HADEP) was formed in 1994 and was closed down in 2003. The Constitutional Court banned its successor, the Democratic Society Party (DTP), in 2009. While the Turkish state made it clear that it would be extremely hard for a party with a pro-Kurdish agenda to exist within the political system, the experiences of these parties also showed the difficulty Kurdish activists had in distancing themselves from the PKK. The pro-Kurdish parties could not formulate policies that would run counter to the PKK's position and refrained from an outright condemnation of PKK activities.[36]

The abolishment of the Kurdish language ban and the growing public recognition of a separate Kurdish identity did not relax state practices over Kurdish linguistic and cultural practices. Two main reasons account for this. First, the broad and ambiguous provisions of laws allowed authorities to legally justify their interventions over Kurdish linguistic and cultural practices. For example, use of the Kurdish language could be prosecuted under the Anti-Terror Law as constituting separatist propaganda or support for the PKK. Second, the local civil and military bureaucracy did not easily endorse the policy changes and showed resistance to their implementation. After Law 2932 was lifted in 1991, most restrictions on the use of the Kurdish language remained de facto in force, largely because the abolition of the law did not influence the behavior of the local state cadres. Operating in a conflict-ridden environment, where they faced the harsh circumstances of the war, toughened the behavior of these officials, who tended to blame the locals for their distress. In addition, unlike the parliamentarians and the members of the government, these local officials were largely insulated from international pressures for the improvement of human rights. The local officials' intransigence to relaxing the cultural restrictions also stemmed from the politicization

---

[36] For more on the pro-Kurdish political parties, see Watts (2010).

of Kurdish cultural elements, such as music, dress, language, and celebrations, in the 1990s. Several examples of such politicization could be given: Newroz, known as the Persian New Year that marks the first day of spring around March 21, began to be celebrated by the Kurds in the Middle East starting in the 1950s. By the 1980s, these celebrations became more public and political events that symbolized Kurdish resistance against state repression. The PKK also used Newroz as a means to propagate and organize mass protest, and the celebrations led to violent conflicts between state security forces and Kurdish activists (Yanık 2006, 287). A genre of Kurdish music developed that glorified and propagated armed struggle and self-determination (Güneş 2012, 263). The usage of red, green, and yellow in combination came to symbolize support for the PKK and Kurdish aspirations for a separate state. Consequently, state officials on the ground came to associate almost every element of Kurdish culture with separatism and did not show much willingness to loosen restrictions on Kurdish cultural expressions. Such politicization led them to see Kurdish cultural demands as a subtle prelude to autonomy and eventually territorial secession. After granting the right to speak Kurdish in state bureaus, the governor-general, Hayri Kozakçıoğlu, for instance, stated that he hoped this right would not turn the Kurdish language into an unarmed means of propaganda (*Hürriyet* 1990a).

The Turkish state's half-hearted relaxation of the restrictions on the Kurdish language did not have an effect on the armed conflict. Between 1991 and 1999 the conflict between the PKK and security forces reached its peak with the highest number of casualties occurring during this period. Weak coalition governments of the 1990s devolved more authority to the military in dealing with the Kurdish conflict. The intensified conflict resulted in the forced evacuation of 3,428 villages and hamlets by security forces and displacement of more than a million Kurds (International Crisis Group 2011, 4). Various forms of legal and extralegal repression were used to intimidate and silence Kurdish activists and their supporters.[37] According to Romano (2006, 88), the indiscriminate violence by the state security forces compared to the PKK's more selective repression helped the PKK's popularity among the Kurds in the 1990s. Similarly,

---

[37] Watts (2010, 96–101) categorizes four different types of repressive measures: "policing" such as detention without trial and searches of pro-Kurdish organizations; "juridical-legal" such as prosecutors' investigations and trials in State Security Courts; "extralegal" such as unknown assailant killings and torture;, and "bureaucratic" such as suspension or interruptions in funding and withholding permission for projects or activities by Kurdish organizations.

Aliza Marcus (1990, 42–44) suggests that people were more frightened of the Turkish army than the PKK and the military's repression gradually turned them against the state.

The next section examines two examples of cultural contestation between the Turkish authorities and the Kurds in the 1990s: the state's interventions into Kurdish music and the giving of Kurdish names to children. These two cases provide further details about the nature of state intervention into Kurdish cultural practices. They underline the difficulties of reconciliation, even at the cultural and symbolic level, once armed conflict starts. They also suggest that the Turkish state has not been a coherent and unitary actor in dealing with the Kurdish issue. Instead, ideological or normative disagreements as well as the different contexts in which state actors operated mattered in the different interpretation and enforcement of laws and policies. As Joel Migdal (2001, 116–117) underlines, the state may not generate a single response to an issue or problem:

> Rather, its outcomes – the formulation and implementation of its policies – are a series of different actions based on the particular calculus of pressures that each engaged component of the state faces in its particular environment of action ... The outcome can just as likely be a sum of ill-fitting responses that stem from the different components of the state as they respond to their various arenas of domination and opposition.

THE CONTROVERSY OVER NAMING

In February 1987, *Nokta*, a weekly news magazine in Turkey, reported that the Office of the Public Prosecutor in Bitlis brought twelve people to court, charging them with giving Kurdish names to their children. The judicial process started after the Bitlis chief of police did a survey of the names that were registered in the public registration office and wrote a report about local naming practices for the Office of the Public Prosecutor. In this report, the police chief wrote that the majority of the population living in Bitlis conserved their local characteristics, that they continued to speak their local language, and that they gave their children Kurdish names. Before the public prosecutor in Bitlis proceeded to sue the parents, he asked for an opinion from the Ministry of the Interior that set up a committee of experts on the issue. The report written by the committee underlined that the names were not Turkish and added, "Over the long term the names that are given to children are very important for our national unity and social structure. Therefore, names that will be given to children should have a character that unites the society." The report also drew attention to Article 16/4 of the Registration Law, which stipulated that names that do not conform to the national culture, moral norms, customs, and traditions and which offend the public cannot be given to children. As a result of this report from the Ministry of the Interior, the public prosecutor applied to the court to annul the Kurdish names. After ten months of the first hearing in court, the judges decided to drop the case, claiming that public prosecutors could not open court cases to annul registered names.[38] This ruling was in conformity with a previous decision of the Court of Cassation (*Yargıtay*), which stipulated that a name's non-Turkish origin could not be a justification of its annulment. This ruling, however, did not bar numerous court cases of a similar kind from being opened in the Kurdish region during the following years.

Throughout the 1980s and 1990s the ban on giving Kurdish names to children was one of the main cultural contestations between the Kurds and the state. For state officials who served in the local areas of conflict, banning Kurdish names was a way to assert state authority over the very private details of people's lives, at a time when they felt the utmost threat against such authority. The local bureaucracy's insistence on the ban, despite the consistent rulings of the Court of Cassation against it, underlines the former's role in instigating the conflict. In turn, names increasingly became a tool for the symbolic creation of Kurdish nationhood and protest. The result was a gradual creation or revival of names of Kurdish linguistic origin and their increasing use among the politicized Kurds to distinguish themselves from the general Turkish public.

As James Scott (1998) points out, state interference in personal naming practices is related to the expansion of state control over the population. States regulate names in order to institutionalize a standard legal system and property regime, to increase the legibility of the population in order to easily identify their citizens, and to fix their identities. As mentioned in Chapter 2, the 1934 Surname Law in Turkey required each Turkish citizen to take a last name. This law not only aimed at increased population legibility for the sake of effective taxation and conscription, but it was also part of the state's project to transform its citizens' identities. That is why Article 3 of the law forbade citizens to use surnames that are related to tribes and foreign ethnicities and races.[39] The state aimed to create a new citizen, who would bear equal rights before the law and whose relationship with the state would be unmediated and direct (Scott *et al*.

---

[38] See *Nokta* (1987a, 16–18; 1988a, 38).
[39] The full text of the law can be found at www.hukuki.net/kanun/2525.13.frameset.asp.

2002, 16). Ethnic groups and tribes were considered as communities that stood between states and citizens.

In the case of the first names, though, the legal requirement was less clear and open to interpretation. In the early republican period, especially in the 1930s when an official nationalist history was being formulated and there were attempts at language purification, there was official encouragement for distinctively Turkish names, but it was not a legal requirement. Article 16/4 of the Registration Law that was passed in 1972 stipulated that names that do not conform to the national culture are impermissible. It was left to the discretion of officers working at the registration offices to decide whether a name ran counter to the national culture or not. Before the military coup in 1980 Kurds could give Kurdish names to their children. Many Kurdish names such as Berfin, Helin, and Kendal were officially registered.[40] Some of the Kurdish activists I interviewed confirmed this and pointed out that negotiating with state officials in the registration offices over a Kurdish name was possible before the 1980s. A disagreement over a name was resolved during such negotiation, without having to go through a judicial process. It was in the contentious environment of the 1980s that Kurdish names increasingly became seen as subversive of national culture and were banned at the local registration offices. According to Sezgin Tanrıkulu, the military regime, which was in power between 1980 and 1983, provided the registration offices a list of Kurdish names to help enforce the ban (Düzel 2003). Transition to multi-party politics in 1983 did not lead to a relaxation of the policies restricting Kurdish cultural practices. With the emergence of the PKK and the armed conflict in the region, there was increased sensitivity on the part of local state officials, such as registrars, public prosecutors, judges, police, and gendarmerie to expressions of Kurdish ethnic identity, including Kurdish names. The 1980 military coup and the revival of the makeover policies also helped increase politicization and mobilization based on Kurdish cultural elements. Consequently, Kurds increasingly embraced Kurdish names as a way to assert their Kurdishness. The armed conflict politicized and increased the value of cultural symbols, such as names, for both sides.

In many instances it was the officials in public registration offices in the Kurdish cities who played a critical role in instigating the contestations

---

[40] See Neşe Düzel's interview with Sezgin Tanrıkulu, a prominent Kurdish rights activist and human rights attorney, in Düzel (2003).

over naming. In 1988, the registration office in Midyat issued a criminal complaint against a parent who gave his children the Kurdish names Valat and Baver. According to the officials, these names were not in conformity with the national culture, customs, and traditions and, therefore, should be erased from the registration records. The civil court of Midyat asked for an opinion from the Ministry of the Interior's General Directorate of Population and Citizenship Affairs. The General Directorate underlined that the names were not of Turkish origin but that according to the Lausanne Treaty, people who belonged to minority groups in Turkey had the right to give foreign names to their children. This was one of the very rare instances when an official institution recognized the Kurdish population as a minority. In fact, the opinion was also based on a wrong interpretation of the Lausanne Treaty, which recognized only non-Muslim Turkish citizens as minority groups in Turkey. In addition, this answer was contradictory to the one that the Ministry of the Interior gave in response to the court in Bitlis a year before. In that year, the ministry underlined that names should conform to the territorial integrity of the state, implying that Kurdish names were not acceptable. In accordance with the answer sent from the Ministry of the Interior, the local civil court of Midyat ruled that the Kurdish names of the children could not be changed (*Nokta* 1988c, 22–23).

A survey of the Court of Cassation decisions with regard to naming shows that the issue became more controversial in the local Kurdish areas during the 1990s. In Turkey, the Court of Cassation is the court of appeals of last resort, which reviews the decisions of the lower courts to ensure standardization in legal practice. If the Court of Cassation does not agree with a decision, it annuls the decision of the lower court and remands the case to the lower court. If the lower court insists on its previous decision, the General Assembly of the Court of Cassation concludes appellate review on the lower court's judgment and makes the final decision on the case.[41] The Court of Cassation's decisions with regard to taking non-Turkish names have been consistently liberal. In all the cases about naming, Kurdish and other foreign names,[42] the court ruled that

---

[41] More information about the Turkish Court of Cassation can be found at www.yargitay.gov.tr. The court decisions are compiled from the Kazancı case law database. For more information on the database, see www.kazanci.com.tr.

[42] The following are a few case examples that involved non-Kurdish names. The 18th Civil Chamber (18. Hukuk Dairesi) of the Court of Cassation heard all these cases. About a man who wanted to retain his original German name after he became Turkish citizen, see Esas no: 1996/2181, Karar no: 1996/2777, March 19, 1996; about the name "Jutta," see

individuals were free to take any name, unless the meaning of the name was insulting, humiliating, or profane. Such rulings, however, were hardly taken into consideration in the conflict-ridden Kurdish areas by the local bureaucratic circles.

In 1990, the Court of Cassation overruled a decision of a lower civil court, which had ruled that the parents involved should annul the Kurdish name, Berivan, that they had given their child. The Court rejected the ruling based on several reasons. It ruled that, procedurally, name annulment cases could not be opened in courts either by public prosecutors or by registration offices but that only individuals could apply to courts in order to change their names. The judges also stated that, since naming their children is a right of parents, no individual could be stripped of a name by a court decision according to the main principles of human rights. In addition, it found the lower court's explanation inadequate as to why the name Berivan did not conform to the national culture, customs, and traditions.[43]

During the 1990s, the Court of Cassation decided on a number of cases that related to individuals who wanted to change their Turkish names to Kurdish ones. In all these cases, the court consistently ruled that first names do not have to be of Turkish origin. In 1993, it canceled a lower court's decision that refused a parent's demand to change his daughter's name from Berrin to the Kurdish name, Berfin. While the lower court refused this demand on the ground that the name was not Turkish, the Court of Cassation stated that the foreignness of a name could not be a justification for its nonconformity with national unity, traditions, and customs.[44] A year later, in a very similar case, the Court of Cassation overruled a decision that did not allow a woman to change her name from Songül to Rojda. In all these cases the Court of Cassation made a decision based on the meaning of the name and whether or not the individual was known within the society by the name he/she wanted to take. Unless the meaning of the name was insulting, defamatory, or profane, it ruled that the lower courts did not have the right to deny that name to the individual even though the name was not Turkish.

In 2000, a father whose daughter's name was Hatice applied to the Court of Cassation to challenge the lower court's refusal to change it

---

Esas no: 1997/3451, Karar no: 1997/4459, May 6, 1997; about the name "Jülyet," see Esas no: 2002/10421, Karar no: 2002/12155, December 16, 2002.
[43] Yargıtay İlamı, T.C. Yargıtay 3. Hukuk Dairesi, Esas no: 8859, Karar no: 516.
[44] Yargıtay İlamı, T.C. Yargıtay 18. Hukuk Dairesi, Esas no: 9708, Karar no: 0832, October 13, 1993.

to a Kurdish name, Mizgin. The lower court denied the name change to Mizgin on the grounds that it did not exist in the Turkish language and had Persian (Kurdish) origin.[45] The court also referred to the opinion of a Turkish language and literature professor who stated that the name had different meanings, one of which could be considered insulting.[46] The General Assembly of the Court of Cassation found the expert's opinion inadequate and subjective. It ruled in favor of the father and stated:

First we should note that the fourth clause of Article 16 of the Registration Law was not written to purify Turkish from words of foreign origin but to avert people from giving names that do not conform to the national culture, moral norms, customs and traditions. Eastern and Southeastern Anatolia is a part of the motherland, where, not only a particular ethnic group, but people with different ethnic origins live as part of our country's reality.

The court acknowledged that many of the names used in Turkey are of Arabic and Persian origin and were ingrained into the Turkish culture and traditions. It was convinced by the father's claim that "Mizgin" is commonly used in his region and stated that the father had legitimate reasons to change his daughter's name.[47]

The attitude of different state institutions towards naming was neither monolithic nor consistent. The Ministry of the Interior sent separate circulars in 1986, 1990, and 1992 stating that officials in registration offices should register names of parents' choice. The circulars also specified that if a name was considered objectionable, registrars should first consult the ministry before informing the public prosecutor (Türkiye İnsan Hakları Vakfı 1993, 171). Nevertheless, state registrars continued to refuse to register Kurdish names, the gendarmerie searched for Kurdish names in order to inform the legal authorities, and local public prosecutors now and then filed suits against parents who gave Kurdish names to their children. Many local courts continued to interpret Article 16/4 of the Registration Law as a ban against Kurdish names. For example, in 1998, the Elazığ

---

[45] Only once in the court's decision is the name's Kurdish origin acknowledged. In the rest of the text, the name is referred to as Persian.

[46] According to the expert's opinion, the name could mean "guest, dining table, hospitable, clean, and urine," depending on the way it was spelled in Persian. One of the reasons why the lower civil court found the name objectionable was because of its probable meaning of "urine." The plaintiff, however, stated that it meant "good news" in his regional language.

[47] T.C. Yargıtay Hukuk Genel Kurulu, Esas no: 2000/18–127, Karar no: 2000/154, March 1, 2000. Also see the previous decision by the Court of Cassation with regard to the same case: Yargıtay Hukuk Genel Kurulu, Esas no: 1999/18–966, Karar no: 1999/1010, December 1, 1999.

registration office refused a father's demand to register his child's name as Laşer Rodi. The administrative court of Malatya approved the registration office's claim two years later. In an interview, the father stated that although his grandmothers' Kurdish names were officially registered, he was not able to register his child's name during the five years since his birth.[48] The local bureaucracy and judiciary continued to resist relaxation of the limitations on Kurdish cultural expressions. They recreated and strengthened these limitations as everyday forms of coercion.

In 2002, the PKK declared that it promoted political uprising as a solution to the Kurdish problem. As Romano (2006, 144) points out, the discourse of the Kurdish insurgency shifted to the language of human rights and democracy as its military strength weakened and as it needed to attract greater international support. In its 8th Congress, the PKK announced KADEK as its only legitimate representative and declared its decision to undertake resistance in the form of civil disobedience. In this context Kurdish names created another crisis. The Ministry of the Interior allegedly sent a secret circular, warning local administrators about an increase in Kurdish naming. After the circular, the Diyarbakır gendarmerie prepared a list of 600 Kurdish names and sent it to the office of the attorney general. In this document it was written that the campaign for Kurdish naming was part of the PKK's attempts at political struggle and that those who insisted on giving Kurdish names to their children acted in accordance with the PKK's directives. Soon after, seven parents were taken to court in Dicle for giving their children Kurdish names. According to the prosecutor's claim, these names were considered inappropriate for national unity, customs, and traditions and offended the public because they were the code names that the PKK militants used.[49] Ironically, a female judge whose name was Kurdish (Şirvan) presided over the court hearing. The prosecutor drew attention to a report sent from the Turkish Language Association stating that the names were not of Turkish origin and "did not conform to Turkish naming habits." The families' attorney underlined that the prosecutor did not have the right to bring name annulment cases to court. The judge recognized the attorney's claim and dismissed the case for procedural reasons. In different parts of Turkey, however, restriction and refusals of Kurdish names

---

[48] T.C. Malatya İdare Mahkemesi, Esas no: 1999/1204, Karar no: 2000/335, April 11, 2000. For the interview, see *Milliyet* (2003).

[49] These names were Berivan, Zilan, Rojda, Baver, Velat, Serhat, Kendal, Zinar, Hebun, Baran, Rojhat, Agit, Zelal, and Zozan. Serhat is a common name used in Turkey. See *Radikal* (2002).

continued. In Ardahan and İzmir, the civil courts even sent files on two fathers to the State Security Courts claiming that the fathers acted in opposition to the Prevention of Terrorism Act. In both cases, the prosecutors of the State Security Courts dismissed the charges. In 2002, a total of seventy-six name annulment cases were brought before the courts in Turkey.[50] This crisis over naming coincided with parliamentary reforms to satisfy European Union (EU) membership criteria and to lift the bans on Kurdish broadcasting and private education.

The mobilization of both state officials and the Kurds with regards to naming in 2002 underlined two parallel processes. First, it represented the resistance of the local bureaucracy and the military to the pro-EU reforms that began to lift restrictions on the use of Kurdish. For them, these initiatives meant state concessions to the Kurdish insurgency and were considered to be the politicians' betrayal of the military-bureaucratic elite. Second, Kurdification of names increasingly became a tool for the creation of Kurdish nationhood and a symbol for protest against the state. In 2007, Diyarbakır Municipality, which had been governed by the pro-Kurdish Democratic Society Party, published a 105-page book that listed Kurdish names. Even after the Turkish Parliament changed the registration law to minimize the contradictory interpretations of the relevant article about naming, the controversy did not come to an end. With the new amendment, only names that disregard moral norms and offend the public could not be given as first names, ending the requirement of conformity with the "national culture" or "Turkish customs and traditions." Soon after the amendment was passed, Kurdish activists organized a campaign for the registration of Kurdish names that included the letters q, x, and w, which do not exist in the official alphabet. They collectively applied to the courts to replace their names with explicit Kurdish names such as Xemgin, Berxwedan, and Warjin. The number of applications reached hundreds. Some of these names also had explicit nationalist connotations such as Şêrwav (warrior), Serxwebun (independence), Welat (motherland), and Serhildan (uprising).[51] Neither the local courts nor the Court of Cassation allowed the registration of Kurdish names with the letters that did not exist in the alphabet. The courts ruled that the spelling of the names should conform to the rules of the Turkish alphabet

---

[50] For more information on the official circular about naming and the several cases in this period, see Türkiye İnsan Hakları Vakfı (2003, 22–26). Also see *Cumhuriyet* (2002) and *Hürriyet* (2002).

[51] For more, see the 2002, 2003, and 2004 annual reports of the Turkish Human Rights Foundation at www.tihv.org.tr.

and that nonconformity could create administrative problems and confusion.[52] The registration of Kurdish names that are spelled with letters in the official alphabet, nevertheless, has created fewer problems since the amendment of the related article in the Registration Law and signifies a serious change in Turkish state policies.[53]

The naming controversy underlines how state policies and minority activism mutually condition one another. The Turkish state's interventions over the years to regulate and control the private lives of the Kurds provided incentives to Kurdish activists to politicize and nationalize many of the cultural expressions, as in the case of Kurdish naming. Kurdish activists increasingly used names as an "ethnic boundary-making strategy" (Wimmer 2008, 991). The use of names as a form of political resistance and as a marker of divisive identity in turn contributed to further official resistance against Kurdish cultural expressions, making the chances of reconciliation between the Kurds and the state more difficult and complicated.

THE CONTROVERSY OVER KURDISH MUSIC

Kurdish music constituted another subject of cultural contestation in the post-1980 period. Even before the 1980s, the state was quite sensitive about the public playing of Kurdish music. In the early years of the republic, the officials of the Turkish state radio traveled in the Kurdish regions to record Kurdish folk songs and translated their lyrics into Turkish. They were played as Turkish songs afterwards. Canip Yıldırım recalls that when Celal Güzelses, a prominent folk singer from Diyarbakır, wanted to record songs in Kurdish in Syria in the 1950s, he was warned by the National Intelligence Agency not to do it.[54]

The real struggle over the public's listening to Kurdish music started in the 1980s. This was a period when the legal ban on the use of Kurdish in general coincided with the cheaper and easier circulation of music as a result of cassette technology. While there was a social push for the expansion of the Kurdish music market, the legal prohibitions created many problems for artists, producers, and increasingly the general Kurdish

---

[52] Yargıtay İlamı, T.C. Yargıtay 18. Hukuk Dairesi, Esas no: 2004/3398, Karar no: 2004/4808, February 25, 2004.
[53] In 2008, a father could register his newborn daughter's name as Helin Kurdistan, which means "nest of Kurdistan," without much difficulty in Şanlıurfa (*Hürriyet* 2009).
[54] For more, see Orhan Miroğlu's interview with Canip Yıldırım in Miroğlu (2005, 120–123).

audience. Circumcision and wedding ceremonies, where Kurdish songs were played, became targets of police raids, governors ordered the confiscation of many Kurdish music cassettes, and the police detained and interrogated people who listened to or played Kurdish songs.[55] In 1987, Beşir Kaya, a folk singer from Diyarbakır, recorded an album of fifteen songs, three of which were love songs in Kurdish. The production company managed to obtain permission for the album's release from the Ministry of Culture and Tourism. Such permission, however, did not stop the police from investigating. The police questioned Kaya and asked him to translate the lyrics of the Kurdish songs. After being convinced that the songs were on love and did not have any political content, they set him free (*Nokta* 1988b, 30). Rahmi Saltuk, a prominent folk singer, was not as lucky. He had to face criminal charges in 1989 after releasing his album that contained three Kurdish songs. The police confiscated the album, which was authorized by the ministry. Saltuk was taken to the criminal court for singing in Kurdish, which constituted a breach of Law 2932 that banned the use of the Kurdish language. The judge's interpretation of the law, however, was different. Based on an expert's opinion, who translated the songs and stated that they did not advocate separatism but were merely folk songs, the judge acquitted Saltuk.[56] According to the judge, the main objective of Law 2932 was to prevent the use and dissemination of languages other than Turkish as a mother tongue. Saltuk's objective, the judge decided, was to increase his record sales by appealing to "a group of individuals in our society who use the Kurdish language."

After the abolition of Law 2932 in 1991, playing Kurdish music in public, on radio, and on TV became legal. Many popular singers from the Southeast started to include Kurdish songs on their albums. Nevertheless, the overturning of the ban did not immediately influence state practice on the ground. The local officials and security forces continued to restrict the playing of Kurdish music. During the 1990s, the state authorities' intolerance for Kurdish music and the growing politicization of Kurdish music reinforced each other. The confusion over whether it was the mere language of the songs, their content, or the objectives of the artists that the authorities should take into account in judging the permissibility of

---

[55] The annual reports prepared by the Human Rights Foundation in Turkey provide brief information on the individual cases that related to the playing of Kurdish music in public. These reports can be found or ordered online on the Foundation's website: www.tihv.org.tr.
[56] T.C. Istanbul 2. Asliye Ceza Mahkemesi, Esas no. 1989/333, Karar no. 1989/333, October 7, 1989.

Kurdish music, was never resolved. A representative of a major music company complained about the inconsistency at the state level with regard to Kurdish music. He drew attention to the lack of coordination among state institutions. He complained that even after the Ministry of Culture authorized an album it could be banned in the entire Southeastern region with an order from a governor (*Nokta* 1994, 84–85). The ban could sometimes be due to the content of the songs and sometimes to the use of the Kurdish language.

The issue became more intricate after private TV channels and radio stations were allowed to broadcast in Turkey in 1990. The Supreme Board of Radio and Television (RTÜK) was founded in 1996 as a regulatory authority, inspecting whether radio and TV broadcasts conform to the Law on the Establishment of Radio and Television Enterprises and Their Broadcasts (Law No. 3984). This law stipulated that the broadcasts should not violate the territorial integrity of the state, the principles of Atatürk, the national and moral values of the community, and the Turkish family structure, and that they should not incite people to violence, terror, or ethnic discrimination. Article 4/t specified that radio and TV broadcasts should be in Turkish. To rule out Kurdish broadcasting in foreign-language news programs, the law stipulated that "only those foreign languages that contributed to the formation of universal products of culture and science" could be used for the purposes of teaching or transmitting the news.[57] The law, however, did not ban playing Kurdish music on TV and radio programs.[58]

The experiences of a radio station in Şanlıurfa in the 1990s underline the resistance of local security officers to any tolerance for Kurdish cultural elements. Karacadağ radio station was established in 1994 by a group of students from Harran University in Şanlıurfa. The radio station was not apolitical; many of its programs consisted of political debates, where critical views about state policies with regard to the Kurdish question were voiced. As a result, its programs were under close scrutiny by the state's security forces. In its music programs, the station broadcast Kurdish songs but was careful to include world music in its repertoire in order to avoid being considered as a pro-Kurdish radio station.[59] Such

---

[57] The full text of the law can be seen at www.hukuki.net/kanun/3984.15.frameset.asp.
[58] See a relevant decision by the highest administrative court, the Council of State, ruling that the playing of Kurdish music on TV did not constitute a breach of law: T.C. Danıştay 10. Daire, Esas no: 1997/3210, Karar no: 2000/244, January 27, 2000.
[59] For more information on the radio station, see *Radikal İki* (1998) and *Cumhuriyet Dergi* (1998).

caution, nevertheless, did not help for very long. In May 1996, the police department, which supervised the radio broadcasts,[60] sent a notification to the public prosecutor's office in Şanlıurfa, informing the prosecutor that the station played several Kurdish songs. The prosecutor did not find the language of the songs to be against the law. He decided to drop the case against the radio station after being convinced that the songs were merely folk songs and did not contain any political message.[61]

A month later, the radio station received a warning from the RTÜK containing the accusation that they had played a Kurdish song that allegedly violated general moral values, social peace, and the Turkish family structure. The translation of the lyrics made by the police in Şanlıurfa suggested that the song violated Article 428 of the Turkish Penal Code, which prohibited "evoking the public's feelings of shame and provoking or abusing feelings of sexual desire in publications, literature, and music." The public prosecutor in Şanlıurfa soon began an investigation and sent the file to the public prosecutor's office in Istanbul for expert examination. The expert's opinion revealed that the police department mistranslated the song's lyrics and added obscene words to it. The expert, who was a faculty member in the Galatasaray University's School of Law, wrote in his report that his translation differed from the police's translation and that he could not find any expressions that could be interpreted as insults to the Turkish Republic or the Turkish security forces. Based on the report from Istanbul, the public prosecutor of Şanlıurfa decided to drop the case.[62] The director of the radio station accused the police of consciously distorting the lyrics of the Kurdish song and adding obscene content to make legal prosecution possible.[63]

In the following months, Radio Karacadağ again faced criminal charges for broadcasting banned Kurdish songs, all of which had permission from the Ministry of the Interior. In a two-year period until 1998, around twenty legal investigations were opened against the radio station about these songs. Many times the police renewed their accusations

---

[60] Due to the incomplete institutionalization of the RTÜK, the police departments were given responsibility to follow the radio broadcasts and inform the RTÜK and the public prosecutors in case a broadcast violated the law.
[61] Şanlıurfa Cumhuriyet Başsavciliği, Takipsizlik Kararı, Karar no: 1996/1191, June 12, 1996.
[62] Şanlıurfa Cumhuriyet Başsavciliği, Takipsizlik Kararı, October 15, 1996.
[63] The prosecutor's decisions, the expert's opinion, the report of the public prosecutor's office in Istanbul, court decisions, and all correspondence between the radio station and the RTÜK are kept by Radyo Net, which was founded two years after Radio Karacadağ was closed down.

concerning the same songs to the prosecutor. In all these cases, the prosecutor decided to drop the charges, being unable to find any grounds for litigation. Radio Karacadağ's experiences indicate the level of harassment and intimidation that Kurdish institutions had to face from state officials.

Increased state efforts to prevent people from listening to Kurdish music during this period coincided with the gradual emergence of a genre of Kurdish music that narrated state repression and glorified armed struggle against the state. It was in this period that music was increasingly politicized and used by Kurdish nationalists to form a nationalist consciousness among the masses and mobilize them to take up arms against the state. Kurdish songs were incomprehensible to most state officers, who served in the conflict-ridden Kurdish areas without speaking the language. Thus, more often than not, lyrics in Kurdish were themselves enough to raise suspicions. State officials' harassment of those listening to Kurdish songs became quite common in these years. A State Security Court case opened against a driver in Diyarbakır in 1999 for playing Kurdish music in his minibus exemplifies this controversy. The driver was taken to the police by a gendarmerie officer who was in civilian clothes among the passengers. Although the officer did not understand Kurdish, he became suspicious about the driver and asked him to stop by a police station after he heard the word "Kurdistan" repeatedly in the lyrics. Eventually, the driver was taken to the State Security Court for agitating against the unity of the state by playing a Kurdish album that contained separatist messages and that praised the PKK's activities.[64] In his defense, the driver's lawyer emphasized that the Ministry of Culture authorized the album and that it would be unfair to penalize someone who listened to an album that was legal and sold freely everywhere. Ultimately, the court sentenced the driver to ten months in prison, based on Article 169 of the Turkish Penal Code, for aiding an armed organization. His sentence was suspended because the driver did not have a criminal record.[65]

The dynamics of these contentions over Kurdish naming and music suggest the complexity of reconciliation at local levels, where violent

---

[64] The lyrics contained lines such as: "The lions of Kurdistan do not know their history/Go to the villages and tell the Kurds that they should take their guns and ammunition/The guerilla sacrifices his life for the sake of the Kurdish honor, entity and wealth/The bombs of Turkish infidels are booming/Kurds! Get up and get ready for the war."

[65] T.C. Diyarbakır 2 No'lu Devlet Güvenlik Mahkemesi, Esas no: 2001/368, Karar no: 2002/131, April 9, 2002.

conflict became a part of everyday life. As Ross (2007, 3) argues, cultural expressions have strong emotional meaning and can exacerbate conflict when they are markers of divisive identity and mutually exclusive positions. For many Kurds, cultural practices became "everyday forms of resistance," in Scott's (1985) terms, against state domination. The bureaucracy's and security forces' prejudices against expressions of Kurdishness continued in the following years and complicated the government attempts to address some of the Kurdish cultural demands.

ATTEMPTS AT RECONCILIATION? STATE–KURDISH RELATIONS IN THE POST-2000 PERIOD

State–Kurdish relations reached a turning point at the end of the 1990s, first with the capture of Abdullah Öcalan in Kenya in February 1999. Öcalan had been in Syria until the end of 1998. Damascus forced him to leave the country after Turkey gave an ultimatum to Syria to expel Öcalan and cease its support of the PKK. After moving briefly from one country to another, including Russia, Italy, and Greece, Öcalan ended up in Kenya where he was eventually captured. This was a serious blow to the PKK, which declared a five-year unilateral ceasefire, leading to a dramatic reduction of armed clashes in the following years. At the end of 1999, another significant development took place. The Helsinki meeting of the European Council, held in December 1999, took key decisions on the enlargement of the EU and declared Turkey a candidate. The prospect of becoming a full member of the EU and the decline in the PKK's armed operations created a political context that pushed the government to address the issue of human rights and to undertake reforms that would have important consequences for Kurdish demands. Between 2001 and 2003, the Turkish parliament passed seven sets of reform packages that encompassed constitutional and legal amendments to meet the EU membership criteria. These amendments also addressed some of the long-awaited Kurdish demands for cultural rights.

The amendments to the broadcasting law allowed for "broadcasting in different languages and dialects Turkish citizens traditionally use in their daily lives" and stipulated that public and private radio and TV stations could provide such broadcasting, including in Kurdish. Another amendment made to the Law on the Teaching of Foreign Languages in 2002 allowed for the establishment of private courses for teaching "different languages and dialects traditionally used by Turkish citizens in their daily lives." With this amendment, the ban on teaching Kurdish in private classes was abolished. A small change in Article 16 of the Registration Law made giving Kurdish names to children easier.[66]

Adding to the increased hopes for change among Kurdish citizens, the 2002 general elections voted every political party that had ruled Turkey during the 1980s and 1990s out of parliament, and brought a new party, the Justice and Development Party (AKP), to power. Many members of the AKP had affiliations with the previously banned Islamic parties but the party identified itself as a moderate conservative party and included people from different political backgrounds in its ranks. It represented a political formation that was outside the Kemalist tradition and emphasized democratization and Turkey's EU membership as its main goals. The party endorsed a discourse of Muslim brotherhood, emphasized the common sufferings of Islamists and Kurds under Kemalism, and criticized the dominance of the military-bureaucratic establishment in Turkish politics. It abolished the State Security Courts and increasingly brought the military under civilian control.[67] In 2005, in his visit to Diyarbakır, the prime minister and leader of the AKP, Recep Tayyip Erdoğan, said that the state committed some mistakes in the past that should be acknowledged and stated that the Kurdish problem should be addressed with further democratization and expanded citizenship rights.[68] The media presented the visit as a turning point in state–Kurdish relations. During the first half of the 2000s, conditions in the Kurdish cities of the Southeast dramatically improved. Kurdish publications were sold openly on the streets, large posters in Kurdish could be seen in many public places, local radio and TV channels could broadcast in Kurdish, and several municipalities that were run by the pro-Kurdish political party could organize conferences on Kurdish language and literature and stage theater plays in Kurdish even without getting permission from the governor's office.[69] In the following years, the AKP government continued to initiate reforms that accommodated Kurdish activists' cultural and linguistic demands that transformed the Turkish state's ethnic politics. Nevertheless, the legal regulations that opened up opportunities for the use of the Kurdish language and their implementation on the ground have been highly contentious. The AKP

---

[66] For detailed information on the recent reforms that related to state–minority relations in general, see Kurban (2003), Oran (2004), and Yıldız (2005).
[67] For a longer discussion of the reforms initiated during the AKP government, see Aktoprak (2010) and Aktürk (2012), chapter 5.
[68] *Radikal*, August 13, 2005.
[69] Interviews with several Kurdish activists and municipality employees in Diyarbakır and Şanlıurfa, May–June 2006.

government's acknowledgment of Turkey's ethnic diversity and Kurdish cultural demands was laden with significant ambiguities and the actual implementation of the reforms encountered serious setbacks.

Kurdish activists underlined that the rights that were granted by the parliament could be limited through administrative regulations by those who were opposed to those rights within different state institutions. Initially, local private TV channels encountered many bureaucratic difficulties when they applied to the RTÜK for permission to broadcast programs in Kurdish. The administrative regulation prepared after the new broadcasting law came into effect frustrated many with the restrictions it imposed on Kurdish broadcasting. Accordingly, programs in the "languages and dialects traditionally used by Turkish citizens in their daily lives" could not aim at teaching children these languages, should always be accompanied by subtitles in Turkish, and could not exceed forty-five minutes a day and four hours a week.[70] The owners of the radio and TV stations found the requirement to send Turkish translations of the Kurdish programs to the RTÜK headquarters in Ankara every week time-consuming and discriminatory. Davut Dursun, a member of the Supreme Council of the RTÜK in 2006, agreed with many of the critiques concerning Kurdish broadcasting. He pointed to the fragmentation at the state level and stated that the rights that were granted by the parliament could be limited through administrative regulations by those who opposed those rights within different state institutions. He also added that along with resistance to liberalization within the state, part of the problem arose from the lack of qualified staff at the RTÜK who could speak Kurdish and supervise the broadcasts. According to him, because of the sensitivity of the issue and the necessity of certain administrative adjustments within the RTÜK, the problems with Kurdish broadcasting would take more time to solve.[71] The translation and subtitling requirements were eventually abolished in 2009.

Offering private courses to teach Kurdish encountered blatant resistance from state authorities. First, there was a legal problem. A regulation of the Ministry of Education that clarified rules for teaching foreign languages required teachers to have a bachelor's degree in education in the language they would teach. Because there were no university departments

---

[70] The content of the programs was first restricted to news, music, and culture. Documentaries that were explicitly about Kurdish culture, for example, were banned as they were considered in violation of the national integrity of the state. In 2006, the time restriction on Kurdish films and music was lifted. For more, see *Radikal*, June 11, 2006.
[71] Interview with Davut Dursun, June 20, 2006, Ankara.

for the Kurdish language, there was practically no one who would be eligible to teach Kurdish in private classes. In the end, the ministry conceded to accept some of the candidates that the private schools proposed after it did background security checks to make sure that the candidates were not involved with the PKK or any other Kurdish nationalist organizations. The administrators of the Kurdish private courses, who got approval from the Ministry of Education after a long struggle that lasted for months, then encountered several obstacles from the local bureaucracy. In Urfa, a school owner was asked to change the name of his school from "Urfa Private Kurdish Language School" to "Urfa Private Kurdish Dialects Language School," on the grounds that Kurdish was not a language but was composed of two local dialects.[72] The opening of other schools was postponed because the buildings did not have a fire escape or the width of the interior doors did not conform to regulations (Oran 2004, 104). Administrators and students of Kurdish schools claimed that they were under close scrutiny by the police. In the end, a total of seven Kurdish language schools were opened in different cities but did not operate for very long. In August 2005, the owners of the seven Kurdish language schools declared in a press conference that they collectively decided to close down their schools because of a lack of demand (Çakan 2005). They stated that a total of 1,027 students got their certificates but there was not enough demand that could financially maintain the classes for the next year. The closure of the schools strengthened Kurdish demands for state support for the teaching of the Kurdish language. Given the poverty of the region, many argued that Kurds could not afford to pay for the private language classes.

In September 2009, the Council of Higher Education (YÖK) permitted graduate study in Kurdish in the new Mardin Artuklu State University at the Institute for Living Languages. In September 2011, YÖK allowed undergraduate study in Kurdish and established a Kurdish language and literature department in Mardin Artuklu University as well as in Muş Alparslan University. This was followed by Prime Minister Erdoğan's statement in June 2012 that elective courses in "living languages and dialects," including Kurdish, would be offered in middle schools for two hours per week.[73] The latest democratization package announced in September 2013 allowed Kurdish education in private schools but disappointed

---

[72] Interview with a founder of a Kurdish course, May 2, 2006, Şanlıurfa.
[73] For more, see www.cnnturk.com/2012/turkiye/06/11/acilimin.yeni.ayagi.kurtce.secmeli. egitim/664491.0/index.html.

Kurdish activists as it failed to address their demands for Kurdish education in public schools. Neither the AKP nor the major opposition parties in the parliament (except the pro-Kurdish Peace and Democracy Party or the BDP) have supported Kurdish public education.[74]

In state media, support for the Kurdish language came in January 2009, when the state-owned TV channel, TRT-6, was established to broadcast in Kurdish twenty-four hours a day. While some Kurdish activists welcomed TRT-6 as a step towards the official recognition of the Kurdish language, others criticized it for being a tool of state propaganda and the pro-Islamic narrative in its programs. Several restrictions over the use of the Kurdish language still remained. Many activists have complained that while TRT-6 uses the letters w, x, and q in its broadcasts freely, Kurdish publishers, municipalities, and private TV channels could be subject to prosecution for their use of these letters.[75] In February 2009, when Ahmet Türk, a parliamentarian of the pro-Kurdish Democratic Society Party, spoke Kurdish in the parliament, state TV immediately cut off broadcasting his speech. Speaking in a language other than Turkish in the parliament was still illegal (*Radikal* 2009). The Law on Political Parties continued to prohibit the use of a language other than Turkish in political party meetings and election campaigns. For this reason several Kurdish politicians were taken to court for using Kurdish in their public speeches. For example, Osman Baydemir, the mayor of Diyarbakır since 2004, was taken to court many times by the public prosecutor on the charge that his use of Kurdish in public speeches violated the Law on Political Parties.[76] In one of these cases, Baydemir was taken to court for saying goodbye in Kurdish after his speech.[77] He was acquitted by the court. Another politician, Reşit Yardımcı, a member of the pro-Kurdish party DEHAP in Şanlıurfa, was not as lucky. He was sentenced to six months in prison for saying "Have a nice day" in Kurdish at the party's provincial congress (*Hürriyet Daily News* 2005). In September 2013, Erdoğan promised to amend the laws on political parties and elections to allow for the use of Kurdish in political campaigns and speeches as well as to legalize the use of the letters x, q, and w.

---

[74] For a very good critical review of the 2013 democratization package and what it means for the Kurdish demands, see Kurban (2013).
[75] See, for instance, www.rizgari.com/modules.php?name=News&file=print&sid=17616.
[76] For the full text of the law in Turkish, see www.mevzuat.gov.tr.
[77] T.C. Hazro Asliye Ceza Mahkemesi, Esas no: 2003/2, Karar no: 2004/5, Karar tarihi: February 24, 2004.

Human rights organizations have consistently demanded clarification of certain articles in the Turkish Penal Code and the Anti-Terror Law that justify the prosecution of individuals who speak, write, and perform in Kurdish. Several Kurds claimed to be subject to random police violence and harassment because of using the Kurdish language on the streets. The former president of the Diyarbakır Bar Association, Sezgin Tanrıkulu, was taken to court for publishing a bilingual Kurdish and Turkish 2007 calendar for the bar association. Performers of Kurdish music continued to be taken to court for making propaganda for a terrorist organization according to the vague articles of the Anti-Terror Law.[78]

Kurdish activists' demands for amendments of the vague and broad provisions of the Anti-Terror Law and the Penal Code have not been addressed in the 2013 democratization package. While the AKP government transformed the state's nation-building policies by opening up freedoms for the cultural and linguistic expressions of Kurdish identity, it maintained a hawkish stance in dealing with the PKK and Kurdish political demands, which in turn jeopardized the free exercise of the cultural freedoms. The PKK ended the ceasefire and resumed its attacks in 2004. Between 2005 and 2010 around 700 police and soldiers, 175 civilians, and 1,400 PKK militants died as a result of the conflict (Milliyet 2010). The escalation of violence pushed the government to resort to more coercive means. In 2006, the AKP government amended the Anti-Terror Law, which was initially passed in 1991, to widen the definition of terror crimes and introduce longer sentences. Human rights organizations and Kurdish activists criticized provisions of these laws for the lack of clarity and specificity that allows the arbitrary application and abuse of the laws by law enforcement officials. Many underline that demands that match the PKK's demands, such as Kurdish education in public schools, can be prosecuted as PKK propaganda (International Crisis Group 2011, 32; Kurban 2013, 6–7). These laws have been used for the arrests of pro-Kurdish politicians, journalists, mayors, activists, publishers, and lawyers due to their alleged membership in or links to the Kurdistan Communities Union (KCK), the urban, political wing of the PKK.[79] The arrests first started in April 2009 and increased dramatically over the years. According to

---

[78] For more on the case of Tanrıkulu, see Turkish Human Rights Foundation's 2009 Human Rights Report, p. 169. Several examples of problems that people encounter using the Kurdish language can also be found in the annual reports of the Turkish Human Rights Foundation.
[79] The KCK was established on the orders of Öcalan in 2005 as an umbrella organization to bring together organizations affiliated with the PKK in Turkey, Iraq, Syria, and Iran.

the official figures, 2,146 people, including 274 elected officials from the pro-Kurdish BDP, were on trial on charges of belonging to the KCK. The exact number of people arrested on charges of being a KCK member is not known and there are different estimates. The BDP claims that 7,000 were arrested in KCK operations (International Crisis Group 2012, 22). The unwillingness of the AKP to acknowledge the difference between the civilian-political wing of the Kurdish movement and the PKK and to formulate policies accordingly continues to set a barrier to the resolution of the conflict. Although the AKP government took important steps to end the comprehensive and intrusive polices of nation-building in Turkey and allowed open discussion of the Kurdish problem in public, it failed to prove its commitment to the political solution of the Kurdish conflict by sending mixed signals to the Kurds and the Turkish public.

CONCLUSION

The transformation of Kurdish opposition from a limited, elite-based, intellectual movement to a mass-based, violent, nationalist uprising in Turkey took place in a relatively short period of time between the end of the 1970s and the end of the 1980s. As Watts (2010, 27) argues, this process cannot be understood as a nationalist revival or reawakening of the already existing nationalist identity of the Kurdish masses: "The problem with this revivalist schema is that it promotes the idea that a kind of preformed, preconstructed political figure – the Kurdish nationalist – burst into the Turkish political system when the conditions permitted it." In the 1950s and 1960s, when the state's interference into Kurdish daily life was minimal, Kurdish nationalism was neither a powerful force among the Kurds nor a well-developed ideology with a coherent set of ideas, symbols, myths, and rituals. It was in the 1980s, with growing state intrusion into Kurds' behavior, values, habits, and lifestyles and its indiscriminate use of overt repression or intimidation, that Kurdish mobilization, led by the PKK, expanded to the masses and started a counter nation-building process that aimed at the construction of an exclusive ethnic identity with a distinctive cultural heritage. State–Kurdish relations had a mutually transformative character. State interventions into Kurdish culture and daily practices over the years influenced the way Kurdish activists imagined their national symbols and pushed them to define or create Kurdish cultural elements in more political and exclusivist terms with clear-cut boundaries that symbolize nationhood. Books on Kurdish history, literature, cuisine, and even flora and fauna were published in the relatively free atmosphere of the 2000s. Kurdish music, names, celebrations, and dress became increasingly politicized. The process of state–Kurdish interaction, however, cannot be explained as a unidirectional one, in which the state shaped Kurdish protest. The Kurdish political and military opposition also had a considerable impact on the power balance within the state. Fighting with the PKK led to the rise of the military as the most powerful actor on the Turkish political scene at the expense of the politicians and contributed to its high level of legitimacy among the Turkish public in the 1990s. The politicization of Kurdish cultural expressions reinforced anti-Kurdish sentiments and practices among state officials, especially at the local bureaucratic levels, and made liberalization of state practices, and therefore possibilities for reconciliation, more difficult.

State–Kurdish relations in the 2000s underline how difficult settling a conflict becomes after long periods of war. Armed conflicts harden identities, polarize societies, hurt mutual trust, and make negotiations and compromises unlikely. The settlement of the Kurdish problem today is much more complicated than it was before the start of the armed conflict. A possible settlement today depends not so much on the state's accommodation of Kurdish cultural and linguistic demands but on solutions to more difficult questions. It is to these more difficult issues that I will turn in the Conclusion.

5

The rise of the Amazigh movement and state cooptation in Morocco

On October 17, 2001, in the presence of his advisors, the members of the government, the leaders of the political parties and unions, and Amazigh activists, King Mohammed VI announced the royal edict (*dahir*) that established the Royal Institute of Amazigh Culture (*L'Institut Royal de la Culture Amazighe*, IRCAM). He defined Moroccan national identity as a composition of different cultural elements, underlined that the Amazigh language constituted a principal element of the national culture, and added that its promotion was a national responsibility. The Royal Institute was charged with the promotion of Amazigh culture in education and media. While redefining Moroccan identity so as to incorporate Berberness, the king was also careful to emphasize the indispensable principles of Moroccan nationalism: Islam, territorial integrity, allegiance to the throne and the king, and attachment to the monarchy. He also stressed that Amazighness belonged to all Moroccans and should not be used for political purposes.[1] The establishment of IRCAM represented the first substantial change in the state's attitude towards its Berber-speaking population from a policy of subtle neglect to explicit recognition and support, albeit with strings attached.

At the beginning of 2007, the monarchy's support of the Amazigh movement took a magnificent visual shape. A massive, hyper-modern building in Hay Ryad, a relatively new neighborhood of Rabat and the city's commercial and business center, became the permanent location of IRCAM (Figure 6). This building of concrete and glass is owned by the

---

[1] For the full text of Muhammad's speech, see *Le Matin du Sahara et du Maghreb* (2001, 1). Translations from French throughout the chapter are made by the present author.

The Amazigh movement and the state in Morocco

FIGURE 6. The new building of IRCAM. Photo by the author.

royal family and attracts the immediate attention of passers-by with its monumental size, unusual architecture, and triangular design. Its luxurious, marble interior contains individual offices for IRCAM researchers who are charged with doing research on Berber language and culture, along with several conference rooms and a library. In the large entrance hall, King Mohammed VI's photograph in traditional Berber outfit welcomes the visitors. The building's massive size gives the impression that it can accommodate every single Amazigh activist in the country.

This chapter examines the rise of Amazigh activism in the post-1980 period and state responses to it. Amazigh activism, which started to voice its particularistic demands in the public space in the 1980s, took on the character of a full-fledged ethnic movement with identifiable goals and a well-developed organizational structure in the 1990s. Unlike the Kurdish movement's development in Turkey, Amazigh activism remained peaceful and conciliatory with limited claims that revolved around cultural rights. The activists have largely been well-educated, multilingual, urban Berbers with strong international ties. Amazigh activism had limited appeal in the rural areas and has not yet taken the form of a nationalist mobilization mainly due to carefully formulated state policies. The Moroccan state refrained from directly and coercively intervening in Berber areas to transform them culturally. As anthropologist David Crawford (2001, 382) states, referring to the Berber villagers living in the High Atlas:

> The government as I asked the question was usually taken to mean the distant and abstract thing, the anonymous gendarmes along the road, or ... the qaid. It did not seem to be the case that people felt particularly oppressed by being Berber in this sense. The perspective of most people in Tagharghist is that in these domains all Moroccans have the same issues and Berbers are not specifically discriminated against.

In addition, unlike in Turkey, the Moroccan monarchy's flexible and loosely defined nationalist ideology made negotiation, compromise, and change easier in state policies when Amazigh activism began to show signs of politicization.

The relationship between the Moroccan state and the Amazigh activists, nevertheless, has been an uneasy one. The state's response towards the rise of Amazigh mobilization under the leadership of an urban-based Berber elite was initially marked by repression and exclusion. Especially during Hassan II's more repressive rule, called the "years of lead" (*les années de plomb*), arrests, tortures, disappearances, and harassment of regime opponents were common. In the 1980s, when Amazigh demands became more visible, Amazigh activists were not immune to state repression. Even during this period, however, the Moroccan state used more selective repression, unlike the Turkish state, whose basic strategy was indiscriminate political exclusion and suppression in dealing with the emergence of an urban-based Kurdish mobilization in the 1950s and 1960s. Towards the end of his rule in the 1990s, Hassan II began to open up the regime and allowed Amazigh activism to be more vocal about its demands and to organize more freely. When Mohammed VI succeeded his father to the throne in 1999, he resorted more to cooptation policies and gradually accommodated the Amazigh demands that hindered the movement's politicization on a nationalist agenda. The monarchy's effective integration of moderate Amazigh activists within the institution of IRCAM helped it extend its reach within the movement. Such cooptation worked against the solidarity of the Amazigh movement, fragmenting the movement further by creating an unresolved debate about the meaning of cooperating with the state. The establishment of IRCAM also increased the king's legitimacy in the eyes of the moderate Amazigh activists and aborted their further radicalization. In fact, the strategy of the integration of Amazigh activists within IRCAM was reminiscent of the monarchy's cooptation of Berber power centers during the first years of its independence.

This process of accommodating Amazigh demands has not been linear and coherent due to the resistance of the political parties and the bureaucratic establishment to the recognition of Berber identity and culture. Their opposition to the accommodation of Amazigh demands demonstrates that even in authoritarian contexts, where state leaders are the ultimate decision makers, governments, political parties, and bureaucracies may not act solely as façades that do not have influence over policy making. The Moroccan case shows that they can actually be effective in bending and reshaping policies at the implementation level in ways that may present a challenge to the leader's decisions.

THE RISE OF AMAZIGH ACTIVISM AND THE INITIAL REPRESSION

It was in the early years of the 1980s that Berber intellectuals started to be more vocal in the public space about their grievances. Two factors created the political opportunities that encouraged them to be more visible to the regime. First, the state gave the first sign that it was willing to openly acknowledge the Berber element within Moroccan culture when the Interior Ministry asked Professor Mohamed Chafik, who was then the director of the Royal College, to prepare a report on the Berber question.[2] This demand came after a series of heated debates in the parliament on Arabization and the Popular Movement's formation of a parliamentary group for the preservation of Berber culture. Chafik's report proposed an Institute for Berber Studies and the creation of a university chair that would undertake academic research on Berber culture and codify and teach the Berber language. As a result of the report, the Moroccan parliament voted for the establishment of such an institute in 1979, but the parliament's decision was never enforced (Lehtinen 2003, 162; Maddy-Weitzman 2011, 96–97). The report and the parliamentary

---

[2] Mohamed Chafik is a venerable and prominent Berber intellectual and activist, who has written extensively on Berber history and culture. He became a Royal Cabinet member responsible for education matters in 1968 and became the Director of the Royal College in 1976. Because of his high state posts, he was close to the official circles along with the royal family and he acted as an intermediary between state officials and the Berber activists during the negotiations over Berber demands in the 1990s. Although some activists today criticize him for being "a man of the state," he is still revered by all because of his works on the Berber culture and language. For more on Chafik, see *Tel Quel* (2002–2003, 24–27).

vote, however, gave hope to Berber intellectuals that they could start a public debate on the marginalization of the Berber culture.

Second, and similar to the spillover effects of Mustafa Barzani's revolt on Kurdish activism in Turkey in the 1960s, the increased contention between the Berbers and the state in Algeria in the 1980s provided inspiration and guidance for many activists and Berber youth in Morocco. In Algeria, there had been a much more political and contentious Berber movement since the early 1970s. This contention culminated in a five-day clash between Berber activists and state forces in March 1980, which left hundreds wounded and between thirty and fifty dead.[3] This confrontation, which came to be known as the "Berber Spring" (*Le Printemps Berbère*), encouraged many activists in Morocco to voice their demands openly. As in Turkey, the ethnic contention in a neighboring country disturbed the state authorities and alerted them about Berber activism in Morocco. An Amazigh activist who was arrested in 1982 recalled that the police asked him during his interrogation whether he had ever been to Algeria (*Tel Quel* 2007).

An important public activity that the Berber activists organized was the "Agadir Summer University" (*l'Université d'Été d'Agadir*), a colloquium that took place in the last two weeks of August 1980 in a predominantly Berber city in Southern Morocco. This meeting was initiated by the leaders of the first Amazigh association, AMREC, with the aim of bringing together Berber intellectuals and researchers from all over the country for discussions on different aspects of the Berber question. It was the first occasion when activists openly discussed Berber identity and their linguistic and cultural rights. It was also during this meeting that the activists discussed the pejorative connotations of the word "Berber," which is a derivation of the word "barbarian," and decided to use the word "Amazigh" instead (Rachik 2006, 26). The participants were careful not to challenge official policies directly because they were scared of regime reprisal. These were the "years of lead" of Hassan II's reign, a time that was characterized by extensive repression and intimidation of political opponents.[4] As the theme of the meeting, "The Popular Culture: Unity in

---

[3] For more on the Berber–state conflict in Algeria, see Maddy-Weitzman (2011) and Layachi (2005).

[4] This period spanned from 1961, when Hassan II achieved complete control over the state, to the early 1990s. Between these years, arbitrary arrests and torture were common and hundreds of outspoken regime dissidents disappeared. One of the most well-known examples is the disappearance of Mehdi Ben Barka, founder of the National Union of Popular Forces (UNFP), in Paris in 1965. Mohamed Oufkir, a Berber who was the right-hand man of Hassan II until 1972, was killed because of his involvement in the coup

Diversity," suggests, the organizers put the emphasis on Moroccan unity and implied that the discussions would not be solely on the Berber identity. The themes of individual sessions (such as "the relations between popular culture and national culture," "traditional Qur'anic schools," "the history of the cultural life of tribes," and "Amazigh language") signaled a non-political, academic, and cultural meeting (Rachik 2006, 29). This event was important in bringing increased contact between Berber activists living in different cities of the country. Although the meeting was completed without state interference, one of the participants claimed that the police tried to kill him by running his car into a truck after one of the sessions (*Tel Quel* 2007).

There were other developments in the early 1980s that indicated the state's tolerance of Berber cultural activities. For the first time an organization that could openly refer to Amazighness was established in Rabat in 1980 with official authorization under the name of the Amazigh Cultural Association. At the end of the same year, Mohamed Chafik gave a speech in the Royal Academy, calling attention to the Berber heritage of Morocco and the necessity to protect the Berber language from extinction (Lehtinen 2003, 162). Between 1980 and 1982, Ouzzin Aherdane, the son of the founder of the Popular Movement, Mahjoub Aherdane, published a bilingual journal titled *Amazigh*, which contained articles on the Berber language, history, arts, and culture. The editorial that Ahmed Alaoui wrote to welcome the publication of the journal *Amazigh* in the semi-official, pro-monarchy newspaper, *Maroc Soir*, could be read as reflecting the monarchy's attitude on the Berber issue.[5] After warning about political Berberism as a project of the colonizers, Alaoui (1980, 1) continued:

Today, however, we are free and independent. Thus, the time has come to liberate ourselves from this complex, to put an end to this rejection, and to restore the Berber culture for the enrichment of our national culture. Because we should not forget that ethnically we are an Arab-Berber people of Arab-Muslim culture. Since the arrival of Islam, and in particular since Idriss I, we have grown into an authentic nation because the two elements of our population are united into a genuine symbiosis, as the two cultures are mixed to form a Moroccan culture that is distinct from the cultures of all other Arab-Muslim countries.

---

attempt of 1972. In addition, his wife along with his children were sent to a secret desert prison, where they were detained until 1991. For more, see Miller (2013), chapter 6.

[5] Alaoui was the king's cousin and a minister, writing the editorial column of the semi-official dailies *Maroc Soir* and *Le Matin du Sahara et du Maghreb*.

Alaoui (1980, 2) emphasized the role of Islam in uniting the two cultures and advocated the necessity of preserving the Berber culture as part of the unique Moroccan national heritage. The message of the palace to the Berber activists was clear. As long as their activities stayed within the cultural framework and did not promote a separatist agenda, the state would tolerate them.

The state's tolerance towards Amazigh activism did not last long, however. Popular unrest due to the deep economic crisis and the state's austerity measures culminated in two riots in 1981 and 1984, in Casablanca and in Nador, respectively. The popular grievances were directly related to the rise in prices of basic commodities and poverty. This popular unrest led by students, unemployed youth, and workers presented a strong challenge to the political system as protestors expressed their bitterness about corruption and the excesses of the ruling elite, including the royal family. The state resorted to more repressive measures to quell this public unrest. The general political atmosphere terrorized and silenced the country's organized groups, including the Berber activists, until the late 1980s (Waltz 1991, 486).

Amazigh was banned in 1982 after it published an article by Ali Sidqi Azaykou questioning the official history of Morocco. Azaykou was a prominent Berber intellectual and poet and, since the 1970s, had written extensively on issues of Arabization, popular culture, and the Moroccan national identity. In the article Azaykou criticized the association of Islam with the Arab culture and argued that Arabization could be regarded as imperialism in Morocco, where the popular culture was actually based on the Berber culture. He wrote that the Moroccans were not totally Arabized and asked for a revision of the official history as a way to do justice to both cultures (el-Khatir 2005, 405; Rachik 2006, 27–28). His depiction of Arabs as conquerors cost him one year's imprisonment for offending the public order (Maddy-Weitzman 2011, 99). Another activist, Hassan Id Belkassm, who was the founder of ANCAP (New Association for Culture and Popular Arts), was arrested for having written his name in Tifinagh characters (an old script of the Berberophone people) in front of the building of his law office. He was not taken to court and was released from prison in a week. According to Belkassm, his arrest was completely arbitrary and the aim of the security forces was to intimidate him from pursuing the issue of Amazigh rights.[6] Both Azaykou and Belkassm advocated shifting Amazigh activism to a more political arena

---

[6] Interview with Hassan Id Belkassm, December 2006, Rabat.

as they believed that the state's support was necessary to put an end to the marginalization of the Berber language and culture. The regime, however, was sensitive about the politicization of Berber activism in the 1980s. The authorities did not allow the second meeting of the colloquium in Agadir planned for 1982. The existing Amazigh organizations either closed down or suspended their activities as a result of official pressures or fear of repression until the late 1980s.

THE ERA OF POLITICAL OPENINGS AND THE DISCURSIVE RECOGNITION OF BERBER IDENTITY

The 1990s was a period of change in Morocco, which came about as a result of an intersection of a number of domestic and international factors. The monarchy was pushed hard to open up the regime by growing domestic demands for social reforms and power sharing, a worsening economic crisis, and increased international pressure on the state for the improvement of human rights. Morocco's economic crisis began in the late 1970s when the price of phosphate, Morocco's primary export, declined and the price of oil increased. The economic problems that followed forced the monarchy to undertake a structural adjustment program sponsored by the International Monetary Fund and the World Bank beginning in 1983. The program led to significant cuts in public expenditures, a devaluation of the currency, and reduced subsidies on many basic goods, increasing mass resentment. Unemployment increased, real wages fell, and prices rose. While the state had hired 40,000 to 50,000 new employees per year before 1983, this number fell to 10,000 between 1983 and 1987. Urban unemployment rose from 11.3 percent in 1980 to 16 percent in 1992 (Lust-Okar 2005, 8–9). Domestic unrest, which became more visible to the monarchy through increased demonstrations and strikes, put pressure on Hassan II to undertake certain political reforms.

The increased economic problems of the regime also coincided with the rise of the Islamic challenge against the monarchy, which was fueled by the 1991 Gulf War (Morocco joined the coalition of forces against Iraq) and the beginning of a conflict between state forces and Islamists in Algeria in 1991. The rise of Islamism increased Hassan II's concerns over his regime's stability. One indicator of the Islamist threat against the monarchy was the considerable growth of the Justice and Charity movement at the end of the 1980s. Its leader, Abdessalam Yassine, was an outspoken critic of the regime as well as the religious credentials of the monarchy. In 1989, Yassine was put under house arrest and his movement was declared illegal. Nevertheless, a demonstration against the Gulf War by thousands of Islamists in Rabat showed that the movement was far from being contained (Waltz 1995, 126).

Increased criticism of human rights practices in Morocco by international organizations, such as Amnesty International as well as several European states, beginning in the late 1980s added to the domestic pressures.[7] The end of the Cold War led to the rising significance of human rights discourse at the international level. Gränzer (1999, 121–125) writes that the collaborative effort of domestic and international human rights organizations in publicizing rights violations by the end of the 1980s forced Hassan II to improve his regime's image and to undertake certain tactical measures. As a result, the 1990s were marked by controlled political liberalization in Morocco. In order to direct the mass discontent into institutionalized channels that could more easily be controlled by the state, freedoms of association and expression were expanded. Although the king did not give up any of his powers and remained as the ultimate decision maker in the political system, he allowed for the burgeoning of civil society as well as a freer and more vocal press, invited opposition parties to join the governing coalition, let the parliament take a more influential role in politics through constitutional amendments (although this did not necessarily mean a decrease in his powers), pardoned more than 400 of Morocco's longest-held political prisoners, and closed down the notorious Tazmamart prison, where prisoners were held for indefinite periods in severe conditions (Waltz 1995, 204, 211). This liberalization process culminated in the appointment of a long-time regime opponent, Abderrahmane al-Youssoufi, the leader of the Socialist Union of Popular Forces (USFP), as prime minister by the king in 1998.

Amazigh activism entered a new phase in the 1990s, like other political movements in Morocco. Increased freedoms of association and the press opened up opportunities for Amazigh activists to establish additional organizations, organize conferences, demonstrations, and sit-ins, and publish their own journals. The 1990s became a period when there was a proliferation of Amazigh associations, both at the national and local levels, and when the movement expanded from an intellectual elite to a larger population of Berber students and newly urbanized youth. The

---

[7] The influence and effectiveness of international pressure and transnational advocacy networks on the liberalization of the political system in Morocco are debatable. For different opinions, see Gränzer (1999) and Malka and Alterman (2006). For more on human rights reforms and political changes in Morocco during the 1990s, see Denoeux and Maghraoui (1998), Layachi (1998), Mayer (1993–1994), and Waltz (1995).

movement gradually shifted from the cultural to the political arena as the activists' demands for the official recognition of the "right of difference" became more pronounced and the first direct contacts between activists and parliamentarians and members of the government started.

While Turkey was also under increasing international pressure, particularly from the European Union, to improve its human rights record and to recognize Kurdish cultural rights in the 1990s, the armed struggle against the PKK prevented accommodation, as I explained in Chapter 4. In other words, by the 1990s the Moroccan and Turkish states encountered very different challenges from these ethnic groups. The Kurdish movement of the 1960s presents a better comparison to the Amazigh movement of the 1990s. Similar to the Amazigh movement, the Kurdish movement of the 1960s was quite fragmented, limited to an urban-based, educated elite, and its demands revolved around cultural rights. Nevertheless, the official attitude towards growing Berber particularism in Morocco was markedly different from the Turkish state's response to the emergence of Kurdish activism in the 1960s. Even when the Kurdish demands revolved largely around the issue of cultural rights, the Turkish state did not provide legitimate channels for expressions of Kurdish demands, as a result of which many activists began to pursue their aims outside the system. In contrast, the Moroccan state tolerated the organization of Amazigh activism and the public expression of its demands, albeit with some unease. In addition, unlike in Turkey, the channels of negotiation with the state elite were left open to moderate Amazigh activists, who would be willing to play by the rules of the game. The monarchy's conventional cooptation strategy vis-à-vis its political opponents gave the moderate activists the chance to negotiate with the state elite.

The differences in these states' attitudes towards similar challenges posed by their ethnic movements can be attributed to the differences in their official nationalist ideologies. In Turkey, a strong nationalist ideology, which aimed at homogenizing the society and which did not recognize the existence of a separate Kurdish entity, foreclosed the kinds of options available to the Moroccan monarchy. In Morocco, the official nationalist ideology was flexible and ambivalent enough to allow for compromise. When the Amazigh movement began to put further pressure on the state for the recognition of difference, the monarchy could adjust its nationalist discourse to accommodate Amazigh identity without having to refute its earlier narrative on Moroccan identity. In addition, the international climate in the 1960s was different from the one in the 1990s. During the Cold War, there was very little international pressure on states to improve their minority rights. As Preece (1997) points out, the issue of minority rights was generally absent from international agreements and the covenants of international organizations during the Cold War, with these rights becoming important only after the end of the Cold War.

Amazigh activism re-entered the political scene in 1991 with the publication of the Agadir Charter, which represented the foundational text that explicitly stated the grievances and demands of the Amazigh movement. The Charter was originally signed by six associations, and later other associations also declared their support for it. Since then the Charter has become an object of pride for many activists, who saw it as a proof of their ability to overcome their differences and undertake collective action. Through this Charter, the activists conveyed three general messages to the public. First, they underlined the indigenousness of the Amazigh culture on Moroccan territory. The text stated that the Berber language was the oldest language in the Maghreb and was spoken as the mother tongue in a territory of five million square kilometers, from the Egyptian–Libyan frontier to the Canary Islands. It criticized the dominance of the Arab-Muslim culture and underlined that the Moroccan culture was in reality composed of the Amazigh, Muslim-Arab, and African cultures. Second, the text listed the complaints of Amazigh activists. It stated that despite the massive participation of the Amazigh people in the armed struggle against the colonizers, Amazigh culture and language were marginalized after independence for the sake of Arabism and linguistic and cultural unity. As a result, it claimed, people living in the rural areas were excluded socio-culturally, and the neglect of their language pushed them into poverty and confined them to the periphery. Finally, the text enumerated the demands of Amazigh activists: the constitutional establishment of Tamazight as an official language alongside Arabic,[8] the establishment of a national institute for the standardization of the Amazigh language, the integration of the Amazigh language and culture in the educational domain, the right to use the Amazigh language in written and visual media, and the encouragement of Amazigh cultural production and language teaching.[9]

The preparation of the Agadir Charter and the absence of any state action against it led to a resurgence of Amazigh activism. By the end of

---

[8] Tamazight refers to one of the three varieties of Berber dialect, which is spoken in the Middle Atlas region. With the efforts of standardization, Tamazight came to mean the standardized version of the Berber language that unites all three variants.
[9] Part of the Amazigh Charter can be found in the appendix of Rachik (2006, 237–241). For more on the demands of the Charter, see el-Khatir (2005, 409).

FIGURE 7. The symbol of the Amazigh movement (letter "z" in Tifinagh script) drawn on a wall in Rabat. Photo by the author.

the 1990s, over forty associations represented the movement (Kratochwil 1999, 154) and this number reached 400 by 2009 (Maddy-Weitzman 2011, 181). These associations organized cultural activities such as exhibitions, concerts, plays, and poetry readings along with academic and political meetings, where members freely discussed government policies and Berber rights. Several Amazigh journals were published with articles in Arabic, French, and Tamazight.[10] Traditional Berber costumes and jewelry as well as the new symbolic productions of Amazigh activism (such as the use of the letter "z" in Tifinagh script that became the symbol of the movement (Figure 7), along with an Amazigh flag in blue, green, and yellow with the Tifinagh letter "z" in the middle) were increasingly worn or used in public by activists, without much fear of official reprisal. Increased contacts were established with Amazigh activists across the border, most importantly in Algeria and France. The 1990s were also the years when a transnational Berber movement developed. The Moroccan Amazigh activists participated in its institutions, such as the

---

[10] A list of these journals can be found in Saib (2004).

World Amazigh Congress, in large numbers.[11] One of the oldest national Amazigh organizations, Tamaynut, became very active in several human rights meetings abroad and its leader, Hassan Id Belkassm, undertook lobbying activities at meetings of the United Nations related to human and indigenous rights.[12]

The state's response to the sudden resurgence of Amazigh activism was twofold. On the one hand, it opened up the political space significantly by allowing for the free expression of the Berber identity in public. On the other hand, it signaled to the activists the consequences of politicization and radicalization, reminding them about the limits of their recognition and legitimacy. A confrontation between state authorities and activists took place in 1994, when members of Association Tilelli (Freedom) carried banners calling for the constitutional recognition of Tamazight and shouted slogans such as "No democracy without Tamazight" and "No to the folklorization of Tamazight" during the May Day parade. Seven of them were arrested on the charges of disturbing public order and threatening state sanctity. It was significant that the detainees were members of Association Tilelli, which operates in a peripheral region close to the Algerian border in Southeastern Morocco. The association represents the more radical wing of the movement, with its activists' uncompromising secularism and highly critical attitude towards the regime. As a way of showing their anti-Arab sentiments, the detainees refused to speak in Arabic during their trials (Alami *et al.* 2004, 23). Amazigh activists along with human rights organizations quickly mobilized, with 400 attorneys volunteering to defend the detainees. While four of the seven were soon released, the other three were sentenced to prison terms of between one and two years (Lehtinen 2003, 181–182). A few months later, they were released by a royal amnesty, which was reminiscent of the pardons accorded to the participants in the Berber revolts in the first years after independence. This conflict served as a signal to the activists of the consequences of challenging state power. For the Amazigh movement, the event epitomized state repression and Amazigh victimhood.

Another indicator, which suggested the regime's uneasiness and sensitivity to the rise of the Amazigh movement, could be seen in the pro-monarchy newspapers' extensive coverage of the "Berber Dahir" on the anniversary on May 16 of its promulgation by the French in 1930. The Berber Dahir recognized the jurisdiction of Berber customary law in the

---

[11] For more on transnational Amazigh activism, see Kratochwil (1999) and Maddy-Weitzman (2006).
[12] Interview with Hassan Id Belkassm, December 2006, Rabat.

Berber areas as opposed to Sharia. It sparked the first anti-colonial protests as the nationalists saw it a blatant attempt to divide Moroccans into two exclusive ethnic categories. Throughout the 1990s, *Le Matin du Sahara et du Maghreb* and *Maroc Soir* suddenly began to direct the public's attention to the issue of the Berber Dahir by allocating extensive coverage (around seven pages) to the subject on the day of its anniversary. In the pre-1990 period, the same newspapers had allocated only a small portion of the day's issue to the Berber Dahir. The extensive coverage in the 1990s included Ahmed Alaoui's editorial, excerpts on the promulgation of the Dahir from the newspapers of the 1930s, and a reprint of a section on the Berber policies of the colonial regime taken from the book *Le Maroc de Demain* written by Paul Marty, a high-level state administrator during the colonial period. The content remained exactly the same each year. The timing of this extraordinary coverage was not a coincidence. It reflected the regime's concerns about Amazigh activism and implicitly warned activists of the colonial roots of ethnic particularism. In his editorial, Alaoui (1992) underlined French motivation in issuing the Berber Dahir to divide Arab–Berber unity by minimizing Islamic laws' jurisdiction. He emphasized that Islam constitutes the basis of the Moroccan nation and reminded the readers that although the Berbers resisted all invasions throughout history, including the Arab incursions, they converted to Islam en masse because it suited their temperament the best. Such discourse can be read as a warning to Amazigh activism, given its highly secularist character.

Alongside these warnings and limitations over Amazigh activism, a process of incremental recognition of Amazigh demands began in the second half of the 1990s. In 1994, a few months after the Tilelli controversy, King Hassan II in his annual Throne Day speech underlined the plural character of Moroccan identity and stated that all Moroccans constituted a united body "with their dialects, identities, personalities, costumes, cultures, and local traditions." The Arab civilization, he continued, did not suppress the Moroccan dialects (referring to both the Moroccan Arabic dialect and Berber dialects) nor did it challenge Moroccan specificity, dress, cuisine, folklore, and architecture. Each Moroccan region preserved its own particularity, he stated, with its own celebrations, costumes, and cuisine. He added that he was not against the use of dialects; on the contrary, he would prefer that Moroccan children mix Moroccan dialects with Modern Standard Arabic instead of mixing Arabic with Western languages. He underlined the importance of Arabic as the language of prayer required for all Muslims. The Moroccans' attachment to

Arabic, he added, should not come at the expense of dialects, which were the symbols of Moroccan authenticity. He declared that the state should consider introducing the teaching of dialects in the school curriculum and continued:

> Preserve your authenticity, your religion, the language of your religion, Arabic ... Maintain the style of dress specific to your region and your tribe. Conserve your dialects, your cuisine, your architecture, your literature, your poetry. Preserve all these values because Morocco of today could not differ from yesterday's Morocco just as the Morocco of tomorrow cannot be different from present Morocco.[13]

The speech underlined that the new emphasis on Berberness had limits. It made clear that while the Amazigh activists' demands were recognized, they were not supposed to challenge the sacred elements of Moroccan nationalism, namely Islam, the king, and Moroccan unity. Although the teaching in schools of the Berber dialects was not put into practice until after his son, Mohammed VI, came to power, this speech was important in reducing tensions and according legitimacy to Amazigh demands. The speech was not in contradiction to the monarchy's earlier depictions of Moroccanness. Nevertheless, it reflected a change in official discourse as it explicitly touched upon a demand by the Amazigh movement. In the following years, the king periodically underlined the importance of Berber identity as a component of Moroccan identity. The government also addressed some of the Amazigh demands. The state-owned television channel started short news bulletins in three Berber dialects and radio broadcasts in these dialects were expanded (Maddy-Weitzman 2001, 32).

CONTAINED CONTENTION: STRATEGIC CONCESSIONS TO PLACATE THE STATE

By granting legitimacy to the Amazigh demand for the right to be different, at least at the discursive level, the king's 1994 speech encouraged activists to contact the political elite directly for the actual implementation of their demands. Several associations formed the National Council of Coordination in 1994 to direct their collective mobilization and kept pressuring the parliament, the government, and the Royal Council by sending them letters, memorandums, and petitions detailing their demands (Rachik 2006, 50–51). The official attempts to address the Amazigh

---

[13] The full text of the speech can be found in the Moroccan daily *L'Opinion* (1994, 1, 3).

question helped form a conciliatory attitude among the activists, who were willing to shape their discourse in a way that would be more acceptable to the state elite. As Lust-Okar (2005, 79) suggests, opponents are likely to moderate their policy demands, but not necessarily their true preferences, when they sense that inclusion in the system is probable. The contrast between Kurdish and Amazigh activists' strategies confirms Lust-Okar's argument. In Turkey, the state's indiscriminate exclusion of Kurdish activists from the political (and cultural) arena marginalized the moderates while opening the way for radicals to mobilize on their true preferences. In Morocco, on the other hand, the Amazigh activists received signals that the accommodation of their demands was possible, particularly through royal channels, as long as they did not challenge the fundamentals of the regime. Such signals provided them incentives to compromise.

The Amazigh activists had to concede on two issues in their interactions with state actors. The first concession was on the idea of Moroccanness. Although the activists did not share a monolithic idea about what it meant to be a Moroccan, there was a general agreement that Morocco should be considered a Berber country with the majority of the population having Berber ancestors. Many Amazigh activists argue that Berber culture is indigenous to the country while the Arab culture had come to the Berber region as an alien culture in the seventh century. As one of the leaders of the movement stated: "The Arab world is clearly not an Arab world. It is an Arabophone world. That must be clarified. It is like if you talk about the Francophone world. It is a real confusion in the nations. Morocco is not an Arabic state. It is an Amazigh state. It is not an Arab state, it is an Arabophone state."[14] The texts that were prepared for presentation to state authorities, nevertheless, did not portray Morocco as predominantly a Berber country but rather presented the Berber culture as only one component of the pluralist Moroccan culture and demanded equality between the Berber and the Arabic languages. The Amazigh Manifesto, which was signed by 229 activists in 2000, for instance, underlined the importance of speaking Arabic for the Berber population and presented it as the "strongest link" between Arabs and Berbers.[15]

---

[14] Interview with Hassan Id Belkassm, December 2006, Rabat.
[15] The Manifesto was highly critical of many state practices and radically challenged the official history presented in the school textbooks. However, it was carefully worded so as not to challenge the place of the king, the role of Islam, and territorial unity. The English translation of the Amazigh Manifesto can be found at www.amazighworld.net/human_rights/morocco/manifesto2000.php.

More importantly, the activists' concessions related to the role of Islam in Morocco. Since its beginning, the Amazigh movement has had a highly secularist character. The Amazigh activists, along with Moroccan feminists, have strongly supported initiatives to free family law from Islamic law and have been the main opponents of the rising Islamic movement.[16] The activists think that the dogmatic interpretation of Islam constituted the main reason behind the marginalization of the Amazigh language and culture as it transformed the Arabic language into a holy language. "The Arabic language is presented as the sacred language, the language of God, and the language of paradise," stated one activist.[17] According to her, political Islam and Pan-Arabism are racist ideologies that recognize only the right of existence of Islam and the Arabic language. As Maddy-Weitzman (2006, 76) underlines, "Modern Berber imagining is bound up with a secular, Western-modern vision of the future." In my interviews, many of the activists were highly critical of the Moroccan state's nonsecular character and advocated the separation of state and religion. Yet, despite the secularist character of the Amazigh movement, the texts that addressed the state elite did not imply any challenges to the Islamic foundation of the regime. On the contrary, they explicitly acknowledged its strong presence. For example, the letter that was sent to the Royal Cabinet in 1996 asked that the following sentence be considered in the revision of the constitution: "The Kingdom of Morocco is an Islamic state whose languages are Tamazight and Arabic and whose identity rests on three components: Islam, Tamazight, and Arabic" (cited in Rachik 2006, 50). The Amazigh Manifesto of 2000, which will be discussed in the next section, was also full of references to God and gave examples from the Qur'an to support its arguments. As Maddy-Weitzman (2007) argued, the Amazigh Manifesto was an attempt "to incorporate Moroccan Islam into Amazigh identity."

According to Hassan Rachik (2006, 50), many of the Amazigh signatories of the petitions sent to the state elite were willing to make certain concessions because they thought that moderate demands would have more chance of being accepted by the king and the government. In my

---

[16] There has been an ongoing tension between the Islamists and the Amazigh activists in Morocco. For instance, the main Islamist Party, the Party of Justice and Development (PJD), has been against the recognition of Tamazight and considered the revival of the Tifinagh alphabet as blasphemy. Many Islamists see the Amazigh movement as an imperialist project aiming to divide the Muslim peoples. For more see, Maddy-Weitzman (2011).

[17] Interview with Meryam Demnati, November 2006, Rabat.

informal conversations with them, some of the activists confirmed that the reason why certain issues were not brought up in the letters submitted to the political elite was tactical. The conciliatory attitude of the Amazigh activists, as contrasted with the increasingly nonconciliatory attitude of the Kurdish activists, indicates their different expectations about state behavior. The Moroccan Berber policies, which have been much more flexible, pragmatic, and ambiguous than the Turkish state policies towards the Kurds, created an expectation of a political opening among the Amazigh activists. In addition, the king's speeches on Moroccan and Berber identity clearly indicated the boundaries of legitimate debate on the issue. In Turkey, however, because of the continuous denial by the Turkish state authorities of even the existence of Kurds as a separate ethnic group, at least up until the 1990s, the state did not allow any space for legitimate debate. This unwillingness weakened its potential ability to steer Kurdish activism in ways that would not present a fundamental challenge to the state.

ACCOMMODATION OF AMAZIGH DEMANDS

In 1998, when Hassan II appointed Abderrahmane al-Youssoufi, the leader of the USFP, the prime minister, the Amazigh activists' hopes of finding some support within the new government increased. This was the first time since independence that the king had allowed his adversary to head the government, although he still continued his strict control over its functioning by appointing the key ministers (ministers of the interior, justice, foreign affairs, and Islamic affairs) from among independent politicians who were loyal to him. The appointment of Youssoufi, who had long been a regime dissident and had been persecuted by the regime for many years (he had been sentenced to death by Hassan II a few decades earlier), was considered an indication of political liberalization. Some of the activists within the Amazigh movement were previous members of the USFP, which had enjoyed the backing of educated, urban Berbers in the 1970s. The party's advocacy of democratization, secularization, and the promotion of civil society were also taken as a potential sign of support for Amazigh demands (Maddy-Weitzman 2001, 35). The Amazigh activists immediately acted to take advantage of the new political opening by starting to contact the USFP members of the government. The outcome of such interactions, nevertheless, was disappointing. When a leading Amazigh activist who was a leading member of the USFP until 1979 talked to the minister of public affairs, Ahmed Lahlimi, in private, the minister warned that the movement should not be impatient as there were not currently many supporters of Amazigh demands within the government. Soon after this private meeting, nevertheless, Prime Minister al-Youssoufi made a symbolic gesture by underlining the Amazigh dimension of national identity in a speech in front of the parliament. This was the first time a prime minister had openly declared in the parliament that he recognized Berber identity.[18]

The shift from symbolic gestures to substantial policy changes, namely the establishment of a Berber Institute and the teaching of Tamazight in schools, came a few years later, after Mohammed VI succeeded his father Hassan II in 1999. The decision was the king's, which came as a result of informal contacts and personal negotiations between certain Amazigh activists and the king's close circles. In fact, the establishment of a Berber Institute under royal tutelage and the incorporation of several Amazigh activists within this institute represented an informal monarchical strategy that the palace has employed when dealing with challengers that had the potential to grow and radicalize. The selective cooptation of moderate regime dissidents has been a conventional instrument of the monarchy in its attempts to control and dominate political challenges to its authority. As discussed in Chapter 3, the state subdued tribal dissidence and achieved its monopoly of power in the countryside after independence by establishing a dense network of patronage through which tribal notables' loyalty to the regime was attained. Starting in the mid-1980s, the monarchy used a similar strategy of cooptation with other political groups in the face of rising social and political demands.

Selective cooptation gives states the ability to fragment challengers and marginalize the radicals of the movement. The state's cooptation of activist elites, through institutionalized patronage networks, can inhibit the growth of a movement due to its fragmenting effects (Snyder 1992). Although cooptation requires the satisfaction of certain demands of the moderate challengers, it also allows states to manipulate activists' demands and strategies: "The inclusion of opposition activists in positions of potential influence within formal politics could drain civil society of the resources it needs to be effective, leaving the government ultimately unchecked, harder to challenge, and more dominant" (Weiss 2006, 50). Lust-Okar (2005, 5) argues that included opposition groups would not want to challenge the system drastically due to their fear of losing their privileges. In addition, she suggests that competition within an opposition

---

[18] Interview with Mounir Kejji, March 2007, Rabat.

group between its moderate and more radical, excluded sections also precludes the moderate section's willingness to demand systemic changes, as they fear that such change may strengthen the radical groups. In short, states that effectively fragment the opposition and create competition within oppositional groups will be more likely to preserve the status quo. In almost every new challenge that the Moroccan regime encountered, its consistent strategy has been to incorporate the moderate representatives of the challenging group within the ranks of a new state institution while punishing the radical regime dissidents. As Denoeux and Maghraoui (1998, 105) underline: "Unlike in the region's more authoritarian states, repression has been used only sparingly and in moderate doses. It usually has targeted only those who advocate violence or cross certain implicit but well-understood 'red lines' (such as questioning the sanctity of the monarchy or the legitimacy of its dominant role in the political system)." The Moroccan monarchy's strategy to deal with rising social and political demands rests not solely on intimidation and repression, but also on incorporation and cooptation. The monarchy resorts to repression if an opponent cannot be coopted.

There have been many institutions that served to incorporate political activists into official channels. In 1990, in the face of rising critiques of the state's human rights record and the formation of human rights organizations in Morocco, Hassan II created a Consultative Council for Human Rights (*Le Conseil Consultatif des Droits de l'Homme*, CCDH), which included representatives from political parties, trade unions, human rights organizations, and the lawyers' association, university professors, as well as four cabinet members, who have always been the personal choice of the king. Similarly, the formation in the 1990s of a vibrant feminist movement represented by dozens of women's associations heightened feminist pressure for a change in the Moroccan family code, leading the king to create an organization, Cell for the Integration of Women in Development (*Cellule Intégration de la Femme au Développement*, CIFD), in which he brought together many feminist activists. These organizations became consultative agencies that were unable (or unwilling) to challenge the king's prerogatives and whose activities led to only modest reforms.[19] The official approval given for the formation of the Justice and Development Party (PJD) by Abdelkrim al-Khatib, an old

---

[19] For more on different consultative bodies created by the monarchy to address the demands of new social movements in the 1990s and their limited capacity, see Denoeux and Maghraoui (1998), Mayer (1993-1994), and Sater (2007).

politician who is known to have had close ties to the palace circles, was also considered another cooptation attempt to curtail the rise of radical Islamism (especially the Justice and Charity movement, which has rejected the political and religious authority of the king)[20] and to provide an integrative enclave for moderate Islamists (Malka and Alterman 2006, 51–52).[21] These organizations, founded through the direct or indirect support of the palace, became mechanisms of control and stability for the monarchy and increased the incentives for activists to moderate their demands. Activists involved in these organizations did so either because they thought changing the system incrementally from within would be a more realistic and less risky option or because they saw these organizations solely as instruments for social prestige and personal advancement. Through these institutions, the king found the means to closely watch the activities of the associative space, to assert his authority as the ultimate decision maker and arbiter of the country, and to marginalize the activists who advocate radical changes of the regime. The establishment of IRCAM can be seen as an attempt to extend the monarchy's patronage network to coopt Amazigh activism.

With Hassan II's death, his 36-year-old son, Mohammed VI, succeeded to the throne in July 1999. Soon after he came to power, the new king gave signals of his support for further liberalization of the regime. He removed Driss Basri, Hassan II's all-powerful and widely reviled interior minister, from office. Basri was known for his highly repressive measures against political opponents and had been in charge of the ministry since the early 1980s. In his speeches, Mohammed VI also underlined the necessity for political reform and democratization (Malka and Alterman 2006, 47). The succession of Mohammed VI soon increased the hopes of many politically active groups, including the Amazigh movement. Through a combination of conciliatory messages and the use of personal networks of influence, the activists managed to negotiate their demands with the highest level of state authority, King Mohammed VI.

The process that led to the establishment of IRCAM began with the preparation of the Amazigh Manifesto by Mohamed Chafik. The activists' choice of Chafik as the Manifesto's author was hardly coincidental.

---

[20] For more on the Justice and Charity movement and the ideas of its leader, Sheikh Abdessalam Yassine, see Maddy-Weitzman (2003), Zeghal (2008), and chapter 5 in Willis (2012).

[21] Waltz (1995, 127) writes that two delegations close to the palace offered certain benefits even to Abdessalam Yassine, the leader of the Justice and Charity movement, in return for his acceptance of the king's authority.

Chafik was a revered figure for both Amazigh activists and those in official circles. He had been the professor of Mohammed VI when he was the director of the Royal College and had contacts with the palace circles. The activists hoped that Chafik's authorship would provide the Amazigh movement with immunity from state persecution.

This twenty-two-page document, which was initially signed by over 200 activists, expressed harsh critiques of past policies; presented a completely new version of history, different from the official history; called upon the state to recognize Amazigh demands;[22] and emphasized the activists' determination to fight against cultural hegemony.[23] Despite its harsh critiques of state policies, the Manifesto also assured the new king of the Amazigh activists' loyalty to the main principles of the regime and signified the movement's willingness to cooperate with the monarch to resolve the conflicts. It was carefully worded so as not to present any accusations against the earlier monarchs with regard to their policies on the Berbers, but rather put the blame on the ambiguously defined "makhzenian circles," who misdirected the sultans based on their "dogmatic religious thinking." The Manifesto accused "the forces of the political right and left," without the slightest critique of Hassan II, for the problems that the Berbers suffered (Arabization, economic marginalization, and attempts to eliminate minorities, as in Turkey and Iraq) during the post-colonial period. Instead, Hassan II was portrayed as a mere victim of the makhzenian circles; he understood the importance of the Amazigh demands but was not able to lead any policy changes because these circles had impeded such changes.[24] To reaffirm that the Amazigh movement does not present an attack against Islamic values and unity, the Manifesto underlined that Amazigh political traditions, particularly the managing of communal affairs in tribal councils (*jemaas*), have been in line with real Islamic principles as practiced by the Prophet Muhammad and the first four caliphs.

The activists were successful in attracting the attention of the palace through their personal contacts. They found a suitable mediator, Hassan

---

[22] The demands of the Manifesto were: constitutional recognition of Tamazight, planning for the economic development of the Amazigh population, the teaching of Tamazight in schools, revision of the national history presented in schools, provision of Tamazight translators in courts and the administration, TV and radio broadcasting in Tamazight, state support for Amazigh arts, and financial help to Amazigh associations and publications.

[23] For a very good analysis of the Manifesto, see Maddy-Weitzman (2007).

[24] See the manifesto at www.amazighworld.net/human_rights/morocco/manifesto2000.php.

Aourid, to convey their message to the king. Aourid, who became the spokesman of the palace after Mohammed VI came to power, had been a classmate of Mohammed VI at the Royal College. He knew the movement quite well as he had conducted research on the Amazigh movement for his dissertation. A prominent activist took the Manifesto to him and asked him to take it to the king. Aourid's mediation was critical. In the following days, the king asked Aourid along with his two other advisors to listen to Chafik and the leading representatives of the movement. During the meeting, the contents of the Manifesto were discussed in depth. Aourid transmitted the king's message to the activists that the king considered the Amazigh question to be a very important national matter.[25] Nevertheless, a year passed after the meeting without any official steps towards the resolution of Amazigh demands. The absence of any official initiative created unrest among some activists who began to push for politicization of the movement and put pressure on other activists to form a political party. In addition, the so-called Black Spring (*le Printemps Noir*) in Algeria,[26] which refers to increased violent confrontations between Algerian state forces and Kabyle activists during the spring of 2001, fueled Moroccan activists' impatience. On May Day 2001, the Berber activists in Morocco shouted angry slogans and carried photos of Algerian Berber martyrs to show their solidarity, as well as signs that read "No to Arabism in Morocco" (Lehtinen 2003, 189–190). With its high level of mobilization and media attention, the demonstration showed to the regime the possibility of the movement's radicalization.

A month later, the activists prepared for a congress that would bring together representatives of several associations from all over the country. They planned to discuss the Manifesto and what their future strategy should be in the absence of further official concessions. The Ministry of the Interior immediately banned the congress, with the police closing off the roads to the town where the meeting was supposed to take place. The attendees were asked to go back home. Professor Chafik intervened and told the activists that they could meet in his house in Meknès on the same day. Soon the punitive measures were followed by a message of accommodation from the king, as long as the activists were willing to negotiate. While the meeting was taking place, Aourid, along with two royal advisors, visited Chafik's house and told him about the king's plans

[25] Interview with an anonymous Amazigh activist.
[26] The protests in Algeria started after an 18-year-old Berber was killed while in police custody. According to estimates, the security forces killed between 100 and 200 people during the events (Maddy-Weitzman 2011, 185).

to establish an institute to develop the Berber language and culture.[27] On October 17, 2001, through a royal edict, Mohammed VI announced the establishment of IRCAM. The king's choice of Ajdir, in the province of Khénifra in the Middle Atlas, to declare his royal edict was highly symbolic as this was the location where Mohammed V, the king's grandfather, had had a meeting with Berber tribal leaders to end the rebellion in 1956 (Maddy-Weitzman 2011, 165). The choice of Ajdir suggested the continuation of the previous policy of negotiation and patronage to address Berber dissent.

The king appointed Mohamed Chafik as the first rector of IRCAM and asked him to nominate activists to work at the institute. It was placed under the direct authority of the king and given only consultative authority. Its thirty-three-member administrative council was composed of seven high-level state officials from the Ministries of Culture, Education, and Communication, selected and appointed directly by the king, along with Amazigh activists from different associations, selected by Chafik and appointed by the king. The decisions of the administrative council are simply advisory to the king and the institute does not have independent policy-making authority. The institute is also dependent on the palace financially, as its annual budget of 70 million dirhams (around $9 million in 2005) is covered by royal funds (Boukhari 2005, 9).

The establishment of IRCAM as an institution tightly linked to the palace soon created a fierce debate within the Amazigh movement, dividing it into two camps, with considerable tension between them. The first camp has been composed of activists who have been referred to as the radicals of the movement and who have refused to work at IRCAM because they have perceived it as the state's attempt to buy off Amazigh activism and to control its demands. They have pointed to the high salaries and luxurious working conditions of the IRCAM employees and have argued that the institute implies only cosmetic change.[28] AZETTA (*Le Réseau Amazighe Pour la Citoyenneté*), which was founded in 2002 as a nationwide organization, for instance, has openly declared its rejection of the *dahir* that established IRCAM. It has also been highly critical of IRCAM activists for not pushing policy changes hard enough. Activists outside of IRCAM, including AZETTA, have also been known for their

---

[27] An account of this process can be found in Alami *et al.* (2004, 20–27). Also see Benchemsi (2001, 18–26).
[28] Today IRCAM has around 300 employees. Out of the 300, 100 are permanent members of staff and 200 are contract employees. Their salaries and working conditions are noticeably superior to those of state employees at comparable levels (Boukhari 2005, 9).

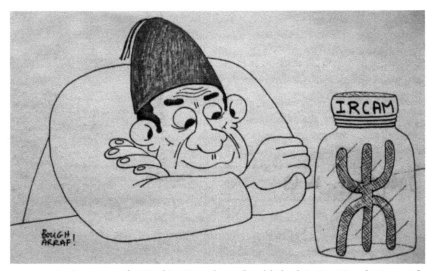

FIGURE 8. A cartoon by Brahim Bougharraf published in *Le Monde Amazigh*, September 2004. It satirizes the establishment of IRCAM as a tool to coopt Amazigh activism. The man with the fez symbolizes the Arabist state. Courtesy of *Le Monde Amazigh*.

uncompromising stance on a number of other issues such as secularization, separation of powers, administrative decentralization, and constitutional recognition of Tamazight as an official language alongside Arabic. The association's explicit critiques and confrontational attitude have not been without cost. Despite the reform in 2002 that made the establishment of associations legally easier,[29] AZETTA could not obtain official recognition for four years after it submitted its files to the local authorities.[30] While the regime provides benefits to those who play by the rules of the game, it openly punishes those who do not cooperate.

The regime has also been reluctant to tolerate the politicization of the Amazigh movement, thus not allowing the establishment of political parties advocating Amazigh identity. The political party law forbids the formation of political parties founded on a religious, linguistic,

---

[29] The 2002 law introduced the principle of simple declaration for the establishment of associations. According to the new law the newly formed organizations should only inform the authorities in order to become legally registered. Nevertheless, as in the case of AZETTA, the authorities may deny a provisional receipt and not register the association. For details, see Kausch (2008, 54).

[30] For more, see AZETTA's declaration on its website at www.reseauamazigh.org/article151.html?lang=fr.

ethnic, or regional basis. The Democratic Amazigh Moroccan Party (*Parti Démocrate Amazigh Marocain*, PDAM) was founded in 2005. The party founders advocated administrative decentralization and regional autonomy as solutions to the underdevelopment of the rural Berber areas. Ahmed Adghirni, who was one of the founders of PDAM, argued that the central state did not have the right to keep the former communal lands, which had been owned by tribes before the French and Spanish colonial regimes confiscated them and turned them into state lands. According to Adghirni, the Moroccan state should have returned these lands to the tribes after independence and allowed them to use these lands' natural resources for their own benefit. He emphasized that Amazigh poverty has been very much related to the exploitation of natural resources on the former tribal lands by the state. The discourse of regional development can be seen as an attempt by the more politically oriented Amazigh activists to break out of their elitist circle and to speak to the larger Berber community, for whom poverty, unemployment, and lack of infrastructure present more immediate problems than cultural and linguistic rights. The party also advocated that all Moroccans were in fact Amazighs, some of whom were Arabized after years of Arab rule, underlining that the party represented all Moroccans, rather than one ethnic community. This claim, however, was not found convincing by the administrative court in Rabat, which declared in April 2007 that the party was illegal and should be dissolved because it was based on an ethnic criterion.[31]

The second camp of Amazigh activists includes those who accept working at IRCAM and believe that policy change is possible only when they cooperate with the state. IRCAM activists hardly have a romanticized view of the king's initiative and are aware of the limited authority of the institute. If the king saw IRCAM as a tool for coopting and controlling the development of the Amazigh movement, the activists collaborated with him for their own ends. As one activist working at IRCAM explained:

There are always extremist associations who told us that nothing can be done with the state, that if you work with the state, they will benefit from it but not us. We told them that we took up our arms and joined the Institute just like militants. We will continue our struggle from within the Institute. It is not only the state that automatically benefits from this process, we can benefit too. The youth started to accuse us of selling out Tamazight and all that. I reply to them

---

[31] Interview with PDAM members, December 10, 2006, Rabat. Also see Adghirni (2006, 5, 13).

by saying, "Give me another solution" and they propose nothing. If you stay outside the system, others will always make decisions for you. By working within the system, you know that one day you will decide.[32]

Many activists incorporated into IRCAM also came to consider the king the only ally of the movement among the political elite. The establishment of IRCAM increased the king's legitimacy (at least in comparison to other political actors in Morocco) in the eyes of these activists. Ahmed Assid, who is a member of the administrative council at IRCAM, vehemently criticizes those who propose an alternative institution completely independent from the state, adding:

> It is necessary to understand that the Amazigh movement is not yet strong and that it is rather fragmented. In addition, we do not have any strong allies. The political parties and part of the civil society is against us. Those who criticize us do not take this into consideration. They do not have political realism ... With the cadre of IRCAM we have the political support of the King. It is what gives us some strength because the parties are not with us.
>
> (*Le Reporter* 2006, 27)

Such perceptions of the king as the sole ally of the movement and the ultimate arbiter became increasingly common among IRCAM employees, who began to encounter resistance from the government as well as the bureaucracy to implementation of IRCAM-initiated policies. As one activist expressed: "When we have a problem, we send letters to the King. We say that we have such and such problems with this ministry ... The King sends an order to the related minister to come to the Institute to work with us."[33] Although the extent to which the king intervenes to ensure the government's collaboration with the Amazigh activists in IRCAM is not clear, there was a clear sense among activists within IRCAM that no policy change could be possible without the king's support, since they had no other political support. Referring to the representatives of the ministries, the same activist added: "We are always obliged to monitor the government because people do not do anything out of conviction. There is no political will. They would have loved it if Tamazight died out."

As in Turkey, the Moroccan state's response to Amazigh activism was far from unitary, with Amazigh activism encountering opposition from different levels of the state. For example, in the mid-1990s, a controversy over giving Berber names to children emerged, when the Interior

---

[32] Interview with an anonymous IRCAM employee.
[33] Interview with an anonymous IRCAM employee.

Ministry, headed by the infamous Driss Basri, who had been the main aide of Hassan II for a long time, sent a circular to the governors with a list of permissible names. Many, but not all, Berber names were included in the list. The list received a strong reaction from Amazigh activists, who argued that it aimed at outlawing the customary naming practices of the Berbers and they challenged this practice through litigation (Houdaïfa 2006, 34–35). A *dahir* proclaimed in November 1996 stipulated that the first name shall be an original Moroccan first name and that it should not create a threat against society's customs or national security.[34] Although the law did not explicitly ban Berber names, many registrars, who were not sympathetic to growing Amazigh demands, rejected Berber names on the grounds that they were not Moroccan names. The controversy continues to this day. While some courts and registration offices allow parents to give Berber names to their children, others reject similar demands. I could obtain only two court decisions that relate to the rejection of Berber names. In each case, the judges rejected the registration of Berber names, but they based their rulings on different justifications. In the first case, the judge proclaimed that the plaintiff could not prove that the name was an Amazigh name, indicating that *de jure* an Amazigh name could be accepted as an original Moroccan name. In the second case, the judge ruled that the name Idir could not be registered because the right transcription is Yeder, as fixed by the Higher Registry Commission in 1997. According to Chafik (2005, 34), such resistance against Berber names indicates the Arabist ideology's popularity within the administration, especially among the local authorities.

Amazigh activists have also been highly critical of the Ministry of Communication and the Ministry of Education for their foot-dragging on helping IRCAM make the Berber culture more visible in education and the media. The lack of support for Amazigh demands was not limited to administrative circles. The majority of the political parties represented in the parliament were either dismissive of their demands or openly against them. The members of the main Islamist party, the Party of

---

[34] The law also stipulated that first names should not be based on the name of a city, village, or tribe. As Hoffman (2000, 97) points out, this law could be interpreted as part of the state's attempt to assert its authority more in the countryside and to break up local and tribal identities in order to strengthen the people's allegiance to the state. The full text of the law can be found in *Bulletin Officiel*, No. 4428 (November 7, 1996), 735. The entire collection of the *Bulletin Officiel*, from 1912 onward, can be retrieved online, through the website of the Secretariat General of the Government: www.sgg.gov.ma/historique_bo.aspx?id=982.

Justice and Development, which won the plurality of the vote in the 2011 elections, thus leading the coalition government, have often expressed their opposition to Amazigh demands, which they considered as divisive of the Muslim *umma* and an attempt to desacralize the Arab language and culture by supporters of the imperialist West.

Since 2003, activists working in IRCAM's seven research centers have tried to initiate policy changes to promote the Berber culture and to create a general consciousness among Moroccans about the country's pre-Islamic, Berber heritage.[35] The main task of IRCAM has been the unification and transformation of three Berber dialects into a standardized, written form and the creation of school textbooks for Tamazight instruction. By the fall of 2003, Tamazight began to be taught as a compulsory class for all students in 300 elementary schools for three hours a week. A representative of the Ministry of Education at IRCAM stated that every elementary school would incorporate Tamazight into its curriculum by 2010.[36] Nevertheless, there have been several problems in the actual implementation of Tamazight education. Many activists at IRCAM point to the lack of willingness of the representatives of the Ministry of Education to cooperate with IRCAM, the shortage of specialized teachers, the lack of adequate training for teachers, the refusal of some school directors to incorporate Tamazight into their school curriculum, and the reluctance of the educational inspectors to address problems with the teachers and school directors.[37] Representatives of the Ministry of Education, however, call attention to the lack of resources, the difficulties of teaching a language that has not yet been standardized, and the absence of parental support in Arab-speaking regions.[38] In 2012, only 15 percent of students in state schools had Tamazight courses (Ali 2012).

[35] The centers concentrate on the following tasks: standardization of Tamazight into a written form and creation of dictionaries; anthropological and sociological analysis of the Berber population; historical and geographical studies on Berbers; development of pedagogical programs, curricula, and materials for teaching Tamazight; translation of Tamazight texts, creation of a documentation center, and integration of Amazigh language and culture into the media; development of scientific research based on computer technology; development of Amazigh art and literature and audiovisual production. For more on each center's responsibilities, see www.ircam.ma.
[36] Interview with an anonymous IRCAM employee.
[37] Several interviews at IRCAM.
[38] Although some of my interviewees mentioned that some Arabic-speaking parents are not satisfied with Tamazight teaching in schools and that the perceptions of Tamazight as an undeveloped language that does not offer any prospects of success in the job market are quite common, there was still not much public debate questioning Tamazight teaching at the time that I conducted my fieldwork. For more on the problems associated with Tamazight teaching in Morocco, see Buckner (2006) and Errihani (2006).

The establishment of IRCAM did not seem to make the Amazigh activists working in this state institution passive and obedient subjects. As IRCAM activists do research, publish books, and organize conferences, they write a Berber history, redefine Berber traditions, and fashion a new Berber imagery. Through these activities, they challenge the prevailing notions of Berberness in Moroccan society. The school textbooks in Tamazight refer to the pre-Islamic history of Morocco, to the Amazigh personalities of the Roman and Byzantine periods. In an attempt to erase the conventional depictions of Berbers as rural, parochial, uneducated, and uncivilized, the main characters in the school textbooks prepared by IRCAM look modern, wear Western clothes, and live in cities. "The Amazighs are not ignorant mountain people, goat herders, and folk dancers in their spare time," says Fatima Agnaou from IRCAM (Lamlili 2006, 24). The Amazigh activists have long been sensitive to the prevalence of a folklorized representation of Berber culture and are critical of the depictions of Berber culture as traditional and archaic. Hence in the ceremony organized by the palace for the king's declaration of appointments to the administrative council of IRCAM, the activists refused to wear traditional Berber clothes and saluted the king by shaking his hand rather than kissing it, as Moroccan state tradition stipulates. In my interviews, activists proudly underlined the symbolic significance of this handshake. For them, the handshake showed to the Moroccan public the democratic and modern face of the Berbers, as represented by the Amazigh movement. It also showed that an alternative and more modern way to relate to the king is possible instead of complete submission as implied by the traditional hand kissing.

In a similar effort, in presentations of Berber traditions and tribal life, IRCAM writers assign them new meanings through incorporating modern notions into their discussions. The Berber "memory work," in Maddy-Weitzman's words (2007), presents traditional tribal institutions as democratic institutions and customary laws as the most egalitarian.[39] Such new imagery, and the emphasis on Westernization, may appeal to urbanized Berbers, whose numbers increase every day, but may also run the risk of alienating Berbers living in the rural areas away from Amazigh activism. Abouzaid (2005, 70–71) points to the critiques of teachers who work in Berber rural areas to the highly secular character of the textbooks and the pictures in them, depicting girls wearing short skirts and

---

[39] For an example, see Rachid (2005), especially part 4, "Rural Social Institutions: Ultimate Fortresses Before Collapse."

boys wearing caps. These teachers complain about the textbooks as being unrepresentative of the lifestyle and values of Berbers in rural contexts. Similarly, Errihani (2006, 152) argues that the rural Berbers' support for the teaching of Tamazight is far from certain: "For many of them, the teaching of Tamazight is nothing but a political act that serves the interests of the urban Amazigh elite, who are often ignorant of the actual conditions of the rural Amazigh."

Since the establishment of IRCAM, the public visibility of the Berber identity has grown. Objects that symbolize the Amazigh movement can be seen in public places more frequently. The symbol of the Amazigh movement, the letter "z" in Tifinagh script (see Figure 7, above), is drawn on walls, worn by people as jewelry, and adorns the rear windows of cars as stickers. This has not seemed to bother the state authorities. Amazigh activists organize conferences, advertise Amazigh arts festivals, and meet activists from other countries in international meetings without encountering much state interference. An annual Amazigh cultural festival is organized with state funds. Even the Amazigh flag, which was adopted by the First Amazigh World Congress in 1997, can be freely carried in demonstrations. A state-funded Amazigh TV channel was launched in January 2010 after intense lobbying efforts by Amazigh activists. So far, these incremental concessions have worked to lower the tension between the state and Amazigh activism.

CONCLUSION

The main objective of this chapter was to underline how the Moroccan monarchy's strategy of cooptation and accommodation of some Amazigh demands were influential in preventing the radicalization and politicization of the movement in general. The recognition of Amazigh demands did not come automatically. In fact, the monarchy's initial response to the rise of the Amazigh movement was characterized more by intimidation than accommodation. Nevertheless, over time the monarchy did not solely rely on repression and intimidation in its efforts to control a growing Berber activism. Its strategy that involved negotiation, compromise, and the extension of cooptation to Amazigh activists curtailed the movement's potential for radicalization. The ambiguity of its nationalist ideology made official concessions to Amazigh activism easier and faster than in the Turkish case. The activists' increasing hopes that their demands were negotiable led them to be open to conciliation.

The Moroccan state's strategy also influenced the way activists interacted with the state. When the activists tried to reach the palace to make their demands heard, when they used personal channels to reach the king, and when they moderated their discourse, they were acting in accordance with the officially propagated image of the monarch as the "supreme arbiter" who intervenes and dispenses justice at crucial moments of societal conflict. The conciliatory attitude of Amazigh activists was informed by this fatherly image of the monarch who grants royal tutelage to his loyal subjects. The Amazigh activists knew from Moroccan political history that cooptation of the political opposition and accommodation of claims are possible as long as activists signal that they would play by the rules of the game and not challenge monarchical rule.

The state's attentiveness to Amazigh demands and its acceptance of ethnic difference in Morocco does not indicate its commitment to liberal multiculturalism and individual rights. The regime does not refrain from punishing those who do not cooperate and continue to oppose the policies of the regime concerning the Berbers. The official recognition of several Amazigh associations was delayed for years even after they submitted all the necessary documents for registration to the local authorities. Security forces continue to harass and intimidate Amazigh activists in demonstrations. But the repressive measures of the state are accompanied by other strategies that prevent an anti-monarchical consensus within the movement. As a poor and authoritarian state in the politically unpredictable and shaky region of North Africa, the Moroccan monarchy produces power and achieves ethnic stability by controlling Amazigh activism through cooptation, selective rewards, and accommodation of its cultural demands. The Moroccan state's initial weakness in terms of its lower coercive power and higher dependence on the support of social power centers has created a state with limited aims as well as a state that has more adaptability to emerging opposition from its society. In that sense, the gradual accommodation of Amazigh demands and the establishment of IRCAM represent more of a continuity in state policy than a radical break.

Conclusion

In this book I underline that state strategies are crucial in the development of ethnic movements. Although initially Kurdish and Berber areas posed similar challenges to the Turkish and Moroccan states, the ethnic movements that were born out of these communities evolved in different ways. The Kurdish identity movement evolved into a large and violent nationalist movement in the world, challenging Turkey's unity in the past three decades, while Berber activism remained an ethnic identity movement whose demands were limited to cultural and linguistic rights. I explained this striking contrast by looking at the different nation-building strategies of the respective states, particularly the scope of their intrusion into people's everyday lives and the range of changes they demand from the ethnic groups that are different from the state's ideal image of the nation. This book demonstrated that the Turkish state, in pursuit of constructing a sense of common national identity, intervened directly and coercively in Kurds' daily practices, demanding changes in everyday behavior, which politicized Kurdish cultural expressions and spurred Kurds' increasing resistance and mobilization around a counter-nationalist project. Although many of the potential conflict-breeding factors have existed in Morocco (underdevelopment of the Berber community, colonial divide-and-rule policies, contentious ethnic conflict in a neighboring state, absence of a democratic system, to name a few), the state has been able to curtail the radicalization of Berber activism and to maintain years of ethnic peace. I argued that this was due to the Moroccan state's cautious and non-intrusive nation-building policies. The Moroccan state has been flexible in defining the boundaries of Moroccan identity and in dealing with Berber dissent. This curtailed the rise of a Berber nationalism and limited the ethnic movement's appeal among the Berber masses. In addition, the Moroccan monarchy's policy of selective repression and cooptation helped form the Berber activists' uneasy and yet peaceful relations with the state.

In both countries the core approach to nation-building that each state took at independence was resilient over decades. State traditions and policies of the past informed the future practices towards Kurds and Berbers. In both countries, however, there was also significant variation in state policies due to fragmentation at the state level or to the way policies were implemented on the ground. In Turkey, there has been waxing and waning of the state's makeover project, depending on which faction had the upper hand within the state and the manner in which policies were enforced by local state officials. Different parts of the state – the military, bureaucracy, political parties, government, and judiciary along with their representatives at the lower levels of the state in local areas – sometimes formulated and implemented conflicting responses in their attempts to transform the Kurdish citizens into their own definition of Turkishness. In Morocco, there has been resistance from the bureaucratic cadres and the political parties in government to the legal expansion of freedoms for Berber linguistic and cultural expressions. The official recognition of the Berber language and culture led to uneven and incomplete changes in actual state policies.

Moroccan and Turkish state policies suggest that nation-building should be conceptualized along a continuum that leads to a variety of possible relationships between states and minorities rather than seen from a dichotomous perspective that characterizes state strategies as civic vs. ethnic or inclusive vs. exclusive. As Brubaker (2004) underlines, it is often impossible to characterize an entire state as civic or ethnic because states endorse a mixture of ethnic and civic policies to different degrees. Brubaker also points to the ambiguities of the definitions of ethnic and civic and argues that both understandings of nationhood are simultaneously inclusive and exclusive, albeit in different ways. This categorization of nationhood also assumes state policies to be monolithic and coherent. States may, however, undertake contradictory and uncoordinated responses that may promote both inclusive and exclusive understandings. While some parts of the state may take an inclusive stance towards cultural and ethnic differences, other parts may propagate more exclusivist strategies. Or, at other times, a policy initiative may have unintended results depending on how it was implemented. In this work I underlined that nation-building should not be considered as a clean and smooth process controlled by an integrated state. In general, the Turkish state operated at one end of the continuum while the Moroccan state operated at the other, but at times, these states' strategies came closer to each other.

Indeed, in the post-2000 period Moroccan and Turkish state policies towards their major ethnic minorities have moved closer along the spectrum of policies. Both states have shown more tolerance for ethno-cultural diversity within their borders by integrating minority languages into the domains of media and education. In both countries Kurdish and Berber cultural expressions have become more visible in public and the official discourses invoke multiculturalism frequently. In Turkey the ideological shift brought by the Justice and Development Party (AKP) that emphasizes "Muslim nationalism," as Jenny White (2013) defined it, as well as growing EU pressure led to a transformation of state practice towards the Kurds. The AKP's new approach to national identity prioritizes Muslim identity more than blood-based Turkish ethnicity and is informed by a reimagined multi-ethnic Ottoman past. As such it resembles the monarchy's narrative of Moroccan nationalism and allows for the recognition of not only Kurdish identity but also other Muslim ethnic minority identities in Turkey, including Arabic, Circassian, and Laz.[1] This new acceptance of Turkey's multi-ethnic reality, however, hardly suggests the end of the Kurdish conflict. With the armed conflict, the Kurdish problem became a more complex and intractable issue that goes far beyond settling cultural rights. Nor in Morocco have Amazigh activists stopped challenging the state. A closer look at the recent developments in both countries shows the ambiguous and contradictory nature of the new state policies as well as their mixed results.

One of the most important changes in state policy under the AKP government has been the beginning of negotiations with the PKK to end the insurgency. While the state, particularly the military, has been in contact with Abdullah Öcalan indirectly through third parties since 1992, after 2005 these talks took the form of direct negotiations led by civilian intelligence officers.[2] The negotiations have led to initiatives to end the conflict over the last few years, but without much success. The ongoing peace process underlines the difficulties of reconciliation after years of armed conflict.

---

[1] For a detailed discussion of this ideological shift, see White (2013) and Aktürk (2012).
[2] For detailed information on the history of negotiations, see Çandar (2012, 56–58).

In the summer of 2009, the AKP government announced an initiative, the so-called "Democratic Opening," that encompassed various proposals for legal and constitutional reforms to improve linguistic and cultural freedoms for the Kurds. Despite the vagueness of the proposals, the initiative received a lot of publicity. During the process, the government organized a series of meetings with intellectuals, journalists, and civil society groups to discuss the Opening. Öcalan provided a roadmap to peace, detailing his proposals to end the conflict. The roadmap included amnesty for PKK militants and suggestions for their integration into Turkish political life, legal and constitutional reforms, and a multinational force that would arrange the withdrawal of PKK insurgents (International Crisis Group 2011, 7). The negotiations between the PKK and the Turkish authorities led to an agreement on the entry into Turkey of a group of PKK members from Northern Iraq. In October 2009, thirty-four PKK members entered Turkey from the Harbur border gate expecting an amnesty. The reception of the PKK members as heroes by thousands of people and the pro-Kurdish Democratic Society Party (DTP) and the following celebrations outraged the Turkish public. According to opinion polls, support for the Opening fell to 27 percent after the return of the PKK members from 69 percent at the beginning of the summer (Cemal 2011, 108). Under heavy attack from the opposition, the government toughened its stance towards the Kurdish movement. Several of the returnees were arrested and given prison sentences ranging from seven to sixteen years.[3] Those who were not arrested returned to Northern Iraq (Çandar 2012, 81). In December 2009, the DTP was closed down for becoming "a focal point of activities against the indivisible unity of the state, the country, and the nation."[4] The failure of the amnesty initiative reinforced the mutual sense of distrust and uncertainty between the Kurdish activists and the state.

The difficulty of resolving ethnic civil wars through negotiated settlements is well known. "Fewer negotiated settlements are signed; if they are signed, they are less likely to be implemented; and even if they are implemented, they are more likely to break down," writes Barbara Walter (2009, 244) in her analysis of bargaining failures. Lack of trust, uncertainty about the adversary's future intentions, and social polarization inhibit the start and continuation of negotiations or hinder credible commitments to settlements after they are made. While states fear that

---

[3] "Kandil ve Mahmur'dan gelen PKK'lılara hapis," *Hürriyet*, October 12, 2011 and "Kandil ve Mahmur'dan gelenlere 61,5 yıl hapis," *Hürriyet*, April 24, 2012.
[4] "Turkish Top Court Bans Pro-Kurdish Party," *BBC News*, December 11, 2009 http://news.bbc.co.uk/2/hi/8408903.stm (accessed October 26, 2013).

insurgent groups will use autonomy and cultural rights to prepare for secession, insurgents refuse to disarm because they fear that states would violate the agreement and repress them once they give up their arms (Downes 2004). Insurgencies face this dilemma particularly in contexts like Turkey where political and legal institutions do not provide strong checks on the actions of the government (Walter 2009, 251).

The peace process in Turkey so far has supported these expectations. A new round of talks with Öcalan started in late 2012 as a result of domestic and regional developments. Turkey's fear of Kurdish independence increased with the worsening of the civil war in Syria and the growing autonomy of the Kurdish-populated regions in Northern Syria. The close links between the PKK and the Democratic Union Party (PYD), which is the dominant Kurdish party in Syria, put pressure on the AKP government to address the Kurdish problem. On the domestic front, the increase in violence between the PKK and security forces also pushed the government.[5] In addition, the AKP needed the pro-Kurdish party deputies' support in the parliament to change the constitution. Altering the 1982 constitution, which was prepared by the military government after the coup, has been on the AKP's agenda for a long time but the government lacked enough votes in the parliament to unilaterally approve a constitution and submit it to a referendum. As a result, the government resumed negotiations with Öcalan, which culminated in the PKK's declaration of a ceasefire in March 2013. In May, the PKK began to withdraw its fighters from Turkey. Soon, however, problems emanating from mutual distrust began to emerge. While Prime Minister Erdoğan insisted that the PKK insurgents disarm while pulling out of Turkey, the PKK declared that the insurgents would keep their arms for self-defense (Arsu 2013). The KCK's executive member Cemil Bayık asked for legal guarantees to protect the withdrawing PKK units from attacks by the Turkish military, observing that during the pullout in 1999 the military attacked the PKK, inflicting severe casualties (*Fırat News* 2013). From the beginning there was a disagreement between the government and the Kurdish camp over how the peace process should proceed. The PKK and the pro-Kurdish Peace and Democracy Party (BDP) asked the government to do its part during the withdrawals by addressing Kurdish demands, including releasing the KCK suspects, changing the constitution to recognize Turkey's ethnic diversity, abolishing the anti-terror law, allowing Kurdish-language

---

[5] Between June 2011 and March 2013, 928 people were killed in this upsurge of violence. See International Crisis Group (2013, 2).

education in public schools, lowering the 10 percent national electoral threshold,[6] improving Öcalan's prison conditions, and abolishing the village guard system. The government accused the PKK of delaying its withdrawal and claimed that only a minority of the PKK's forces had left the country. At the beginning of September 2013, the PKK announced that it had halted its withdrawal due to the government's failure to undertake reforms (*Today's Zaman* 2013). Although Erdoğan announced a democratization package at the end of September, the reforms were far from addressing the critical Kurdish demands. The package included some of the Kurdish demands such as lifting the ban on election propaganda in languages other than Turkish, restoring the old names of villages and provinces, increasing penalties for hate crimes, removal of the pledge of allegiance in elementary schools, revoking the ban on the use of the letters x, q, and w, and permission for private schools to teach in languages other than Turkish; however, it did not address the anti-terror law or Kurdish-language education in public schools. It was vague on the issue of lowering the 10 percent national electoral threshold as the prime minister announced that the issue would be discussed in parliament.[7] In response, the KCK expressed its frustration with the democratization package and warned the government of a possible suspension of the ceasefire. To advance the peace process it demanded the recognition of "democratic autonomy," a vague term that suggests decentralization and local autonomy, recognition of Kurdish identity in the constitution, and the recognition of Kurdish-language education (*Hürriyet Daily News* 2013).

As the rocky peace process in Turkey suggests, once ethnic wars start, they become exceedingly difficult to end. Today the resolution of the Kurdish conflict requires successful bargaining over the demobilization of the PKK and integration of PKK militants into Turkey's economic and political life, as well as over an administrative arrangement to address Kurdish demands for local autonomy. While there has not yet been a serious public backlash over the accommodation of Kurdish cultural demands, a discussion of federalism or a general amnesty for the PKK militants or Öcalan is likely to create major opposition from the Turkish

---

[6] Turkey's electoral law requires a party to receive a minimum of 10 percent of the national vote to secure representation in parliament. Such a high threshold has forced the pro-Kurdish party members to run as independents in the elections to enter parliament. The threshold has caused significant problems for fair competition in the elections for the pro-Kurdish parties. For a longer discussion, see International Crisis Group (2011, 20–21).
[7] See Kurban (2013).

public. In the absence of strong checks on government behavior, such as an independent judiciary or a strong media, which can hold the government accountable and guarantee the enforcement of a possible peace agreement, the PKK will be reluctant to disarm. Although Turkey has gone a long way in its attempts to address the Kurdish problem, the resolution of the conflict seems quite unlikely in the foreseeable future at the time of writing.

Since February 2011, the Moroccan monarchy has been under growing pressure from street protests, which mobilized as part of the Arab Spring, demanding democratization, an independent judiciary, and the protection of human rights in Morocco. The Amazigh activists have been an integral part of the demonstrations, known as the "February 20 movement," openly carrying Amazigh flags and banners written in Tamazight. As is usual in Moroccan political history, instead of resorting to outright repression, the monarchy responded to the protests with immediate promises of political reform. A constitutional reform commission appointed by the king amended the constitution. While the new constitution incorporated many human rights provisions that were not recognized in the previous constitution, such as the rights to life, a fair trial, physical and moral integrity, protection of privacy, access to information, and health care, it fell short of addressing the demands for democratization. The constitution did not make any substantial changes in the executive powers of the king. While the new constitution no longer characterizes him as "sacred," he is still the highest religious authority as the "commander of the faithful." The royal decrees (*dahir*) are incontestable. The king retains the power to appoint the head of the government and government ministers, to dissolve the parliament, command the military, and preside over the Higher Judicial Council (Madani *et al.* 2012). Although its critics denounced the new constitution as merely bringing cosmetic changes (Benchemsi 2012), the king's immediate response and promise of reform along with the deeply divided nature of the opposition slowed down the protests.

One of the most important changes that the new constitution brought was making Tamazight an official language alongside Arabic. The new constitution explicitly recognizes the ethnic and religious diversity in the country and defines Moroccan unity as a convergence of Arab-Islamic, Amazigh, and Saharan components, enriched by the African, Andalusian, Jewish, and Mediterranean cultures.[8] What concrete policies

---

[8] The full text of the constitution in French can be accessed at www.maroc.ma.

Conclusion

the constitutionalization of Tamazight will bring is not clear as its actual implementation awaits a law to be passed by the government headed by the Islamist Justice and Development Party that opposes Amazigh demands. However, the constitutionalization of Tamazight once again underlines the plasticity of Moroccanness, as defined by the monarchy.

The recognition of Tamazight as an official language did not stop Amazigh activists from pushing the regime further. They have publicized the discriminatory practices of state officials against Berbers, organized conferences that question official history, and lobbied for the expansion of Tamazight education and integration of Tamazight in official domains. In March 2013, Rachid Raha, the publisher of *Le Monde Amazigh*, wrote an open letter to the king, criticizing the government and complaining that the constitutionalization of Tamazight has not yet led to any practical consequences.[9] Today many Amazigh activists also advocate a wide range of political objectives that go beyond linguistic and cultural rights. They believe that recognition of diversity can only be meaningful in a fully democratic system. They are vocal in their demands for democratization, separation of powers, judicial independence, and increasing rights for women. Some call attention to the regional disparities in development and question the state's appropriation of communal lands.[10] Others demand the secularization of the state. Rachid Raha, for instance, explicitly criticizes the religious foundations of the monarchy. He argues that the monarchy should not legitimize itself through religious credentials and that there should be a complete separation of religion and state.[11] Another prominent member of the movement and a researcher at IRCAM, Ahmed Assid, takes issue with the content of school textbooks of religion, arguing that religious education in Morocco is outdated and teaches values that contradict basic human rights. Such remarks by Amazigh activists have provoked significant reaction from Morocco's Islamist movement (Saadouni 2013). Amazigh activism continues to be a vibrant opposition movement and has been an integral part of the "February 20 Movement," protesting against widespread corruption, lack of civil liberties and democracy, and high unemployment. The ability of the "February 20 Movement" to challenge the regime is yet uncertain. It will depend on several factors, such

---

[9] For the French translation of the letter, see www.depechedekabylie.com/contribution/125705-amazighite-respect-de-la-constitution-et-democratisation-du-maroc.html (accessed December 10, 2013).

[10] See, for instance, the 2013 declaration by AZETTA: www.amazighworld.org/human_rights/index_show.php?id=4161 (accessed January 5, 2014).

[11] Interview with Rachid Raha, March 9, 2007, Rabat.

as its ability to forge a broad-based alliance, stay united, and develop effective strategies of protest over the long term. It will also depend on the outcomes of regime change in the Arab world, as well as, obviously, the economic situation of the country.

Four major implications emerge from this study. First, it underlines that there are different paths to state- and nation-building, which have different consequences for state–minority relations. The European model of the nation-state was not simply exported to non-European contexts. This study builds on and challenges the Eurocentric models of state-building, which see state centralization as a process in opposition to local strongmen, particularly as a result of the state's pacification through coercion. Post-colonial Moroccan political history shows that the European model of the nation-state was not simply imported to non-European contexts because there are alternative paths to state and nation-building. Faced with a highly fragmented society and a weak state structure in 1956, the monarchy, in centralizing its authority and expanding its rule over the society, allied with the tribal authorities and rural notables by integrating them into the state's administrative structure and providing them with material advantages, rather than attacking their power base. The Moroccan example contradicts the assumption of most of the state-building literature, by suggesting that modern state-building can occur without eliminating local power centers or without a major clash between a consolidating state and local social forces.

Second, I argue that nation-building can actually hurt state-building by weakening a state's ability to exercise effective social control and legitimize its rule. Although the predominant conceptions of nation-building posit that building a homogeneous nation is essential to building a strong state, this study shows that top-down attempts at homogenization may actually weaken a state's ability to expand and legitimize its rule. In Turkey, the state elite's insistence on social homogeneity and its forceful intrusions into the Kurdish society have curtailed, paradoxically, its ability to penetrate the Kurdish regions. The Turkish state's rigidities and uncompromising attitude in its relations with the Kurds turned into a major constraint on the exercise of state authority in the Kurdish regions. This book highlights that state- and nation-building processes might not always be mutually reinforcing.

Third, this study underlines that state strength and weakness may have ironic and unintended consequences. My case studies suggest that state weakness and strength are not absolute categories but should be conceptualized as contextual and variable. In Morocco, the state's initial weakness in terms of its lower coercive and administrative power and higher dependence on the support of social power centers gave the regime its major strength: adaptability. Such weakness has forced the state to be more flexible and made it more capable of preventing conflict and sustaining stability than states that have more coercive and autonomous power, like Turkey. It has created a state with limited aims in shaping its society, at the expense of state-led economic and social development, as well as a state that for its survival has been more adaptable to changing circumstances and emerging challenges.

Finally, this study shows that the institutional and ideological legacies of states shape modern state and nation formation. It discusses the significant consequences of the Ottoman reforms of state centralization and Westernization for the institutional and ideological shape of the Turkish Republic. In the Moroccan case, the historical legacy of a weak central authority and a strong tribal society, coupled with the colonial experience, influenced its post-colonial nation-building policies. This approach is in line with Bayart's (1991, 54) idea of "historical trajectory," which suggests that the ruptures in states' histories "take on their critical significance as a result of their own distinct histories." In Turkey, the historical trajectory of a strong center led to attempts at the "extreme makeover" of society that paradoxically weakened the state by increasing resistance in Kurdish areas. In Morocco, by contrast, the historical trajectory of a weak state led to a more accommodating and flexible nation-building that has allowed the Moroccan state to gradually assert its rule over society.

Bibliography

Archives

BCA Başbakanlık Cumhuriyet Arşivi (Prime Ministry's Republican Archives, Turkey)
Catalogue numbers of archival documents used in the book:
490.01: Cumhuriyet Halk Partisi (Republican People's Party)
030.10: Başbakanlık Muamelat Genel Müdürlüğü (Prime Ministry General Directorate of Documentation)

Newspapers and periodicals

Turkey
Bulletin de Liaison et d'Information, Institut Kurde de Paris
Cumhuriyet (Istanbul)
Demokrat Türkiye (Urfa)
Diyarbakır Sesi (Diyarbakır)
Diyarbakır Söz (Diyarbakır)
Hürriyet (Istanbul)
Milliyet (Istanbul)
Nokta (Istanbul)
Özgürlük Yolu (Ankara)
Radikal (Istanbul)
TBMM Zabıt Ceridesi (Journal of Proceedings of the Turkish Grand National Assembly)
Urfa İçin Hizmet (Urfa)
Yankı (Istanbul)
Yeni Akış (Ankara)
Yeni Gündem (Istanbul)
Morocco
Amazigh: Revue Marocain D'Histoire et De Civilisation (Rabat)
Bulletin d'Information de L'Institut Royal de la Culture Amazighe (Rabat)

Bulletin Officiel (Rabat)
Jeune Afrique/L'Intelligent (Paris)
Le Journal Hebdomadaire (Casablanca)
Le Matin du Sahara et du Maghreb (Rabat)
Le Monde Amazigh (Rabat)
Le Petit Marocain (Rabat)
Le Reporter (Casablanca)
L'Opinion (Rabat)
Maroc Soir (Rabat)
Revue Tifinagh (Rabat)
Tamunt (Rabat)
Tel Quel (Casablanca)

List of interviewees

On Turkey
Abdullah Demirbaş, June 2006, Diyarbakır.
Abdullah Keskin, September 2006, Istanbul.
Abdullah Yıldız, April 2006, Şanlıurfa.
Ali Akıncı, June 2006, Diyarbakır.
Ali Fuat Bucak, April 2006, Şanlıurfa.
Ayfer Yürük, June 2006, Diyarbakır.
Canip Yıldırım, June 2006, Ankara.
Cemal Doğan, June 2006, Diyarbakır.
Cengiz Çandar, August 2006, Istanbul.
Cevahir Sadak Düzgün, May 2006, Diyarbakır.
Davut Dursun, June 2006, Ankara.
Edip Polat, June 2006, Diyarbakır.
Evrim Alataş, May 2006, Diyarbakır.
Filiz Buluttekin, May 2006, Diyarbakır.
Hamit Bozarslan, May 2007, Paris.
İsmail Dağ, May 2006, Şanlıurfa.
Mehmet Baykara, September 2006, Istanbul.
Mehmet Kuyurtar, May 2006, İzmir.
Melike Coşkun, June 2006, Diyarbakır.
Mesut Yeğen, June 2006, Ankara.
Mithat Sancar, June 2006, Ankara.
Muhsin Kızılkaya, June 2009, Istanbul.
Nebahat Akkoç, June 2006, Diyarbakır.
Nedret Bilici, May 2006, Diyarbakır.
Ömer Kurt, May 2006, Şanlıurfa.
Orhan Miroğlu, June 2006, Ankara.
Ruşen Arslan, August 2006, Istanbul.
Şefik Beyaz, September 2006, Istanbul.
Sezgin Tanrıkulu, May 2006, Diyarbakır.
Tarık Ziya Ekinci, August 2006, Istanbul.
Ümit Fırat, August 2006, Istanbul.

On Morocco
Abdellah Kassi, December 2006, Rabat.
Abderrahmane Lakhsassi, November 2006, Rabat.
Abdulkareem Afoulay, November 2006, Rabat.
Ahmed Adghirni, December 2006, Rabat.
Ahmed Arehmouch, December 2006, Rabat.
Ahmed Boukouss, March 2007, Rabat.
Ahmed Assid, October 2006, Rabat.
Ali Amahan, April 2007, Rabat.
Amina Bouayach, March 2007, Rabat.
Amina Ibnou-Cheikh, December 2006, Rabat.
Fatima Agnaou, February 2007, Rabat.
Hamid Lihi, December 2006, Rabat.
Hammou Azday, April 2007, Rabat.
Hassan Id Belkassm, December 2006, Rabat.
Ibrahim Akhiyat, October 2006, Rabat.
Meryem Demnati, November 2006, Rabat.
Mohamed Ajaajaa, April 2007, Meknés.
Mounir Kejji, March 2007, Rabat.
Mustapha Buziani, December 2006, Rabat.
Mustapha Qadéry, April 2007, Rabat.
Omar Chiban, March 2007, Rabat.
Ouzzin Aherdane, January 2007, Rabat.
Rachid Raha, March 2007, Rabat.
Saida Kouzzi, March 2007, Rabat.

Books and articles

Abouzaid, Myriam. 2005. *L'Aménagement de la Langue Amazighe au Maroc: Enjeux et Réception Auprès des Enseignants*. MA thesis, Université Stendhal, Grenoble III.
Abrahamian, Ervand. 1982. *Iran Between the Two Revolutions*. Princeton University Press.
Adghirni, Ahmed. 2006. "Mémorandum au Sujet de la Constitution Adressé par le PDAM au Roi Mohammed VI." *Le Monde Amazigh*, July–August.
Ahmad, Feroz. 1993. *The Making of Modern Turkey*. London, New York: Routledge.
Aït Mous, Fadma. 2006. "Réseau Associatif Amazigh: Émergence et Diffusion." In *Usages de l'Identité Amazighe au Maroc*, edited by Hassan Rachik, 129–161. Casablanca: Imprimerie Najah el Jadida.
Akekmekçi, Tuba and Muazzez Pervan, eds. 2010. *Doğu Sorunu: Necmeddin Sahir Sılan Raporları (1939–1953)*. Necmeddin Sahir Sılan Arşivi-1. Istanbul: Tarih Vakfı Yurt Yayınları.
Aktar, Ayhan. 2000. *Varlık Vergisi ve Türkleştirme Politikaları*. Istanbul: İletişim Yayınları.
Aktoprak, Elçin. 2010. "The Kurdish Opening and the Constitutional Reform: Is There Any Progress?" *European Yearbook of Minority Issues* 9: 643–667.

Aktürk, Şener. 2012. *Regimes of Ethnicity and Nationhood in Germany, Russia, and Turkey*. New York: Cambridge University Press.
Alami, Younès, Omar Brouksy, and Nadia Hachimi Alaoui. 2004. "Que Veulent Les Berbères?" *Le Journal Hebdomadaire*, October 30–November 4.
Alaoui, Ahmed. 1980. "Defense et Illustration de la Culture Berbère." *Maroc Soir*, March 27.
  1992. "Il y a 62 Ans le Dahir Berbère." *Maroc Soir*, May 16.
Ali, Siham. 2012. "Morocco Expands Tamazight Teaching." *Magharebia*, September 12. Available at http://magharebia.com/en_GB/articles/awi/features/2012/09/12/feature-04 (accessed October 2, 2013).
Anderson, Benedict. 1991. *Imagined Communities: Reflections on the Origin and Spread of Nationalism*. London: Verso.
Anderson, Lisa. 2000. "Dynasts and Nationalists: Why Monarchies Survive." In *Middle East Monarchies: The Challenge of Modernity*, edited by Joseph Kostiner, 53–69. Boulder, CO: Lynne Rienner.
Anter, Musa. 1999. *Hatıralarım (1–2)*. Istanbul: Avesta Yayınları.
Arslan, Ruşen. 2006. *Şeyh Said Ayaklanmasında Varto Aşiretleri ve Mehmet Şerif Fırat Olayı*. Istanbul: Doz Yayınları.
Arsu, Şebnem. 2013. "Kurdish Rebel Group to Withdraw from Turkey." *New York Times*, April 26. Available at www.nytimes.com/2013/04/26/world/europe/kurdish-rebel-group-to-withdraw-from-turkey.html?_r=0 (accessed September 9, 2013).
Ashford, Douglas E. 1959. "Politics and Violence in Morocco." *The Middle East Journal* 13 (1): 11–25.
  1961. *Political Change in Morocco*. Princeton University Press.
Aslan, Senem. 2007. "Citizen, Speak Turkish! A Nation in the Making." *Nationalism and Ethnic Politics* 13 (2): 245–272.
  2009. "Incoherent State: The Controversy over Kurdish Naming in Turkey." *European Journal of Turkish Studies* 10. Available at http://ejts.revues.org/4142.
  2011. "Everyday Forms of State Power and the Kurds in the Early Turkish Republic." *International Journal of Middle East Studies* 43 (1): 75–93.
  2013. "Negotiating National Identity: Berber Activism and the Moroccan State." In *The Everyday Life of the State: A State-In-Society Approach*, edited by Adam White, 176–188. Seattle, WA: University of Washington Press.
Ataman, Muhittin. 2002. "Özal Leadership and the Restructuring of Turkish Ethnic Policy in the 1980s." *Middle Eastern Studies* 38 (4): 123–143.
Avar, Sıdıka. 2004. *Dağ Çiçeklerim: Anılar*. Fourth Edition. Ankara: Öğretmen Dünyası Yayınları.
Aygün, Hüseyin. 2011. *Dersim 1938 ve Zorunlu İskan*. Fifth Edition. Ankara: Dipnot.
Balta, Evren. 2004. "Causes and Consequences of the Village Guard System in Turkey." Unpublished paper. Available at http://web.gc.cuny.edu/dept/rbins/IUCSHA/fellows/Balta-paper.pdf (accessed August 3, 2012).
Barkey, Henri J. and Graham E. Fuller. 1997. "Turkey's Kurdish Question: Critical Turning Points and Missed Opportunities." *The Middle East Journal* 51 (1): 59–80.

Barkey, Karen. 1994. *Bandits and Bureaucrats: The Ottoman Route to State Centralization*. Ithaca, NY: Cornell University Press.

1997. "Thinking about Consequences of Empire." In *After Empire: Multiethnic Societies and Nation-Building*, edited by Karen Barkey and Mark Von Hagen, 99–114. Boulder, CO: Westview.

Bayart, Jean-François. 1991. "Finishing With the Idea of the Third World: The Concept of the Political Trajectory." In *Rethinking Third World Politics*, edited by James Manor, 51–71. London: Longman.

Bayrak, Mehmet, ed. 1994. *Açık-Gizli/Resmi-Gayriresmi Kürdoloji Belgeleri*. Ankara: Özge Yayınları.

Bedirhan, Celalet Ali. 1997. *Kürt Sorunu Üzerine: Kürtlerin Sürgün Edilmesi ve Dağıtılması Yasası*. Translated by Taylan Doğan. Istanbul: Avesta Yayınları.

Belge, Ceren. 2011. "State Building and the Limits of Legibility: Kinship Networks and Kurdish Resistance in Turkey." *International Journal of Middle East Studies* 43 (1): 95–114.

Ben Kaddour, Abdaslam. 1972. "The Neo-Makhzan and the Berbers." In *Arabs and Berbers: From Tribe to Nation in North Africa*, edited by Ernest Gellner and Charles Micaud, 259–267. Lexington, MA: Lexington Books.

Benchemsi, Ahmed R. 2001. "Berbères: La Victoire Tranquille." *Tel Quel*, November 12–18.

2006. "Le Culte de la Personnalité." *Tel Quel*, July 29–September 8.

2012. "Morocco: Outfoxing the Opposition." *Journal of Democracy* 23 (1): 57–69.

Beşikçi, İsmail. 1992. *Doğu Anadolu'nun Düzeni: Sosyo-Ekonomik ve Etnik Temeller*. Ankara: Yurt Kitap-Yayın.

Boone, Catherine. 2003. *Political Topographies of the African State: Territorial Authority and Institutional Choice*. Cambridge University Press.

Bora, Tanıl. 1986. "Adını Bilmesek de Bizim Köyümüzdür," *Yeni Gündem* 3 (29): 26–27.

Boukhari, Karim. 2005. "Amazighs: Bilan d'une Ouverture." *Tel Quel*, October 29–November 4.

Boum, Aomar. 2007. "Dancing for the Moroccan State: Ethnic Folk Dances and the Production of National Hybridity." In *North African Mosaic: A Cultural Reappraisal of Ethnic and Religious Minorities*, edited by Nabil Boudraa and Joseph Krause, 214–237. Newcastle-upon-Tyne: Cambridge Scholars Publishing.

Bourqia, Rahma. 1999. "The Cultural Legacy of Power in Morocco." In *In the Shadow of the Sultan: Culture, Power, and Politics in Morocco*, edited by Rahma Bourqia and Susan Miller, 243–258. Cambridge, MA: Harvard Center for Middle Eastern Studies.

Bozarslan, Hamit. 1988. "Les Revoltés Kurdes en Turquie Kémaliste (Quelques Aspects)." *Guerres Mondiales* 151: 121–136.

1996. "Political Crisis and the Kurdish Issue in Turkey." In *The Kurdish Nationalist Movement in the 1990s*, edited by Robert Olson, 135–153. Lexington, KY: University Press of Kentucky.

1997. *La Question Kurde: États et Minorités au Moyen-Orient*. Paris: Presses de Sciences Po.

2001. "Human Rights and the Kurdish Issue in Turkey: 1984–1999." *Human Rights Review* 3 (1): 45–54.

2003. "Some Remarks on Kurdish Historiographical Discourse in Turkey (1919–1980)." In *Essays on the Origins of Kurdish Nationalism*, edited by Abbas Vali, 14–39. Costa Mesa, CA: Mazda Publishers.
  2008. "Kurds and the Turkish State." In *The Cambridge History of Turkey, vol. IV: Turkey in the Modern World*, edited by Reşat Kasaba, 333–356. New York: Cambridge University Press.
Brass, Paul R. 1985. "Ethnic Groups and the State." In *Ethnic Groups and the State*, edited by Paul R. Brass, 1–56. Totowa, NJ: Barnes and Noble.
  1991. *Ethnicity and Nationalism: Theory and Comparison*. New Delhi, Newbury Park, CA: Sage Publications.
Brewer, John. 1990. *The Sinews of Power: War, Money and the English State, 1688–1783*. Cambridge, MA: Harvard University Press.
Brockett, Gavin D. 1998. "Collective Action and the Turkish Revolution: Towards a Framework for the Social History of the Atatürk Era, 1923–38." *Middle Eastern Studies* 34 (4): 44–66.
Brown, Michael E. 1997. "The Impact of Government Policies on Ethnic Relations." In *Government Policies and Ethnic Relations in Asia and the Pacific*, edited by Michael E. Brown and Šumit Ganguly, 511–576. Cambridge, MA: MIT Press.
Brubaker, Rogers. 1996. *Nationalism Reframed: Nationhood and the National Question in the New Europe*. New York: Cambridge University Press.
  2004. *Ethnicity Without Groups*. Cambridge, MA: Harvard University Press.
Brubaker, Rogers and David Laitin. 1998. "Ethnic and Nationalist Violence." *Annual Review of Sociology* 24: 423–452.
Bucak, Mustafa Remzi. 1991. *Bir Kürt Aydınından İsmet İnönü'ye Mektup*. Istanbul: Doz Yayınları.
Buckner, Elizabeth. 2006. "Language Drama in Morocco: Another Perspective on the Problems and Prospects of Teaching Tamazight." *The Journal of African Studies* 11 (4): 421–433.
Burkay, Kemal. 2001. *Anılar Belgeler*. Stockholm: Roja Nû Yayınları.
Burke III, Edmund. 1972. "The Image of the Moroccan State in French Ethnological Literature: A New Look at the Origin of Lyautey's Berber Policy." In *Arabs and Berbers: From Tribe to Nation in North Africa*, edited by Ernest Gellner and Charles Micaud, 175–199. Lexington, MA: Lexington Books.
Byman, Daniel. 1997–1998. "Explaining Ethnic Peace in Morocco." *Harvard Middle Eastern and Islamic Review* 4 (1–2): 1–29.
Çağaptay, Soner. 2004. "Race, Assimilation, and Kemalism: Turkish Nationalism and the Minorities in the 1930s." *Middle Eastern Studies* 40 (3): 86–101.
  2006. *Islam, Secularism, and Nationalism in Modern Turkey: Who Is a Turk?* London, New York: Routledge.
Çakan, Şeyhmus. 2005. "Artık Kürtçe Kurs Yok." *Radikal*. August 2. Available at www.radikal.com.tr/haber.php?haberno=160362 (accessed August 10, 2007).
Çalışlar, Oral. 2009. "En çok şehit Şırnak'tan." *Radikal*, September 5.
Çandar, Cengiz. 2012. *"Leaving the Mountain": How May the PKK Lay Down Arms?* Istanbul: TESEV Publications. Available at www.tesev.org.tr/%E2%80%98leaving-the-mountain%E2%80%99--how-may-the-pkk-lay-down-arms-freeing-the-kurdish-question-from-violence/Content/377.html (accessed September 25, 2013).

Cemal, Hasan. 2003. *Kürtler*. Istanbul: Doğan Kitap.
  2011. *Barışa Emanet Olun! Kürt Sorununa Yeni Bakış*. Istanbul: Everest Yayınları.
Chafik, Mohamed. 2005. Interview by Driss Ksikes. *Tel Quel*, June 18–24.
Charrad, Mounira. 2001. *States and Women's Rights: The Making of Postcolonial Tunisia, Algeria, and Morocco*. Berkeley, CA: University of California Press.
Cizre Sakallıoğlu, Ümit. 1997. "The Anatomy of the Turkish Military's Political Autonomy." *Comparative Politics* 29 (2): 151–166.
Claisse, Alain. 1987. "Makhzen Traditions and Administrative Channels." In *The Political Economy of Morocco*, edited by William Zartman, 34–58. New York: Praeger.
Çolak, Yılmaz. 2004. "Language Policy and Official Ideology in Early Republican Turkey." *Middle Eastern Studies* 40 (6): 67–91.
Coram, A. 1972. "Note on the Role of the Berbers in the Early Days of Moroccan Independence." In *Arabs and Berbers: From Tribe to Nation in North Africa*, edited by Ernest Gellner and Charles Micaud, 269–276. Lexington, MA: Lexington Books.
Corrigan, Philip and Derek Sayer. 1985. *The Great Arch: English State Formation as Cultural Revolution*. Oxford: Basil Blackwell.
Crawford, David. 2001. *Work and Identity in the Moroccan High Atlas*. PhD dissertation, University of California Santa Barbara.
  2002. "Morocco's Invisible Imazighen." *The Journal of North African Studies* 7 (1): 53–70.
Csergo, Zsuzsa. 2007. *Talk of the Nation: Language and Conflict in Romania and Slovakia*. Ithaca, NY: Cornell University Press.
Cumhuriyet. 1991a. "Kürtçe Mağdurları." January 28.
  1991b. "Kürtçe Kaset Tartışması." February 4.
  2002. "Şirvan'dan Baran'a onay." May 22.
Cumhuriyet Dergi. 1998. "Makul Olun, Kapanmayın." February 1.
Daadaoui, Mohamed. 2011. *Moroccan Monarchy and the Islamist Challenge*. New York: Palgrave Macmillan.
Demirel, Ahmet. 2011. "Representation of the Eastern and Southeastern Provinces in the Turkish Parliament During the National Struggle and Single-Party Era." *New Perspectives on Turkey* 44: 73–102.
Demokrat Türkiye. 1961a. "Şapka Kanununa Muhalefet." February 13.
  1961b. "Şehir Haberleri: Şapka Kanununa Muhalefet." March 9.
Denoeux, Guilain and Abdeslam Maghraoui. 1998. "King Hassan's Strategy of Political Dualism." *Middle East Policy* 5 (4): 104–131.
Deutsch, Karl W. 1966. *Nationalism and Social Communication*. Cambridge, MA: MIT Press.
Devrimci Doğu Kültür Ocakları Dava Dosyası I. 1975. Ankara: Komal Yayınları.
Diken, Şeyhmus. 2005. *İsyan Sürgünleri*. Istanbul: İletişim Yayınları.
Downes, Alexander. 2004. "The Problem with Negotiated Settlements to Ethnic Civil Wars." *Security Studies* 13 (4): 230–279.
Dündar, Fuat. 1999. *Türkiye Nüfus Sayımlarında Azınlıklar*. Istanbul: Doz Yayınları.

Düzel, Neşe. 2003. "Bakan İşkence Davasını Engelledi." *Radikal*. August 25. Available at www.radikal.com.tr/turkiye/bakan_iskence_davasini_engelledi-681023 (accessed September 9, 2008).
Eickelman, Dale F. 1987. "Religion and Polity in Society." In *The Political Economy of Morocco*, edited by William Zartman, 84–97. New York: Praeger.
Eisenstadt, Shmuel Noah. 1973. *Traditional Patrimonialism and Modern Neopatrimonialism*. Beverly Hills, CA: Sage Publications.
  1978. *Revolution and the Transformation of Societies: A Comparative Study of Civilizations*. New York: The Free Press.
Ekinci, Tarık Ziya. 2010. *Lice'den Paris'e Anılarım*. Istanbul: İletişim Yayınları.
Erdem, Tarhan and Selçuk Erez, eds. 1963. *Kuruluşlarının Yıldönümü Halkevleri (1932–1951–1963)*. Istanbul: Cumhuriyet Halk Partisi İstanbul İl Gençlik Kolu Yayını.
Errihani, Mohammed. 2006. "Language Policy in Morocco: Problems and Prospects of Teaching Tamazight." *The Journal of African Studies* 11 (2): 143–154.
Fearon, James D. and David D. Laitin. 2003. "Ethnicity, Insurgency, and Civil War." *American Political Science Review* 97 (1): 75–90.
Fırat News. 2013. "Bayık: Legal Assurance Needed for Withdrawal." April 2. Available at http://en.firatnews.com/news/news/bayik-legal-assurance-needed-for-withdrawal.htm (accessed September 9, 2013).
Frey, Frederick W. 1965. *The Turkish Political Elite*. Cambridge, MA: MIT Press.
Gellner, Ernest. 1969. "The Great Patron: A Reinterpretation of Tribal Rebellions." *European Journal of Sociology* 10 (1): 61–69.
  1972a. "Patterns of Rural Rebellion in Morocco During the Early Years of Independence." In *Arabs and Berbers: From Tribe to Nation in North Africa*, edited by Ernest Gellner and Charles Micaud, 361–374. Lexington, MA: Lexington Books.
  1972b. "Political and Religious Organization of the Berbers of the Central High Atlas." In *Arabs and Berbers: From Tribe to Nation in North Africa*, edited by Ernest Gellner and Charles Micaud, 59–66. Lexington, MA: Lexington Books.
  1981. *Muslim Society*. New York: Cambridge University Press.
  1983. *Nations and Nationalism*. Oxford: Blackwell.
Grandguillaume, Gilbert. 1983. *Arabisation et Politique Linguistique au Maghreb*. Paris: Editions G.-P. Maisonneuve et Larose.
Gränzer, Sieglinde. 1999. "Changing Discourse: Transnational Advocacy Networks in Tunisia and Morocco." In *The Power of Human Rights: International Norms and Domestic Change*, edited by Thomas Risse, Stephen C. Ropp, and Kathryn Sikkink, 109–133. New York: Cambridge University Press.
Gündoğan, Azat Zana. 2005. *The Kurdish Political Mobilization in the 1960s: The Case of the "Eastern Meetings."* MA Thesis, Ankara: The Middle East Technical University.
Güneş, Cengiz. 2012. "Explaining the PKK's Mobilization of the Kurds in Turkey: Hegemony, Myth, and Violence." *Ethnopolitics* 12 (3): 247–267.

Gunter, Michael M. 1990. *The Kurds in Turkey: A Political Dilemma*. Boulder, CO: Westview Press.
Gurr, Ted Robert. 2000. *Peoples Versus States: Minorities at Risk in the New Century*. Washington, DC: US Institute of Peace.
Hammoudi, Abdellah. 1997. *Master and Disciple: The Cultural Foundations of Moroccan Authoritarianism*. University of Chicago Press.
Hanioğlu, M. Şükrü. 2008. *A Brief History of the Late Ottoman Empire*. Princeton University Press.
Hansen, Thomas Blom and Finn Stepputat. 2001. "Introduction. States of Imagination." In *States of Imagination: Ethnographic Explorations of the Postcolonial State*, edited by Thomas Blom Hansen and Finn Stepputat, 1–38. Durham, NC: Duke University Press.
Hart, David M. 1972. "The Tribe in Modern Morocco: Two Case Studies." In *Arabs and Berbers: From Tribe to Nation in North Africa*, edited by Ernest Gellner and Charles Micaud, 25–58. Lexington, MA: Lexington Books.
    1999. "Rural and Tribal Uprisings in Post-colonial Morocco, 1957–60: An Overview and a Reappraisal." *The Journal of North African Studies* 4 (2): 84–102.
Hatt, Doyle G. 1996. "Establishing Tradition: The Development of Chiefly Authority in the Western High Atlas Mountains of Morocco, 1890–1990." *Journal of Legal Pluralism and Unofficial Law* 37/38: 123–154.
Hattabi, Jamal. 2005. *Les Constitutions du Royaume du Maroc*. Casablanca: Les Editions Maghrébines.
Hechter, Michael. 2000. *Containing Nationalism*. Oxford University Press.
Hobsbawm, Eric. 1989. *The Age of Empire 1875–1914*. New York: Vintage.
Hoffman, Katherine E. 2000. "Administering Identities: State Decentralization and Local Identification in Morocco." *The Journal of North African Studies* 5 (3): 85–100.
Horowitz, Donald L. 1985. *Ethnic Groups in Conflict*. Berkeley, CA: University of California Press.
Houdaïfa, Hachim. 2006. "Raciste Liste." *Le Journal Hebdomadaire*, March 11–17.
Huntington, Samuel P. 1968. *Political Order in Changing Societies*. New Haven, CT: Yale University Press.
Hurewitz, Jacob Coleman. 1969. *Middle East Politics: The Military Dimension*. New York: F.A. Praeger.
Hürriyet. 1986a. "Sayım Kitapçığına Kürtçe Nasıl Girdi?" June 19.
    1986b. "SHP'nin Doğu Raporu." September 5.
    1990a. "Resmi Dairelerde Kürtçe Konuşulabilir." June 13.
    1990b. "ANAP'li Halim Aras'a Kürtçe Soruşturması." June 28.
    2002. "Kadın Hakim Şirvan'dan Berivan'a Beraat." May 22.
    2009. "Kürdistan Kimlikte." October 28.
Hürriyet Daily News. 2005. "DEHAP Member Sentenced for Saying 'Good Day' in Kurdish." November 10. Available at www.hurriyetdailynews.com/default.aspx?pageid=438&n=dehap-member-sentenced-for-saying-good-day-in-kurdish-2005-10-11 (accessed October 10, 2007).

2013. "KCK Disappointed over Democratization Package, Gives Government Three Demands." October 10. Available at www.hurriyetdailynews.com/kck-disappointed-over-democratization-package-gives-govt-three-demands.aspx?pageID=238&nID=56064&NewsCatID=338 (accessed December 10, 2013).
İçduygu, Ahmet and Özlem Kaygusuz. 2004. "The Politics of Citizenship by Drawing Borders: Foreign Policy and the Construction of National Citizenship Identity in Turkey." *Middle Eastern Studies* 40 (6): 26–50.
İçduygu, Ahmet, Yılmaz Çolak, and Nalan Soyarık. 1999. "What Is the Matter With Citizenship? A Turkish Debate." *Middle Eastern Studies* 35 (4): 187–208.
İçişleri Bakanlığı. 1981. *Türkiye Mülki İdare Bölümleri, 1 Kasım 1980 Durumu*. Genel Yayın No: 408, Seri III, Sayı 4, Ankara.
İnsel, Ahmet, ed. 2001. *Kemalizm*. Modern Türkiye'de Siyasi Düşünce II. Istanbul: İletişim Yayınları.
International Crisis Group. 2011. *Turkey: Ending the PKK Insurgency*, Europe Report No. 213. Available at www.crisisgroup.org/en/regions/europe/turkey-cyprus/turkey/213-turkey-ending-the-pkk-insurgency.aspx (accessed May 4, 2012).
2012. *Turkey: The PKK and a Kurdish Settlement*, Europe Report No. 219. Available at www.crisisgroup.org/en/regions/europe/turkey-cyprus/turkey/219-turkey-the-pkk-and-a-kurdish-settlement.aspx (accessed December 20, 2013).
2013. *Crying "Wolf": Why Turkish Fears Need Not Block Kurdish Reform*, Europe Report No. 227. Available at www.crisisgroup.org/en/regions/europe/turkey-cyprus/turkey/227-crying-wolf-why-turkish-fears-need-not-block-kurdish-reform.aspx (accessed December 20, 2013).
Judson, Pieter M. 2006. *Guardians of the Nation: Activists on the Language Frontiers of Imperial Austria*. Cambridge, MA: Harvard University Press.
Kapferer, Bruce. 1988. *Legends of People, Myths of State: Violence, Intolerance, and Political Culture in Sri Lanka and Australia*. Washington, DC: Smithsonian Institution Press.
Karpat, Kemal. 1963. "The People's Houses in Turkey." *The Middle East Journal* 17: 55–67.
Kasaba, Reşat. 1993. "Populism and Democracy in Turkey, 1946–1961." In *Rules and Rights in the Middle East: Democracy, Law, and Society*, edited by Ellis Goldberg, Reşat Kasaba, and Joel S. Migdal, 43–68. Seattle, WA: University of Washington Press.
1994. "A Time and a Place for the Nonstate: Social Change in the Ottoman Empire During the 'Long Nineteenth Century'." In *State Power and Social Forces: Domination and Transformation in the Third World*, edited by Joel S. Migdal, Atul Kohli, and Vivienne Shue, 207–230. Cambridge University Press.
2009. *A Moveable Empire: Ottoman Nomads, Migrants, and Refugees*. Seattle, WA: University of Washington Press.
Kausch, Kristina. 2008. *Morocco: Negotiating Change with the Makhzen*. Working Paper. Madrid: FRIDE. Available at www.fride.org (accessed May 2, 2008).

Kaya, Ferzende. 2003. *Mezopotamya Sürgünü: Abdülmelik Fırat'ın Yaşam Öyküsü*. Istanbul: Anka Yayınları.

Keyder, Çağlar. 1987. *State and Class in Turkey: A Study in Capitalist Development*. London: Verso.

el-Khatir, Aboulkacem. 2005. *Nationalisme et Construction Culturelle de la Nation au Maroc: Processus et Réactions*. PhD Dissertation, Écoles des Hautes Études en Sciences Sociales.

Khoury, Philip S. and Joseph Kostiner. 1990. "Introduction: Tribes and the Complexities of State Formation in the Middle East." In *Tribes and State Formation in the Middle East*, edited by Philip S. Khoury and Joseph Kostiner, 1–22. Berkeley, CA: University of California Press.

King, Gary and Langche Zeng. 2001. "Replication Data for Improving Forecasts of State Failure." Available at http://gking.harvard.edu (accessed September 10, 2013).

Kirişci, Kemal. 2000. "Disaggregating Turkish Citizenship and Immigration Practices." *Middle Eastern Studies* 36 (3): 1–22.

Kirişci, Kemal and Gareth M. Winrow. 1997. *The Kurdish Question and Turkey: An Example of a Trans-state Ethnic Conflict*. London, Portland, OR: Frank Cass.

Klein, Janet. 2007. "Kurdish Nationalists and Non-Nationalist Kurdists: Rethinking Minority Nationalism and the Dissolution of the Ottoman Empire, 1908–1909." *Nations and Nationalism* 13 (1): 135–153.

Koca, Hüseyin. 1998. *Yakın Tarihten Günümüze Hükümetlerin Doğu-Güneydoğu Anadolu Politikaları*. Konya: Mikro Yayınları.

Koçak, Cemil. 2003. *Umumi Müfettişlikler (1927–1952)*. Istanbul: İletişim Yayınları.

Kohn, Hans. 1967. *The Idea of Nationalism: A Study in Its Origins and Background*. New York: Collier Books.

Kratochwil, Gabi. 1999. "Some Observations on the First World Amazigh Congress." *Die Welt des Islams* 39 (2): 149–158.

Kudat, Ayşe. 1975. "Patron–Client Relations: The State of the Art and Research in Eastern Turkey." In *Political Participation in Turkey: Historical Background and Present Problems*, edited by Engin Akarlı and Gabriel Ben-Dor, 61–87. Istanbul: Boğaziçi University Publications.

Kurban, Dilek. 2003. "Confronting Equality: The Need for Constitutional Protection of Minorities on Turkey's Path to the European Union." *Columbia Human Rights Law Review* 151 (35): 151–214.

2013. "Not a Roadmap for Peace." SWP Comments, German Institute for International and Security Affairs. Available at: www.swp-berlin.org/fileadmin/contents/products/comments/2013C35_kun.pdf (accessed December 25, 2013).

Kutlay, Naci. 1994. *49'lar Dosyası*. Istanbul: Fırat Yayınları.

1998. *Anılarım*. Istanbul: Avesta Yayınları.

Kymlicka, Will. 1995. *Multicultural Citizenship: A Liberal Theory of Minority Rights*. Oxford: Clarendon Press.

Laitin, David. 1992. *Language Repertoires and State Construction in Africa*. New York: Cambridge University Press.

1998. *Identity in Formation: The Russian-Speaking Populations in the Near Abroad.* Ithaca, NY: Cornell University Press.
Lamlili, Nadia. 2006. "La Bataille du Tamazight." *Tel Quel*, September 9–15.
Lawrence, Adria. 2007. *Imperial Rule and the Politics of Nationalism.* PhD Dissertation, University of Chicago.
Layachi, Azzedine. 1998. *State, Society, and Democracy in Morocco: The Limits of Associative Life.* Washington, DC: Center for Contemporary Arab Studies, Georgetown University.
  2005. "The Berbers in Algeria: Politicized Ethnicity and Ethnicized Politics." In *Nationalism and Minority Identities in Islamic Societies*, edited by Maya Shatzmiller, 195–228. Montreal: McGill-Queen's University Press.
Lehtinen, Terhi. 2003. *Nation à la Marge de l'État: La Construction Identitaire du Mouvement Culturel Amazigh dans l'Espace National Marocain et au-delà des Frontières Étatiques.* PhD Dissertation, Paris: Écoles des Hautes Études en Sciences Sociales.
Le Matin du Sahara et du Maghreb. 2001. "L'amazighité Appartient à Tous les Marocains." October 18.
Le Monde. 1984. "Le Prison de Diyarbakır: aux Extrêmes de l'Odieux." March 17.
Le Reporter. 2006. "Entretien avec Ahmed Aâssid." April 20.
Leveau, Rémy. 1976. *Le Fellah Marocain: Défenseur du Trône.* Paris: Presses de la Fondation Nationale des Sciences Politiques.
  1993. "Reflections on the State in the Maghreb." In *North Africa: Nation, State, and Region*, edited by George H. Joffé, 247–265. New York: Routledge.
Lewendî, Malmîsanij and Mahmûd Lewendî. 1989. *Rojnamegeriya Kurdi li Kurdistana Bakur û li Tirkiyê, 1908–1981.* Uppsala, Sweden: Wesanên Jîna Nû.
Lewis, Bernard. 1968. *The Emergence of Modern Turkey.* Second Edition. London: Oxford University Press.
Lewis, William H. 1960. "Rural Administration in Morocco." *The Middle East Journal* 14 (1): 45–60.
Linz, Juan J. 1993. "State Building and Nation Building." *European Review* 1 (4): 355–369.
L'Opinion. 1994. "41ème Anniversaire de la Révolution du Roi et du Peuple." August 22.
Lucas, Russell E. 2004. "Monarchical Authoritarianism: Survival and Political Liberalization in a Middle Eastern Regime Type." *International Journal of Middle East Studies* 36 (1): 103–119.
Lust-Okar, Ellen. 2005. *Structuring Conflict in the Arab World: Incumbents, Opponents, and Institutions.* Cambridge University Press.
  2006. "Elections under Authoritarianism: Preliminary Lessons from Jordan." *Democratization* 13: 456–471.
Lust-Okar, Ellen and Amaney A. Jamal. 2002. "Rulers and Rules: Reassessing the Influence of Regime Type on Electoral Law Formation." *Comparative Political Studies* 35 (3): 337–366.
McDowall, David. 1996. *A Modern History of the Kurds.* London: I.B.Tauris.
Madani, Mohamed, Driss Maghraoui, and Saloua Zerhouni. 2012. *The 2011 Moroccan Constitution: A Critical Analysis.* Stockholm: International

Institute for Democracy and Electoral Assistance. Available at www.idea.int/publications/the_2011_moroccan_constitution (accessed December 15, 2013).

Maddy-Weitzman, Bruce. 2001. "Contested Identities: Berbers, 'Berberism' and the State in North Africa." *The Journal of North African Studies* 6 (3): 23–47.

  2003. "Islamism, Moroccan-Style: The Ideas of Sheikh Yassine." *Middle East Quarterly* 10 (1): 43–51.

  2006. "Ethno-politics and Globalization in North Africa: The Berber Culture Movement." *The Journal of North African Studies* 11 (1): 71–83.

  2007. "Berber/Amazigh Memory Work." In *The Maghrib in the New Century: Identity, Religion and Politics*, edited by Bruce Maddy-Weitzman and Daniel Zisenwine, 50–71. Gainesville, FL: University Press of Florida.

  2011. *The Berber Identity Movement and the Challenge to North African States*. Austin, TX: University of Texas Press.

Malka, Haim and Jon B. Alterman. 2006. *Arab Reform and Foreign Aid: Lessons From Morocco*. Washington, DC: CSIS Press.

Malkki, Liisa H. 1995. *Purity and Exile: Violence, Memory, and National Cosmology among Hutu Refugees in Tanzania*. University of Chicago Press.

Mann, Michael. 1986. "The Autonomous Power of the State: Its Origins, Mechanisms, and Results." In *States in History*, edited by John A. Hall, 109–136. New York: Basil Blackwell.

Marais, Octave. 1972. "The Political Evolution of the Berbers in Independent Morocco." In *Arabs and Berbers: From Tribe to Nation in North Africa*, edited by Ernest Gellner and Charles Micaud, 277–283. Lexington, MA: Lexington Books.

  1973. "The Ruling Class in Morocco." In *Man, State, and Society in the Contemporary Maghrib*, edited by I. William Zartman, 181–200. New York: Praeger Publishers.

Marcus, Aliza. 1990. "Hearts and Minds in Kurdistan." *Middle East Report* 163: 41–42, 44.

  2007. *Blood and Belief: The PKK and the Kurdish Fight for Independence*. New York University Press.

Marley, Dawn. 2004. "Language Attitudes in Morocco Following Recent Changes in Language Policy." *Language Policy* 3 (1): 25–46.

Marx, Anthony. 2002. "The Nation-State and Its Exclusions." *Political Science Quarterly* 117 (1): 103–126.

Matur, Bejan. 2011. *Dağın Ardına Bakmak*. Istanbul: Timaş Yayınları.

Mayer, Ann Elizabeth. 1993–94. "Moroccans: Citizens or Subjects? A People at the Crossroads." *NYU Journal of International Law and Politics* 26: 63–105.

Mezran, Karim. 2002. *Negotiating National Identity: The Case of the Arab States of North Africa*. Rome: Antonio Pelicani.

  2007. *Negotiation and Construction of National Identities*. Leiden, Boston: Martinus Nijhoff Publishers.

Micaud, Charles. 1972. "Conclusion." In *Arabs and Berbers: From Tribe to Nation in North Africa*, edited by Ernest Gellner and Charles Micaud, 433–438. Lexington, MA: Lexington Books.

Migdal, Joel S. 1988. *Strong Societies and Weak States: State–Society Relations and State Capabilities in the Third World.* Princeton University Press.
———. 2001. *State in Society: Studying How States and Societies Transform and Constitute One Another.* Cambridge University Press.
Migdal, Joel S., Atul Kohli, and Vivienne Shue, eds. 1994. *State Power and Social Forces: Domination and Transformation in the Third World.* Cambridge University Press.
Miller, Susan Gibson. 2013. *A History of Modern Morocco.* New York: Cambridge University Press.
Milliyet. 2003. "Rodi'nin Adı Yok." February 13.
———. 2010. "26 Yılın Kanlı Bilançosu." June 24.
Miroğlu, Orhan. 2005. *Hevsel Bahçesinde Bir Dut Ağacı: Canip Yıldırım'la Söyleşi.* Istanbul: İletişim Yayınları.
Muller, Mark. 1996. "Nationalism and the Rule of Law in Turkey: The Elimination of Kurdish Representation During the 1990s." In *The Kurdish Nationalist Movement in the 1990s,* edited by Robert Olson, 173–200. Lexington, KY: University Press of Kentucky.
Mutlu, Servet. 2001. "Economic Bases of Ethnic Separatism in Turkey: An Evaluation of Claims and Counterclaims." *Middle Eastern Studies* 37 (4): 101–135.
Natali, Denise. 2005. *The Kurds and the State: Evolving National Identity in Iraq, Turkey, and Iran.* Syracuse University Press.
Nokta. 1986. "Düşünemeyecek Kadar Sporla Meşgul Ediyorum." October 26.
———. 1987a. "Zozan Oldu Suzan." February 15.
———. 1987b. "Bir Kürt Sorunu Var." May 9.
———. 1988a. "Zozanların Yasağı da Kalktı." February 14.
———. 1988b. "Arabeskin Kürtçesi." March 27.
———. 1988c. "Resmi Bir Itiraf: Kürtler Azınlıktır." June 19.
———. 1990. "Kürtçeye Özgürlük." June 3.
———. 1991. "10 Milyon Kürt Yarattık." February 10.
———. 1994. "Kürtçe Sözlü Hafif Türk Müzigi." May 1–7.
Nugent, David. 1994. "Building the State, Making the Nation: The Basis and Limits of State Centralization in 'Modern' Peru." *American Anthropologist* 96 (2): 333–369.
Öktem, Kerem. 2008. "The Nation's Imprint: Demographic Engineering and the Change of Toponyes in Republican Turkey." *European Journal of Turkish Studies* 7. Available at http://ejts.revues.org/2243 (accessed October 17, 2009).
Okutan, Nuri. 1964. "Kıyafet." *Demokrat Türkiye,* April 6.
Olson, Robert. 1989. *The Emergence of Kurdish Nationalism and the Sheikh Said Rebellion, 1880–1925.* Austin, TX: University of Texas Press.
Olson, Robert, ed. 1996. *The Kurdish Nationalist Movement in the 1990s.* Lexington, KY: University Press of Kentucky.
Olzak, Susan. 2006. *The Global Dynamics of Racial and Ethnic Mobilization.* Stanford University Press.
Onur, Necmi. 1979. *Unuttuğumuz Doğu.* Istanbul: Serhat Dağıtım Yayınları.
Oran, Baskın. 2004. *Türkiye'de Azınlıklar: Kavramlar, Lozan, İç Mevzuat, İçtihat, Uygulama.* Istanbul: TESEV Yayınları.

Özgen, Neşe. 2003. *Van-Özalp ve 33 Kurşun Olayı, Toplumsal Hafızanın Unutma ve Hatırlama Biçimleri*. Istanbul: TUSTAV.
Özgürlük Yolu. 1977a. "Dergimiz ve Yayınlarımız Üzerinde Artan Baskılar," 2 (23), April.
  1977b. "Kürtçe Yayın Yapma Hakkı Engellenemez," 3 (30), November.
Özoğlu, Hakan. 2001. "Nationalism and Kurdish Notables in the Late Ottoman–Early Republican Era." *International Journal of Middle East Studies* 33 (3): 383–409.
  2004. *Kurdish Notables and the Ottoman State: Evolving Identities, Competing Loyalties, and Shifting Boundaries*. Albany, NY: State University of New York Press.
Öztürkmen, Arzu. 1994. "The Role of People's Houses in the Making of National Culture in Turkey." *New Perspectives on Turkey* 11: 159–181.
Palazzoli, Claude, ed. 1974. *Le Maroc Politique: de L'Indépendance à 1973*. Paris: Sindbad.
Preece, Jennifer Jackson. 1997. "Minority Rights in Europe: From Westphalia to Helsinki." *Review of International Studies* 23: 75–92.
el-Qadéry, Mustapha. 1995. *L'État National et les Berbères: Le Cas du Maroc. Mythe Colonial et Négation Nationale*. PhD Dissertation, Université Paul Valéry, Montpellier III.
Rachid, Lhoussain. 2005. *The Memory Imprint: Amazigh Landmarks in the National Culture*. Translated by Mohamed Ouakrime. Rabat: Publications de l'IRCAM.
Rachik, Hassan. 2003. *Symboliser la Nation: Essai sur l'Usage des Identités Collectives au Maroc*. Casablanca: Editions Le Fennec.
  2006. "Construction de l'Identité Amazighe." In *Usages de l'Identité Amazighe au Maroc*, edited by Hassan Rachik, 13–66. Casablanca: Imprimerie Najah el Jadida.
Radikal. 2002. "Baran, Serhat Yasaklı." March 4.
  2009. "Ahmet Türk Meclis'te Kürtçe Konuştu, Yayın Kesildi." February 24. Available at www.radikal.com.tr/politika/ahmet_turk_mecliste_kurtce_konustu_yayin_kesildi-923251 (accessed March 9, 2009).
Radikal İki. 1998. "Yirmiiki Dilden Müzik." January 25.
Resmi Gazete. 1983. "Türkçeden Başka Dillerde Yapılacak Yayınlar Hakkında Kanun." No. 18199, October 22.
Robins, Philip. 1993. "The Overlord State: Turkish Policy and the Kurdish Issue." *International Affairs* 69 (4): 657–676.
Rollinde, Marguerite. 2003. "La Marche Verte: un Nationalisme Royal aux Couleurs de l'Islam." *Le Mouvement Social* 202: 133–151.
Romano, David. 2006. *The Kurdish Nationalist Movement: Opportunity, Mobilization, and Identity*. Cambridge University Press.
Ross, Marc Howard. 2007. *Cultural Contestation in Ethnic Conflict*. New York: Cambridge University Press.
Saadouni, Mohamed. 2013. "Comments About Islam Spark Morocco Firestorm." *Magharebia*, May 7. Available at http://magharebia.com/en_GB/articles/awi/features/2013/05/07/feature-04 (accessed October 10, 2013).

Sabahi, Seyed Farian. 2001. "The Literacy Corps in Pahlavi Iran (1963–1979): Political, Social, and Literary Implications." *Cahiers d'Études sur la Méditerranée Orientale et le Monde Turco-Iranien* 31: 191–222.
Safran, William. 2004. "Introduction: The Political Aspects of Language – Special Issue: Language, Ethnic Identity, and the State." *Nationalism and Ethnic Politics* 10 (1): 1–14.
Saib, Jilali, ed. 2004. *La Presse Amazighe État des Lieux et Perspectives d'Avenir.* Rabat: Publications de l'IRCAM.
Sater, James N. 2007. *Civil Society and Political Change in Morocco.* New York: Routledge.
Sayarı, Sabri. 1977. "Political Patronage in Turkey." In *Patrons and Clients in Mediterranean Societies*, edited by Ernest Gellner and John Waterbury, 103–113. London: Duckworth.
Scott, James C. 1985. *Weapons of the Weak: Everyday Forms of Peasant Resistance.* New Haven, CT: Yale University Press.
    1998. *Seeing Like a State: How Certain Schemes to Improve the Human Condition Have Failed.* New Haven, CT: Yale University Press.
    2009. *The Art of Not Being Governed: An Anarchist History of Upland Southeast Asia.* New Haven, CT: Yale University Press.
Scott, James C., John Tehranian, and Jeremy Mathias. 2002. "The Production of Legal Identities Proper to States: The Case of the Permanent Family Surname." *Comparative Studies in Society and History* 44 (1): 4–44.
Seddon, David. 1981. *Moroccan Peasants: A Century of Change in the Eastern Rif, 1870–1970.* Folkestone: Dawson.
Sirles, Craig A. 1999. "Politics and Arabization: The Evolution of Postindependence North Africa." *International Journal of the Sociology of Language* 137 (1): 115–129.
Snyder, Jack. 2000. *From Voting to Violence: Democratization and Nationalist Conflict.* New York, London: W. W. Norton & Company.
Snyder, Richard. 1992. "Explaining Transitions from Neopatrimonial Dictatorships." *Comparative Politics* 24 (4): 379–399.
Soifer, Hillel. 2008. "State Infrastructural Power: Approaches to Conceptualization and Measurement." *Studies in Comparative International Development* 43: 231–251.
Somer, Murat. 2004. "Turkey's Kurdish Conflict: Changing Context, and Domestic and Regional Implications." *The Middle East Journal* 58 (2): 235–254.
Spruyt, Hendrik. 2002. "The Origins, Development, Possible Decline of the Modern State." *Annual Review of Political Science* 5: 127–149.
Süphandağ, Kemal. 2001. *Ağrı Direnişi ve Haydaranlılar.* Istanbul: Fırat Yayınları.
Tapper, Richard. 1990. "Anthropologists, Historians, and Tribespeople on Tribe and State Formation in the Middle East." In *Tribes and State Formation in the Middle East*, edited by Philip S. Khoury and Joseph Kostiner, 48–73. Berkeley, CA: University of California Press.
Tekeli, İlhan. 1990. "Osmanlı İmparatorluğu'ndan Günümüze Nüfusun Zorunlu Yer Değiştirmesi." *Toplum ve Bilim* 50: 49–71.

Tel Quel. 2002–2003. "Hommage à Mohammed Chafik." December 28–January 10.
2007. "Histoire: Les Années de Plomb Version Amazighe." February 10–16.
Tezel, Yahya Sezai. 1982. *Cumhuriyet Dönemi İktisadi Tarihi*. Ankara: Yurt Yayınevi.
Tibi, Bassam. 1990. "The Simultaneity of the Unsimultaneous: Old Tribes and Imposed Nation-States in the Modern Middle East." In *Tribes and State Formation in the Middle East*, edited by Philip S. Khoury and Joseph Kostiner, 127–152. Berkeley, CA: University of California Press.
Tilly, Charles. 1992. *Coercion, Capital, and European States, AD 990–1990*. Cambridge, MA: Basil Blackwell.
  1994. "States and Nationalism in Europe 1492–1992." *Theory and Society* 23 (1): 131–146.
Today's Zaman. 2013. "Terrorist PKK Halts Withdrawal From Turkey, Maintains Cease-Fire." September 9. Available at www.todayszaman.com/news-325823-terrorist-pkk-halts-withdrawal-from-turkey-maintains-cease-fire.html (accessed December 10, 2013).
Toksoy, Nurcan. 2007. *Halkevleri: Bir Kültürel Kalkınma Modeli Olarak*. Ankara: Orion Yayınevi.
Toprak, Binnaz. 1981. *Islam and Political Development in Turkey*. Leiden: Brill.
Torunlu, Lamia. 1993. "Özal ve Kürtler." *Nokta*, April 17.
Tozy, Mohammed. 1993. "Islam and the State." In *Polity and Society in Contemporary North Africa*, edited by I. William Zartman and William M. Habeeb, 102–122. Boulder, CO: Westview Press.
Turan, Murat. 2011. *CHP'nin Doğu'da Teşkilatlanması (1923–1950)*. Istanbul: Libra.
Türkiye İnsan Hakları Vakfı. 1993. *Örneklerle Türkiye İnsan Hakları Raporu 1992*. Ankara: Türkiye İnsan Hakları Vakfı Yayınları.
  2003. *Örneklerle Türkiye İnsan Hakları Raporu 2002*. Ankara: Türkiye İnsan Hakları Vakfı Yayınları.
Türköz, Meltem F. 2004. *The Social Life of the State's Fantasy: Memories and Documents on Turkey's 1934 Surname Law*. PhD Dissertation, University of Pennsylvania.
Ülker, Erol. 2008. "Assimilation, Security, and Geographical Nationalization in Interwar Turkey: The Settlement Law of 1934." *European Journal of Turkish Studies* 7. Available at http://ejts.revues.org/2123 (accessed September 5, 2009).
UNDP (United Nations Development Programme). 2013. *Human Development Report*. Available at http://hdr.undp.org/en/2013-report (accessed January 2, 2014).
Üngör, Uğur Ümit. 2011. *The Making of Modern Turkey: Nation and State in Eastern Anatolia, 1913–1950*. Oxford University Press.
United Nations Economic Commission for Africa. 2010. *Land Policy in Africa: North Africa Regional Assessment*. Available at www.uneca.org/publications/land-policy-africa-north-africa-regional-assessment (accessed January 20, 2014).
Urfa İçin Hizmet. 1982a. "Okuma-Yazma Öğrenenlere Tohumluk ve Kredi Tahsisinde Öncelik Verilecek." December 10.

1982b. "Yatılı Okullarda Yemek Öncesinde, 'Tanrımıza Hamdolsun Milletimiz Varolsun' Denecek." November 3.
Van Bruinessen, Martin. 1984. "The Kurds in Turkey." *MERIP Reports* 121: 6–12, 14.
1992. *Agha, Shaikh, and State: The Social and Political Structures of Kurdistan*. London: Zed Books.
Varlık, M. Bülent, ed. 2010. *Umumi Müfettişler Toplantı Tutanakları-1936*. Ankara: Dipnot Yayınları.
Venema, Bernhard and A. Mguild. 2002. "The Vitality of Local Political Institutions in the Middle Atlas, Morocco." *Ethnology* 41 (2): 103–117.
Vinogradov, Amal and John Waterbury. 1971. "Situations of Contested Legitimacy in Morocco: An Alternative Framework." *Comparative Studies in Society and History* 13 (1): 32–59.
Vu, Tuong. 2010. "Studying the State Through State Formation." *World Politics* 62 (1), 148–175.
Wagner, Daniel A. and Abdelhamid Lotfi. 1980. "Traditional Islamic Education in Morocco: Sociohistorical and Psychological Perspectives." *Comparative Education Review* 24 (2): 238–251.
Waldner, David. 1999. *State Building and Late Development*. Ithaca, NY: Cornell University Press.
Walter, Barbara. 2009. "Bargaining Failures and Civil War." *Annual Review of Political Science* 12: 243–261.
Waltz, Susan. 1991. "Making Waves: The Political Impact of Human Rights Groups in North Africa." *The Journal of Modern African Studies* 29 (3): 481–504.
1995. *Human Rights and Reform: Changing the Face of North African Politics*. Berkeley, CA: University of California Press.
Waterbury, John. 1970. *The Commander of the Faithful: The Moroccan Political Elite – A Study in Segmented Politics*. New York: Columbia University Press.
Watts, Nicole F. 2000. "Relocating Dersim: Turkish State-Building and Kurdish Resistance, 1931–1938." *New Perspectives on Turkey* 23: 5–30.
2010. *Activists in Office: Kurdish Politics and Protest in Turkey*. Seattle, WA: University of Washington Press.
Weber, Eugen J. 1976. *Peasants into Frenchmen: The Modernization of Rural France, 1870–1914*. Stanford University Press.
Wedeen, Lisa. 1999. *Ambiguities of Domination: Politics, Rhetoric, and Symbols in Contemporary Syria*. University of Chicago Press.
Weiss, Meredith Leigh. 2006. *Protest and Possibilities: Civil Society and Coalitions for Political Change in Malaysia*. Stanford University Press.
White, Jenny. 2013. *Muslim Nationalism and the New Turks*. Princeton University Press.
Willis, Michael J. 2012. *Politics and Power in the Maghreb: Algeria, Tunisia and Morocco from Independence to the Arab Spring*. New York: Columbia University Press.
Wimmer, Andreas. 2008. "The Making and Unmaking of Ethnic Boundaries: A Multilevel Process Theory." *American Journal of Sociology* 113 (4): 970–1022.

Wimmer, Andreas, Lars-Erik Cederman, and Brian Min. 2009. "Ethnic Politics and Armed Conflict: A Configurational Analysis of a New Global Dataset." *American Sociological Review* 74: 316–337.

World Bank. Various Years. *World Development Indicators*. Available at http://data.worldbank.org/indicator (accessed January 3, 2014).

Wyrtzen, Jonathan. 2009. Constructing Morocco: The Colonial Struggle to Define the Nation, 1912–1956. PhD Dissertation, Georgetown University.

    2011. "Colonial State-Building and the Negotiation of Arab and Berber Identity in Protectorate Morocco." *International Journal of Middle East Studies* 43 (2): 227–249.

Yacine, Rachida. 1993. "The Impact of the French Colonial Heritage on Language Policies in Independent North Africa." In *North Africa: Nation, State, and Region*, edited by George Joffé, 221–232. London: Routledge.

Yalçın-Heckmann, Lale. 1990. "Kurdish Tribal Organization and Local Political Processes." In *Turkish State, Turkish Society*, edited by Andrew Finkel and Nükhet Sirman, 289–312. London, New York: Routledge.

Yanık, Lerna K. 2006. "Nevruz or Newroz? Deconstructing the Invention of a Contested Tradition in Contemporary Turkey." *Middle Eastern Studies* 42 (2): 285–302.

Yeğen, Mesut. 1996. "The Turkish State Discourse and the Exclusion of Kurdish Identity." In *Turkey: Identity, Democracy, Politics*, edited by Sylvia Kedourie, 216–229. London, Portland, OR: Frank Cass.

    2004. "Citizenship and Ethnicity in Turkey." *Middle Eastern Studies* 40 (6): 51–66.

    2007. "Turkish Nationalism and the Kurdish Question." *Ethnic and Racial Studies* 30 (1): 119–151.

Yeni Gündem. 1986a. "Tunceli: Valinin Türk Yaylası." February 21–March 9.

    1986b. "İrşad Çıkarması." November 9–15.

    1988. "Eziyet Resmi Görev mi Oldu?" October 14–20.

Yıldırım, Tuğba, ed. 2010. *Doğu Anadolu'da Toplumsal Mühendislik. Dersim-Sason (1934–1946)*. Necmeddin Sahir Sılan Arşivi-2. İstanbul: Tarih Vakfı Yurt Yayınları.

    2011. *Kürt Sorunu ve Devlet: Tedip ve Tenkil Politikaları (1925–1947)*. Necmeddin Sahir Sılan Arşivi-3. İstanbul: Tarih Vakfı Yurt Yayınları.

Yıldız, Ahmet. 2001. *Ne Mutlu Türküm Diyebilene*. İstanbul: İletişim Yayınları.

Yıldız, Kerim. 2005. *The Kurds in Turkey: EU Accession and Human Rights*. London: Pluto Press.

Yılmaz, Hale. 2013. *Becoming Turkish: Nationalist Reforms and Cultural Negotiations in Early Republican Turkey, 1923–1945*. Syracuse University Press.

Yücel, Müslüm. 1998. *Tekzip: Kürt Basın Tarihi*. İstanbul: Aram Yayınları.

Zahra, Tara. 2008. *Kidnapped Souls: National Indifference and the Battle for Children in the Bohemian Lands, 1900–1948*. Ithaca, NY: Cornell University Press.

Zarakol, Ayşe. 2011. *After Defeat: How the East Learned to Live with the West*. Cambridge University Press.

Zartman, I. William. 1964. *Morocco: Problems of New Power*. New York: Atherton Press.
  1987. "King Hassan's New Morocco." In *The Political Economy of Morocco*, edited by I. William Zartman, 1–33. New York: Praeger.
Zeghal, Malika. 2008. *Islamism in Morocco: Religion, Authoritarianism, and Electoral Politics*. Translated by George Holoch. Princeton, NJ: Markus Wiener Publishers.
Zürcher, Erik J. 1998. *Turkey: A Modern History*. London: I.B.Tauris.
  2004. "Institution Building in the Kemalist Republic: The Role of the People's Party." In *Men of Order: Authoritarian Modernization under Ataturk and Reza Shah*, edited by Erik J. Zürcher, 98–112. London, New York: I.B.Tauris.
  2007. "The Ottoman Legacy of the Kemalist Republic." In *State and the Subaltern: Modernization, Society and the State in Turkey and Iran*, edited by Touraj Atabaki, 95–110. London: I.B.Tauris.
  2010. *The Young Turk Legacy and Nation Building: From the Ottoman Empire to Atatürk's Turkey*. London: I.B.Tauris.

Index

Adghirni, Ahmed, 189
Agadir Charter, 174
Agadir Summer University, 168–169
Ağrı rebellions, 47–48
Aherdane, Mahjoub, 89, 90, 93, 169
Aherdane, Ouzzin, 169
Alaoui, Ahmed, 169–170, 177
Alevi, 50, 51, 133
Algeria, 14, 168, 171, 175, 186
Amazigh (journal), 169, 170
Amazigh activism
   Agadir Charter, 174
   Agadir Summer University, 168–169
   Berber activism in Algeria, influence of, 168
   concept of Moroccanness, 179
   concessions for dialogue with the state, 178–181
   emergence of, 111–112, 165–166, 167–168, 172–173
   February 20 movement, 202, 203–204
   from within IRCAM, 189–190
   ongoing political objectives, 203–204
   politicization of, 170–171
   relationship with the state, overview, 166–167
   resurgence, 1990s, 174–176
   role of Islam in Morocco, 180
   state repression of, 170–171
   state tolerance of, 167–170
   symbol of the Amazigh movement, 175, 176, 194
   see also Berber movement; state–Berber relations

Amazigh Manifesto, 2000, 179–180, 184–187
Amazigh organizations, 112–113
Anderson, Lisa, 16–17
Anter, Musa, 121–122
Anti-Terror Law (Turkey), 135, 141, 161–162
Aourid, Hassan, 185–186
Arabic language
   in the Amazigh Manifesto, 179, 180
   and Arabization, 27, 85–86, 107–109, 111
   and linguistic centralization, 11, 27, 85, 107
   and Moroccan identity, 27, 177–178, 179–180
   as sacred, 108–109, 180
   speakers of, Morocco, 84–85
Arabization, Morocco
   Arabic language, 27, 85–86, 107–109, 111
   Berber ethnic identity and, 85–86, 107–108
   as imperialism, 170
   Istiqlal Party policies, 85–86
   monarchy's non-promotion of, 106, 108–109
areas of dissidence
   difficult geography of, 10–11
   distinct culture, 11
   local elites, 5–6
   tribal regions, 6–7
Ashford, Douglas E., 26, 85, 86, 92, 93, 95
Assid, Ahmed, 190, 203

Index

Association Tilelli, 176, 177
Atatürk, Mustafa Kemal
  on linguistic uniformity, 62
  success of, 19, 37, 81, 83
  on traditional dress, 71–72
  on Westernization, 69
  see also Kemalism
Avar, Sıdıka, 36–37, 61, 78, 120
Aytuna, Hasip A., 42, 55, 61, 76
Azadi (Kurdish nationalist organization), 44
Azaykou, Ali Sidqi, 170–171
AZETTA (*Le Réseau Amazighe Pour la Citoyenneté*), 187–188

Barkey, Karen, 19, 23
Barzani, Mustafa, 13–14, 121–122, 125, 168
Basri, Driss, 184, 191
Belge, Ceren, 53, 138
Belkassm, Hassan Id, 170–171, 176, 179
Ben Barka, Mehdi, 93, 108
Berber Dahir, 12–13, 176–177
Berber language
  dialects, 11, 85–86, 90, 106
  naming of children, 190–191
  protection of, 169
  teaching of dialects, 177–178, 192
Berber movement
  demands for recognition, 27–28
  overview of, 2–3
  relationship with the state, 26, 27–28
  Royal Institute of Amazigh Culture (IRCAM), 164–165, 166, 184, 187–195, 203
  tribal uprisings, post-independence, 92, 93–96
  see also Amazigh activism; state–Berber relations
Berber Spring, Algeria, 168
Berbers
  under the Alawite dynasty, 8–9
  within areas of dissidence, 5
  cultural marginalization, 107–108
  culture, state tolerance of, 109–110
  difficult geographical location, 10–11
  distinct culture, 11
  under French colonial rule, 9–10, 83
  resistance to state domination, 1–2
  as tribal society, 7, 8–10
  see also rural notables (Berber); state–Berber relations

bilad al– makhzen, 4, 8, 85
bilad al-siba, 4, 8–9, 85
Boone, Catherine, 97–98
Bozarslan, Hamit, 44, 45, 48, 118, 124, 132, 133, 136
Brewer, John, 30–31
Brubaker, Rogers, 11, 28, 33, 40, 197
bureaucracy, and linguistic homogenization, 58–60
Burkay, Kemal, 125, 126, 128

Çağaptay, Soner, 48, 49, 51, 57, 58, 59, 62, 63
centralization, state
  Istiqlal Party policies, 86–87
  linguistic homogenization and, 11, 20–22, 58–60, 67–69
  relationship with local power centers, 23–25, 29, 31
Chafik, Mohamed, 184–185, 186–187
Charrad, Mounira, 6, 9, 25, 84, 86, 90–91, 96, 97, 101
cinema, Turkish, 66–67
colonialism
  Berbers under French colonial rule, 9–10, 83, 84, 88–89
  ethnic identities and conflict, 12–13
  French rule of Morocco, 9–10, 12–13, 81–82, 83
Commander of the Faithful, 102–103, 202
Court of Cassation, Turkey, 144, 146–148, 150–151
Crawford, David, 3, 10, 166
cultural autonomy, areas of dissidence, 11
cultural homogenization, state-building, 11, 20–22

Demirel, Süleyman, 139
Democracy Party (DEP), 141
Democratic Amazigh Moroccan Party (PDAM), 189
Democratic Opening (Turkey), 199–202
Democratic Party (DP)
  authoritarianism of, 121
  elections, 1950, 119–120
  formation, 114
  Kurdish support for, 118, 119
  oppression of Kurdish activism, 121–122
  policies for Kurdish inclusivity, 120
Democratic Society Party (DTP), 141, 150, 160, 199

Dersim
    autonomy of and state control
        policies, 50–51
    rebellion, 1937, 51–52
    see also Tunceli
despotic power, 30
detribalization (Morocco), 98–99
detribalization (Turkey)
    as key nation-building policy, 41–43
    policy reversal, RPP, 119
    post-1925 rebellion, 46
    resettlement policies, 48–50, 53–54
direct rule
    conflict with social actors, 6, 22
    within modern states, 6
divide-and-rule policies
    construction of ethnic categories, 12–13
    French colonial practices in Morocco, 9, 25–26, 88–89, 176–177
Diyarbakır, 54, 58, 65, 66, 77, 118, 121, 124, 131, 132, 134, 137, 149, 150, 151, 152, 155, 157, 160, 161
Diyarbakır Military Prison, 132
Doğan, Avni, 46–47, 59–60, 77–78
dress
    Kurdish traditional, freedom to wear, 120
    nationalism and traditional dress, Morocco, 104–105
    Westernization of the Kurds, 70, 72–74

education
    Kurdish language courses, 156–157, 158–160
    in the People's Houses, 75, 76
    and Turkish language dissemination, 64–65
Eisenstadt, Shmuel Noah, 24, 25
Ekinci, Tarık Ziya, 65, 73, 79, 121, 125
Elazığ, 55, 58, 74–75, 148–149
Elazığ Girls' Institute, 36–37, 61, 120
emirates (Kurdish), 7–8
Erdoğan, Recep Tayyip, 157, 159, 160, 200, 201
Ertan, Muhtar, 55, 60, 72
Esendal, Memduh Şevket, 59, 64, 74
ethnic conflict
    colonialism and, 12–13
    intra-ethnic conflict, 14
    negotiated settlements and, 199–200
    political system and, 13
    support from ethnic brethren, neighboring states, 13–14

ethnic identity
    Amazigh, promotion by IRCAM, 193–194
    Arabization, Morocco, 85–86, 107–108
    concept of, 33
    intra-ethnic conflict, 14
    Kurdish nationalism and, 40
    Kurdish people and Turkishness, 63–64
    state-led nationalism and, 21, 122
    support from ethnic brethren, neighbouring states, 13–14
    see also Moroccanness; Turkishness
European model, nation-state building, 23, 24, 204
extreme makeover, 4, 15–16, 35, 37, 56, 68–69, 116, 205

al-Fassi, Allal, 85–86, 109
February 20 movement, Morocco, 202, 203–204
feminist movements, Morocco, 183
France
    alliances with Berber rural notables, 83, 84, 88–89
    colonial rule of Morocco, 9–10, 12–13, 81–82, 83
    nation-building policies, 21
    relationship with the Sultan, 91
functionalist approaches, state-centric, 29–30

Gellner, Ernest, 9, 25, 67, 87, 88, 96, 103, 111, 124–125
gendarmerie, abuses of power, 54–56
Gulf War (1991), 140, 171–172
Gurr, Ted Robert, 10, 13, 14
Güven, Kenan, 133

Hammoudi, Abdellah, 101, 103, 104, 105
Hart, David M., 9, 25, 85, 88, 94, 95, 96
Hassan II of Morocco
    acceptance of rural status quo, 100–101
    consolidation of political power, 98
    on Moroccan identity, 107, 177–178
    patronage network of, 101–102
    response to international criticism of human rights, 172
    years of lead, 166
Hat Law (Turkey), 72–73, 123
Hechter, Michael, 5, 6, 22, 23, 58
Hobsbawm, Eric, 20–21
human rights
    during the Cold War, 173–174

in Morocco, 172, 183, 202
in Turkey, 136, 139, 156, 161, 173
identity, cultural
　Muslimhood and Turkishness, 56–57
　through language, 63
indirect rule
　empires and feudal states, 5–6
　transition to direct rule, 22
infrastructural power, 30
İnönü, Erdal, 139
Inspectorates General, RPP
　in the Dersim region, 51
　establishment of, 48
inspectors' reports, RPP
　gendarmerie abuses of power, 54–56
　non-Turkish-speaking Kurds, 59
International Crisis Group, 29, 142, 161, 162, 199
interventionist policies (Kurdish regions)
　during military rule, 123
　Kurdish names for children, state ban on, 143–151, 157
　music, state ban on, 142, 151–155
　post-military coup 1980, 130–131
　relaxation of, post-1961 elections, 123–124
　and rise of the PKK, 129–130, 136
　single-party era, Turkey (1923–50), 37–38
　see also Westernization of the Kurds
interventionist policies (Morocco)
　lack of intervention in Berber areas, 26, 106, 109–110, 165–166, 196–197
　state's minimal intervention in society, 105–106
　see also Istiqlal Party
Iran, 14, 17, 47, 64, 120, 129, 161
Iraq, Kurdish nationalism in, 13–14, 43, 121, 122, 125, 140
Islam
　Islamist challenge to Moroccan monarchy, 171–172, 183–184
　Muslimhood and Turkishness, 56–57, 132–133, 198
　nationalism and, Morocco, 87–88, 102–104, 107, 169–170, 177, 180
　popular, tolerance for in Morocco, 105–106
　power of the Kurdish ulema, 44
　religious education, Morocco, 203
Istiqlal Party
　anti-colonial involvement, 81–82
　Arabization policies of, 85–86
　conflict with Berber rural notables, 89, 92–93
　contrasted with the Popular Movement, 90
　detribalization policies, 98–99
　membership of, 85
　nationalism and Islam, 87–88
　post-independence policies, 26, 81
　power struggle with Mohammed V, 82–83, 91–92
　split within, 96–97
　state centralization, 86–87

jellaba, 80, 104–105
journals, Kurdish, 128
Justice and Charity Movement (Morocco), 171–172, 183–184
Justice and Development Party (AKP) (Turkey) election win, 157
　see also state–Kurdish relations
Justice and Development Party (PJD) (Morocco), 183–184, 192, 203

KADEK, 149
Karabekir, Kazım, 42–43
Kasaba, Reşat, 8, 18, 43, 123
Kaya, Şükrü, 58
Kemalism, 39, 122–123, 133, 157
Klein, Janet, 40
Kurdish activism
　administrative obstacles to rights granted, 158–159
　military oppression of, 127, 132
　overview of, 2
　political oppression of, 121–122, 141–142
　politicization of, 121–122, 125, 126–127
　pro-Kurdish parties, 140–141, 160, 161–162
　radicalization of, 127–128
　separation from the Turkish left, 126–127
　support for the Turkish Labor Party, 125–126
　urban-based intellectual elite, 115, 117–118, 120–121, 173
　see also Kurdish movement; Kurdistan Workers Party (PKK)
Kurdish autonomous region
　during Ottoman period, 7–8
　Treaty of Sèvres, 43, 62

Kurdish culture
  ban on Kurdish names for children, 143–151, 157
  as expression of resistance, 155–156
  military repression of, 1980s, 131, 133–135, 138
  music, politicization of, 142, 155
  politicization of, 141–142, 162–163
  relaxation of restrictions on, 139–140, 156–157
Kurdish language
  broadcasting in, 156, 158, 160
  courses in, 156–157, 158–160
  dialects, 11, 156–157, 159
  as disloyalty to the Turkish state, 62–63
  Law 2932, 134–135, 139, 141, 152
  laws against spoken Kurdish, 160–161
  politicalization of, 133–134
  relaxation of restrictions on, 141, 156–157
  state repression of, 61–62, 65
  suppression of under the military regime, 133–135
  use of the Kurdish alphabet, 150–151
  use of Kurdish names for children, 143–151, 157
Kurdish movement
  Ağrı rebellions, 47–48
  compared to Amazigh movement, 28, 115, 173
  Dersim rebellion, 51–52
  Sheikh Said Rebellion (1925), 44–48, 50, 60, 72, 79, 118
  state's intolerance for, 28, 31, 115–116, 126–127, 135, 140–141, 161–162
Kurdish people
  within areas of dissidence, 1–2, 5
  cultural expression as state threat, 131, 138
  deportations to Western Turkey, post-rebellion, 46, 48
  as distinct culture, 11
  during the Ottoman era, 7–8
  ethnic identity of and Turkishness, 63–64
  geographical location, 10–11
  intra-ethnic conflict, 14
  land reforms and resettlements, 49, 53–54
  militarization of Kurdish regions, 54–56, 79
  non-local government representatives, 46–47
  non-Turkish-speaking, 58
  separate identity, recognition of, 139–140
  state's view of, 38
  as tribal society, 7–8
  urbanization of, 124–125
  see also interventionist policies (Kurdish regions)
Kurdism, 40, 47, 121–122, 126, 132, 133
Kurdistan Communities Union (KCK), 161–162, 200, 201
Kurdistan Workers Party (PKK)
  armed conflict, 142–143, 156, 161, 163
  call for civil disobedience, 149–150
  foundation and support for, 129
  negotiations to end the insurgency (Democratic Opening), 198–202
  Öcalan, Abdullah, 129, 131, 156, 198–199
  state interventionist policies and growing support for, 129–130, 136
  support for, 1980s, 137
  use of force, 136–137
Kutlay, Naci, 121, 122, 123, 125

Laitin, David, 10, 20, 33, 40, 58, 115
land reforms
  Morocco, 100–101
  Turkey, 53–54
Lausanne Treaty, 146
Law on Political Parties (Turkey), 160
Law on the Maintenance of Order (Turkey), 45
Leveau, Rémy, 27, 101, 106
Liberation Army (Morocco), 5, 82, 84, 89, 91, 92–93, 110
linguistic homogenization, 11, 20, 58–60, 61, 67–69
local power centers (Berber)
  inclusion in nation-building, 81
  power reduction, Istiqlal policies, 86
  strength of tribal loyalties, 83–84
  tribal alliances with French colonials, 83, 84, 88–89
local power centers (Kurdish)
  detribalization attempts, post-1925 rebellion, 41–43, 46
  non-native placement of state officials, 46–47
  suspicion of, Turkish Republic formation, 20
local power centers, state centralization and, 23–25, 29, 31

Lust-Okar, Ellen, 16–17, 99, 126–127, 171, 179, 182–183
Lyoussi, Lahcen, 93–94

Maddy-Weitzman, Bruce, 2, 9, 14, 16, 82, 96, 99, 167, 168, 170, 175, 176, 178, 180, 181, 184, 185, 186, 187, 193
Mann, Michael, 6, 30
marabouts (holy men), 88, 105
Marais, Octave, 86–87, 100, 106
Marcus, Aliza, 129, 132, 136, 137, 142–143
Mardin, 54, 58, 65, 66–67
Mardin Artuklu State University, 159
Middle East, nation-building strategies, 16–17
Migdal, Joel S., 32, 38, 143
military action (Morocco), suppression of rebellions, Rif region, 95–96
military, the
  manpower, Ottoman empire, 18–19
  as measure of state power, 30–31
  military coup, May 1960 (Turkey), 123
  military coup, March 1971 (Turkey), 127
  military coup, September 1980 (Turkey), 130
  national service and language dissemination (Turkish), 64–65
military action (Turkey)
  armed conflict with PKK, 136–138, 142–143, 156, 161, 163
  Dersim rebellion, 51–52
  militarization of Kurdish regions, 54–56, 79
  suppression of Kurdish rebellions, 30–31, 47–48, 51–52
military regime 1980s (Turkey)
  oppression of Kurdish people, 132
  promotion of Islam (Turkish-Islamic Synthesis), 132–133
  repression of Kurdish culture, 131, 138
  repression of Kurdish language, 133–135
Mohammed V of Morocco
  alliance-building with the Berber rural notables, 94, 95, 96–97, 110–111, 182–183
  Muslimhood and Moroccanness, 106–107
  power struggle with Istiqlal Party, 91–97
  as symbol of nationalism, 91–92
Mohammed VI of Morocco
  founding of the Royal Institute of Amazigh Culture, 164–165
  liberalization policies of, 184
  support for IRCAM, 189–190
monarchy
  abolition of in Turkey, 82–83
  governing strategies, compared to republics, 16–17
monarchy (Morocco)
  alliance-building with the Berber rural notables/Amazigh activists, 94, 95, 96–97, 110–111, 182–183
  constitutional powers of, 202
  cooptation strategies, 182–184
  cult status of, 103–104
  promotion of traditional dress, 104–105
  sacred nature of, 102–104, 202, 203
  tolerance of popular Islam, 105–106
  use of national ceremonies, unifying role, 104
  see also individual kings
Moroccan Association for Research and Cultural Exchange (AMREC), 112, 168
Moroccanness
  Amazigh concessions on the idea of, 179
  ambiguous notions of, post-independence, 26–27
  flexibility of, 173
  Muslim identity and, 102–103, 106–107
  nationalism and Islam, 87–88, 102–104, 107, 169–170, 177, 180
  nationalism and traditional dress, 104–105
  pluralism of, 177–178
  retraditionalization of state practices, 104–105
Morocco
  under the Alawite dynasty, 8–9
  constitution, 109, 202–203
  economic crises, 170, 171
  Feast of the Throne, 91, 96
  French colonial rule of, 5, 9–10, 12–13, 81–82, 83
  human rights discourse and liberalization, 172
  Islamic challenge to, 171–172
  parliament, 99, 105, 167, 172, 178, 182, 191, 202
  political liberalization, 181–182
  renewal of allegiance ceremony (*bay'a*), 80, 104

Morocco (cont.)
  retraditionalization of state practices, 104–105
  social structure, post-independence, 83–84
  socio-economic indicators, 28–29
  see also nation-building (Morocco)
Mouvement Populaire, see Popular Movement (MP)
Muhammad Reza Shah, 17

names
  ban on Kurdish names for children, 143–151
  Berber names for children, 190–191
  The Registration Law (Turkey), 143–144, 145, 148, 150–151, 157
  The Surname Law (Turkey), 49–50, 144–145
National Union of Popular Forces (UNFP), 96–97, 108, 110, 111
The National Unity Committee, 123
nationalism
  creation of, neopatrimonial regimes, 24–25
  national identity, forming, 1
  state-led, 20–22
nationalism (Kurdish)
  autonomous region, post-World War I, 43
  emergence of, 39–40, 162
  and ethnic identity, 40
  symbolic capital of, 129–130
  see also Kurdish activism; Kurdish movement
nation-building (Morocco)
  inclusion of tribal structure, 25–26, 83–84
  overview of, 4, 16, 80–81
nation-building (Turkey)
  detribalization of the Kurds, 41–43
  Kurdish assimilation by transformative state, 37–38, 79
  nation-building strategies (extreme makeover), 4, 15–16
  see also Westernization of the Kurds
nation-building strategies
  comprehensiveness of, 3, 15
  as a continuum, 197–198
  defined, 3
  intrusiveness of, 3, 15
  monarchies/republics, Middle East, 16–17

neopatrimonial model, 24–25
  in relation to state-building, 3–4, 17–18, 20–22, 29–30, 204
  role of cults of state leaders, 103
neopatrimonialism, 24–25
Newroz (New Year), 139, 142
Nugent, David, 22
Nuri, İhsan, 47

Öcalan, Abdullah, 129, 131, 156, 198, 199, 200, 201
Özmen, Abidin, 43
Ottoman Empire
  concentration of state power, 18
  Kurdish relations with, 7–8
  legacy and Turkish state-building, 18–20, 31–32
  military man power, 18–19
  modernization of, 18–20
  social pluralism of, 57, 58
ou Bihi, Addi, 93–94
Özal, Turgut, 139
Özoğlu, Hakan, 7, 43

Peace and Democracy Party (BDP), 160, 161–162, 200–201
People's Democracy Party (HADEP), 141
People's Houses (People's Chambers)
  closure of, 120
  educational role, 75, 76
  failure of the Westernization policies, 76–77
  organization of, 71
  role in nation formation, 39
  role in promoting women in society, 74
  role in Westernization, 70–71
  sports promotion, 75–76
  Turkish language classes, 66
People's Labor Party (HEP), 140–141
Popular Movement (MP)
  foundation of, 89
  policies, 89–90
  within the Moroccan political system, 99, 111
power, state
  despotic power, 30
  infrastructural power, 30
  and social control, 30–31

Rachik, Hassan, 168–169, 170, 178, 180

radio
    Kurdish language, 156, 158
    promotion of Turkish language, 67, 76–77
Raha, Rachid, 203
Reform Plan for the East (1925, Turkey), 60
Republican People's Party (RPP)
    detribalization policy reversal, 119
    quest for Kurdish support, political alliances, 52–53, 118–119
    see also Inspectorates General, RPP; single-party era (Turkey) (1923–50)
republics, contrasted to monarchies, 16–17
The Resettlement Law, 49
resettlement policies (Turkey), 49, 53–54
Revolutionary Eastern Cultural Hearths, 126, 127
Reza Shah, 17
Rıza, Seyit, 51
Royal Institute of Amazigh Culture (IRCAM)
    Amazigh activism within, 189–190
    establishment of, 164–165, 182–184, 186–187
    promotion of Berber language and culture, 192
    work redefining Berber identity/culture/history, 193–194
rural notables (Berber)
    alliance with French colonial powers, 83, 84, 88–89
    alliance-building with the monarchy, 94, 95, 96–97, 110–111, 182–183
    conflict with the Istiqlal Party, 89, 92–93
    integration into the political system, 99–100, 111
    tribal lands and maintenance of status quo, 100–101
    tribal uprisings, post-independence, 93–96

Said, Sheikh, 44–45, 118
Sakallıoğlu, Ümit Cizre, 130, 135
Saudi Arabia, nation-building policies, 17
Scott, James, 10, 11, 50, 59, 144, 156
secularization (Turkey), 18, 44, 70
Sheikh Said Rebellion (1925), 44–48, 50, 60, 72, 79, 118
single-party era (Turkey) (1923–50)
    authoritarianism, post-1925 rebellion, 45

    bureaucratic expansion, 48
    nation-building policies, 56
    state's view of the Kurds, 38, 42–43
    state tribal relationship, 52–53
    transformative state and Kurdish assimilation into, 37–38
Social Democratic Populist Party (SHP), 139, 140
Socialist Union of Popular Forces (USFP), 108, 172, 181–182
state autonomy, 4, 17–18, 30–31, 47
state–Berber relations
    Amazigh concessions for inclusion, 178–181
    cooptation strategies, 26–27, 32, 35, 97, 102, 110, 166–167, 173, 182–184, 194–195
    flexibility and stability, 26, 27–28, 83–84, 110–111, 173, 196–197, 205
    intolerance of Amazigh activism, 170–171
    political liberalization and, 181–182
    recognition of Amazigh demands, late 1990s, 177–178
    response to activism, 1990s, 176–177
    state institutions' opposition to Amazigh activism, 190–192
    state intolerance of Amazigh politicization, 188–189
    tolerance of Berber cultural activism, 167–170, 173
    see also Amazigh activism; Berber movement
state-building
    centralization and internal conflict, 22–23
    defined, 17–18
    homogeneous culture and, 11
    in relation to nation-building, 3–4, 17–18, 20–22, 29–30, 204
    linguistic homogenization, 11–12
    role of local elites, 5–6
    strategies, 3–4, 196–197
    tribal regions and, 6–7
state-building (Morocco)
    historical legacy, 32
    monarchy's strategy for, 97–98, 102
    overview of, 25–26
state-building (Turkey)
    legacy of Ottoman state institutions, 18–20, 31–32
    suspicion of local power centers, 20

state employees
  denigration of the Kurds, 77–78
  non-native placement in Kurdish regions, 46–47, 60
state in society approach, 32–33
state–Kurdish relations
  Democratic Opening, 199–202
  emergence of Kurdish nationalism, 162
  hawkish stance towards PKK, 161–162
  overview of, 37–39, 114–116, 181
  reforms recognizing Kurdish demands, 157–161
  see also Kurdish activism; Kurdish movement
state-led nationalism model, 20–22
state of emergency (Turkey), 136–137
State Security Court (Turkey), 135–136, 150, 155, 157
Supreme Board of Radio and Television (RTÜK), 153–154, 158
The Surname Law, 49–50, 144–145

Tamaynut, 112, 176
Tamazight
  constitutionalization of, 174, 176, 180, 188, 202–203
  teaching of in schools, 182, 192–194
  use of, 175, 189, 190, 202
Tanrıkulu, Sezgin, 145, 161
television
  in Berber dialects, 178
  Kurdish broadcasts, 156, 160
Tibi, Bassam, 6, 7
Tilly, Charles, 5, 20, 21, 23, 48, 58
Tozy, Mohammed, 88, 105
Treaty of Sèvres, 43, 62
tribal regions, state-building and, 6–7
TRT-6 (Kurdish language state TV channel), 160
Tugaç, Hüsamettin, 114
Tunceli, 51, 55, 64, 133, 136
  see also Dersim
Tunceli Law, 51
Turkey
  1950 elections, 119
  army, 18–19
  candidature for EU membership, 156
  concerns over territorial integrity, 43, 62–63
  constitution, 1982, 135–136
  failure to create homogeneous national identity, 29–30
  military coup, May 1960, 122–123
  military coup, September 1980, 130
  Muslim nationalism, 198
  political polarization, 1970s, 128
  republic foundation, 5
  secularization reforms, 18, 44, 70, 72
  socio-economic indicators, 28–29
  state power and failure of social control, 31
  transition to democratic system, 117
  urbanization of, 124
  see also nation-building (Turkey); state-building (Turkey)
Turkification, 44, 58, 123, 130
Turkish History Thesis, 63
Turkish Islamic Synthesis, 132–133
Turkish Labor Party (TLP), 125–126
Turkish language
  dissemination through education and military service, 64–65
  ethnic identity and, 57–58, 61–62, 63, 67–69
  linguistic centralization and, 11
  policies to promote among the Kurds, 65–67
  resettlement policies and, 49
  urbanization and Kurdish speakers, 124
Turkishness
  as defined through language, 63, 67–69
  ethnic identity and, 57–58, 61–62, 63, 67–69
  Kurdish assimilation into, 56–57
  Kurdish people and Turkishness, 63–64
  and Muslimhood, 56–57
  promotion of, 1982 constitution, 135–136

Üngör, Uğur Ümit, 20, 42, 45, 49
Urfa, 114, 123, 124, 133, 159

Van Bruinessen, Martin, 7, 8, 10, 44, 129, 132
village guards, Turkey, 137–138

Wahhabism, 17
Walter, Barbara, 199–200
War of Liberation, Turkey, 19–20
Waterbury, John, 18, 26, 82, 83, 84, 85, 87, 88, 89, 91, 94, 96, 97, 98

Watts, Nicole F., 2, 50, 51, 52, 124, 127, 130, 137, 141, 142, 162
Wedeen, Lisa, 103
Westernization of the Kurds
    education, 75
    everyday life, 69–70
    Kurdish resistance to, 79
    outward appearance/dress, 70, 72–74
    policy failure, 76–77
    promotion of women's public role, 74
    role of the People's Houses, 70–71
    sports promotion, 75–76
    state policies on, 78–79
    see also interventionist policies (Kurdish regions)
Willis, Michael J., 14, 184
Wimmer, Andreas, 6, 21, 28, 151
women
    increased public role, Turkey, 74
    People's House, Urfa region, official ceremony with women present, 74
    veiling, Westernization policies, 73–74
World War I, 5, 18–19, 43, 50, 57
World War II, 19, 53, 82, 117
Wyrtzen, Jonathan, 9, 83, 93

Yassine, Abdessalam, 171–172
Yeğen, Mesut, 8, 10, 38, 42, 57, 140
Yıldırım, Canip, 121, 122, 125, 151
al-Youssoufi, Abderrahmane, 172, 181

Zana, Mehdi, 125, 134
Zazaki, 11, 50
Zürcher, Erik J., 19, 39, 45, 70, 71, 82, 87, 117, 121, 130

For EU product safety concerns, contact us at Calle de José Abascal, 56–1°,
28003 Madrid, Spain or eugpsr@cambridge.org.

www.ingramcontent.com/pod-product-compliance
Ingram Content Group UK Ltd.
Pitfield, Milton Keynes, MK11 3LW, UK
UKHW020926110825
461507UK00029B/229